THE PHILLIES READER

THE Phillies READER

Edited by Richard Orodenker

Temple University Press

Philadelphia

Temple University Press, Philadelphia 19122
Copyright © 1996 by Temple University

Printed in the United States of America

♾ The paper used in this publication meets the
requirements of the American National Standard for Information
Sciences—Permanence of Paper for Printed Library Materials,
ANSI Z39.48-1984

Text design by Erin Kirk New

Library of Congress Cataloging-in-Publication Data

The Phillies reader / edited by Richard Orodenker.
     p.   cm.
ISBN 1-56639-503-8 (alk. paper)
1. Philadelphia Phillies (Baseball team)—History.   I. Orodenker,
Richard.
GV875.P45P486   1996
796.357'64'0974811—dc20   96-26884

This book is dedicated to the memory

of my late beloved uncle, Samuel Orodenker—

in whose arms I wearily saw my first Phillies game in 1960—

and to my son, Todd Andrew Orodenker, age nine,

who appears determined to carry on

the family tradition

◆

Contents

◆ ◆ ◆

THE PHILLIES READER

Introduction

❖ ❖ ❖

One of baseball's most enduring traits, wrote the late Tom Meany, a New York sportswriter and frequent Phillies-basher, is that "the game doesn't lack for kind words. People argue baseball and read about baseball as avidly as they ever did." That observation came at a time, not unlike the present, when many people had stopped going to see games (though increasing numbers of folks watched baseball on television and continued to listen to it on the radio).

Meany was describing what baseball calls the "hot stove league" (defined technically by baseball lexicographer Paul Dickson as the "term for the gab, gossip, and debate that takes place during the winter months when baseball is not being played"); but whatever seasonal cycle or emotional crisis baseball happens to be in at any given moment, baseball fans always want to read and talk baseball. Baseball enthusiasts will argue about things that didn't even happen in their lifetimes. Fans born in the 1970s fret over the fact that Phillies manager Gene Mauch started Bunning-Short-Bunning-Short-Bunning in five out of seven games in 1964's "Year of the Blue Snow" just as those of us who lived through the whole ordeal recall it like a first root canal.

In its literature and lore, however, baseball usually connects with and remembers the past in more gratifying ways. "Writing is exciting," wrote Marianne Moore, "and baseball is like writing." Donald Hall, who calls baseball writing "proseball," notes that "in proseball as in baseball we undergo the splendor of triumph and the agony of defeat. But even when the style is ghastly, full of booted grounders and bases on balls, often the stories are magnificent."

Baseball narratives are often linked to vernacular models—and particularly to the clubhouse quote (such as Danny Ozark's famous quip after a tenth consecutive defeat, "Even Napolean had his Watergate"). One may also call to mind Ring Lardner's fictional epistles of the semi-literate busher Jack Keefe ("I don't remember now what I says to him but I says something you can bet on that. You know me Al") or a real-life Casey Stengel's theater-of-the-absurd-like testimony before the Senate Subcommittee on Anti-trust and Monopoly ("Of course, we have had some bad weather, I would say that they are mad at us in Chicago, we fill the parks"). But there is also the baseball of novels, poems, essays, histories, and, above all, the sports page—what I have called elsewhere "America's literature of the breakfast table." Baseball fans may not be very discriminating readers, but their love of the game and its rich lore and traditions makes reading about baseball a joy and a necessity, especially for the folks who don't get enough baseball between spring training and the World Series.

Phillies fans ("those miserable fans," as Jim Brosnan described them) might well be baseball's most discerning audience, on and off the field. For many years, they had little to cheer about. But whatever their heroics or ignominies, the Phillies have always made, in the parlance of journalists, "good copy" and entertaining reading. What's more, major events, famous and infamous, have occurred on Phillies' soil (from Baker Bowl to the Vet) or wherever the team may have ventured—from Ebbets Field in 1950, where Dick Sisler's home run won the pennant at the last minute, to the Edgewater Beach Hotel in Chicago, where Eddie Waitkus got shot.

Having won only one pennant between the dead ball and lively ball eras, the Phillies were largely ignored by the mainstream press, especially when they were the Futile Phillies of the 1930s. It wasn't until after that second pennant in 1950 that one publisher, G. P. Putnam's Sons, considered the team worthy of inclusion in its team histories series. *The Philadelphia Phillies* (1953), written by veteran New York sportswriter and Philly native Fred Lieb and Phillies pitcher turned *Inquirer* sports reporter Stan Baumgartner, became an instant classic. Meany's 1953 article for *Collier's*, "Baseball Needs Three Big Leagues to Survive," had the Phils moving to Baltimore (with whom the Phillies had a working agreement) in a hypothetical (and now slightly prophetic) major league realignment.

The Baltimore Phillies? No way. It was Connie Mack's Athletics who moved, heading west to Kansas City a few years later. The Phils are still here, "As much a part of the Philadelphia scene as the statue of William Penn," as the A's once insisted they were. Since Meany's time Philadelphia has seen three pennants, one World Championship, and several division titles. But mere success now and then these past thirty years hasn't kept the Phils out of the annals of great baseball literature.

The Phillies Reader taps into the rich mine of literature about the team produced from the end of the nineteenth century to the end of the twentieth. The writings included here document many things besides baseball: the cultural life of the city and, more so, the nation; the history of a Philadelphia institution that has been around since 1883; the social issues of the day; and profiles of some extraordinary and unusual individuals.

I actually began the research for this book a long time ago, when I was a boy. Hoping to find baseball books, I would search through the used books bin at Leary's Bookstore on Ninth Street or in the stacks at the Central Library in Philadelphia's Logan Square. I would look for hours on end at microfilm of old sports pages, where I might encounter firsthand the myths I had only heard about (was it true that William Baker put up a fifteen-foot screen on the right-field fence at Baker Bowl to keep Chuck Klein's home run production—and hence Klein's salary—from reaching, in Fred Lieb's words, "Ruthian dimensions"?).

Baseball is not myth, of course, but its history transforms quickly into myth. Myths, students in my American Studies class at Penn State like to think, are simply falsehoods or tall-tales ("It's only a myth that Babe Ruth called his home run shot in 1932"); but, more properly, myths are narratives that, regardless of veracity, contain elements of truth and core beliefs that followers of a culture (in this case, baseball culture and, by extension, American culture) hold dear. Whether or not Ruth called his shot (he probably didn't) doesn't really matter. The fact is that, knowing "Babe Ruth" as we do, it is not inconceivable that he *could have;* furthermore, it is not so bad a thing to believe that he actually did call his shot (or perform some other amazing feat) because believing the myth lends coherence and stability to our shared values and beliefs (say, our faith in heroes or leaders), which also reflect who we are and what we hope to achieve as a people. Weighty stuff for a game with a stick and a ball.

One long-suffering myth holds that the Futile Phillies of yore were the perennial doormat of the National League (when eight teams were all there were). When does the era of the Futile Phillies begin and end? I start it with the Grover Cleveland Alexander trade in 1918 and end it with the sale of the team to Robert M. Carpenter, Jr., in late 1943. There were many futile years after 1943 (1944, for instance, when the Phils—or Blue Jays, as they tried to rename themselves—were nine games out of first place at the All-Star break and still in last place) and a not-so-bad year or two before '43 (if you can call fourth place "not-so-bad")—and despite pennants in 1983 and 1993, the last ten or twelve years haven't been exactly peachy—but the term "Futile Phils" is generally applied to the Phillies of that span of a quarter century, in which star players came and went (for much needed franchise cash) and seventh or eighth place was a sure bet. As J. Roy Stockton, sports editor of the *St. Louis Post-Dispatch,* wrote in "Them Phillies—Or How to Make Failure Pay" (1941), which appeared in the pages of the *Saturday Evening Post* (published in Philadelphia's Washington Square): "Each spring, when the sap in the trees is about ready to run . . . 287 or so baseball experts are asked to prognosticate on the order of the finish of the major league baseball clubs at the end of the season. Invariably, when the news services carry the consensus, there is a tag line reading, '287 out of 287 picked the Phillies to finish last.' And the faithful Phillies never stump the experts."

Nonetheless, nobody ever hated the Phillies, not the way you could hate the Yankees. You could, however, make merciless fun of the Phillies with impunity—though you were more likely to describe them, as Meany once did in 1941 on the eve of a crucial series for Brooklyn, as "nice fellers, who never harmed anybody, and aren't going to start now, I hope."

The myth (or no myth if you look at the record) persisted even after the Whiz Kids' one-year triumph in 1950. The Futile Phillies seemed to rise again from the ashes left by the afterglow of a solitary pennant. The Phillies did not play badly in the 1950 World Series (just well enough to lose, wrote Jimmy Cannon); but the myth endured. The

Series even prompted a bit of doggerel from the pen of Tim Cohane, *Look* magazine's sports editor: "The youthful Granville / Is no Maranville" (a two-generation allusion: to shortstop Granny Hamner, who made a costly error in the eighth inning of the third game of the 1950 World Series, and to Rabbit Maranville, a colorful character and terrific shortstop, who lasted 1912–35, mostly with the Boston Braves). For the next two decades Philadelphia would be tagged the City of Losers, drummed in further by the debacle of '64. When the Phillies lost three straight ignominious playoff rounds between 1976 and 1978, they re-emerged as the typographically impaired "Phutile Phils." The World Championship in 1980 rewrote that chapter, maybe once and for all; but readers will discover the myth of the Futile Phillies (does the name Mitch Williams ring a bell?) alive and well throughout the pages of this volume.

The tone of *The Phillies Reader* is literary—or, as sportswriters after the fashion of Mr. Dooley used to put it, *lit'ry*. The man behind Mr. Dooley, Finley Peter Dunne, a late-nineteenth-century baseball writer for the *Chicago Daily News,* and later a widely popular newspaperman and the editor of *Collier's,* served as editor for Philadelphia's—and the twentieth century's—first great sportswriter, Charles Dryden. Dryden left his mark wherever he traveled—and he ventured from West Coast to East (working in Philadelphia from 1899 to 1905), finally landing in Chicago, where he laid the groundwork for Ring Lardner, Heywood Broun, Damon Runyon, and other important early figures of American sportswriting. Lardner became a seminal figure in American letters, and he credited Dryden as a major influence. Lardner put all the Phillies lore he knew into "Sick 'Em" (1914), a short story he wrote for the *Saturday Evening Post.* The story concerns how real-life catcher Pat Moran and manager Red Dooin, with the help of the (unreliable) narrator, scheme to get the best out of a pair of fictitious, highly-touted rubber-armed rivals named Smitty and Fogarty, who are pressed into greater service because "Alexander strained his souper and Rixey got a pair o' busted fingers." By pitting one pitcher's bloated psyche against the other's, the three men get Smitty and Fogarty so jealous of each other that one pitcher outdoes the other every time one of them is on the mound. Dooin "prob'ly ruined both o' them guys for the next season by workin' 'em in the shape they was in," but that doesn't matter. The manager really doesn't want either of them around any longer, and they've served their purpose by getting the Phillies into the "World's Serious" with Washington (wrong team, a year early, but a good prediction). The Phillies have appeared in other fiction as well, most prominently the juvenile baseball novels of Frank O'Rourke (*The Team* [1949], *Never Come Back* [1952], and *Bonus Rookie* [1950], which anticipates the Whiz Kids' pennant-clincher against Brooklyn several months ahead of schedule). The Phils also turn up for five paragraphs in Damon Runyon's one and only baseball short story, "Baseball Hattie" (1936), in which several circa-1920 Phillies "refuse to take their departure" after calling the umpire "a scoundrel and a rat and a snake in the grass, and also a baboon."

Heywood Broun was also not one to let a good Phillies quip pass him by. Richard Kluger, in his massive book on the *New York Herald Tribune,* quotes this piece of classic Brouniana from 1913: "[Bareback Joe] Oeschger was in the box for Philadelphia, but his delivery is not nearly as difficult as his name. He was hit so hard that Charlie Dooin was driven at last to send in another pitcher of such obscurity that he was not even indicated on the scorecard. Matteson was the newcomer. He lacks more than a few letters of being a Mathewson."

The Phillies Reader is also a historical anthology of sorts, though not every great event in Phillies history is represented here and a few of the ones we wish we could forget certainly are; but I've placed a greater emphasis on theme: the Futile Phils, the Ben Chapman–Jackie Robinson incident, the Whiz Kids, the 1964 debacle). Not all the names encountered here will be familiar ones. In the 1930s and 1940s Phillies players were "dispatched . . . as perfunctorily as a supermarket rejecting a case of moldy lettuce" (to borrow a line Sandy Grady once used to describe an itinerant one-time Philly pitcher named Johnny Klippstein). "When a good ballplayer went to the Phillies," Kirby Higbe remembers in *The High Hard One* (1967, Viking), "he would hustle and bear down in the hope he would be sold to a good ballclub." Casey Stengel wasn't a Philly for very long, but he is of interest for obvious reasons. If Phillies lore passes through baseball, a lot of baseball lore also passes through the Phillies. When Stengel removed Whitey Ford for Allie Reynolds in the final game of the 1950 World Series, he was heard to say to reporters: "I'm sorry I had to take the young man out but as I have been telling you, the Philadelphias is hard to defeat, and I am paid by my employer to defeat them, which is why I went for the feller with the big fastball. Have a nice winter."

This book is also not just a collection of writings by local sportswriters, though I think the best of them are present and accounted for: Dryden, Horwits, Lewis, Hochman, Grady, Dolson, Merchant, Cushman, Conlin, Stark. In the early days of sports reporting, beat reporters generally covered only the home games. When Chuck Klein hit his four home runs in one game against the Pirates in 1936, the story was covered (quite colorfully) probably by a Pittsburgh correspondent.

As an anthology of the best writing about the best team in the best sport, *The Phillies Reader* comprises writers from all over the United States: Atlanta, San Francisco, St. Louis, and, yes, even the place Tug McGraw said they could stick it. The book is offered with Phillies fans in mind, but it also means to please the large audience of baseball fans.

Of the out-of-town authors appearing in this volume, Furman Bisher, long-time sports editor of the *Atlanta Constitution and Journal,* got to know Gene Mauch when Mauch was managing the Atlanta Crackers (a much better team name than the Braves, I think). Roger Kahn's beat for the *New York Herald Tribune* was the Brooklyn Dodgers and later the New York Giants for a few years during what he calls "The Era"—that is, the late 1940s to the late 1950s, when baseball was pretty much a Big Apple affair. He later served as sports editor at *Newsweek,* where the great John Lardner wrote his wonderful column, "John Lardner's Week." Joe Williams, of the long-defunct *New York World Telegram,* was another nationally syndicated columnist; his take on Game Two of the 1950 World Series is the kind of biased New York writing Phillies fans love to hate. But it's *good* writing, nonetheless, by a sportswriter that Jim Murray, no slouch himself, put in the same company "with legendary figures like Ring Lardner, Damon Runyon, Grantland Rice, and the rest." And more than a few readers might forget that a young Red Smith (assuming you remember an *old* Red Smith) got his big break (if you can call it that) on the old *Philadelphia Record;* at least that's where Stanley Woodward found him and plucked him from to write for the late, lamented *New York Herald Tribune,* which had, arguably, the finest sports department ever. Smith, like Dryden, was good no matter what—or for whom—he was writing (that includes his stint for *Women's Wear Daily*). Dip into his columns at any point in his career and you'll come up with something worth your time and effort. Ditto Sandy Grady. Smith would become famous for his leads, and the "Smith touch was evident," wrote his biographer Ira Berkow, in the first lead Smith wrote while covering a Phillies game—"As early as the third inning yesterday, Jimmy Wilson was casting longing glances toward a third-base box where gleamed the incredibly pink dome of James A. Farley, surrounded by deserving Democrats. A little earlier, posing with a baseball for news photographers, Big Jim had exhibited all the form of a top-flight pitcher, which was more than Mr. Fabian Kowalik was doing at the moment."

Another purpose of this book is to give readers a sense of the varying styles that have marked baseball writing since the late nineteenth century: the quaint, Victorian sentences in the manner of Henry Chadwick (called the father of baseball, but more likely the grandfather of baseball writing); the iconoclastic wit of Leonard Dana Washburn, Charles Dryden, and the Chicago School of baseball writing; the "Gee Whiz" and "Aw, Nuts!" repertoires; the gracious, if unimaginative, sportswriting epitomized by the *New York Times*'s, Arthur Daley who in 1956 won a Pulitzer Prize coveted by the more deserving Smith and Cannon, neither of whom liked Daley's writing (or each other's, for that matter). Add to this the "conversation" piece, fashioned in the late 1930s and 1940s by Frank Graham of the *New York Sun,* as well as the "ghost-written" and "as-told-to" staples of baseball literature. New journalism and literary journalism, which W. C. Heinz and others pioneered in the early 1950s, came of age in the early 1960s and carry through to the present (see the essay here by Pat Jordan, for example), as has chipmunk journalism (the in-your-face, everything-on-the-record approach that refuses to take the sport so seriously) and total immersion journalism (see Bruce Buschel's piece, which concludes this volume). Finally, there is what Stanley Woodward called the "on-the-button" school of journalism—that is, solid spot reporting accompanied by a sense of humor and good, plain English. There are a lot of examples of that kind of writing also to be found in *The Phillies Reader.*

As I said, readers looking for a purely hometown perspective or a rehash of Rich Westcott and Frank Bilovsky's invaluable *The New Phillies Encyclopedia* (1993, Temple University Press) will have to turn elsewhere. If reading how Joe DiMaggio finally got the better of Robin Roberts makes you stew, well, then you're in the wrong book and, probably, the wrong sport. Another point to remember is this: any one of the "famous" young men of Manhattan could have worked for one of the Philadelphia newspapers (why they would have wanted to is another matter entirely). If Smith had stayed in Philadelphia, he might have written that "art of fiction is dead / Reality has strangled invention" stuff for Dick Sisler instead of Bobby Thomson. For the record, Smith wrote in 1950 that the Phillies, "in the tenth inning of the 155th game[1] of their season, all snarled up in a strangling tie with the team that had closed eight laps on them in a fortnight, . . . were knocked kicking into the championship by the bat of Dick Sisler." Furthermore, Philadelphia sportswriters have achieved a standard of excellence along with a degree of humility. As Frank Dolson wrote on the night the Phillies clinched the pennant in 1980, "Hemingway would struggle over this one. Shakespeare would grope for words to describe it and give up in despair. Grantland Rice would be in over his head. I don't have a chance."

Think of *The Phillies Reader* as what we used to call a bedside table book. That means it's the kind of book you can pick up and put down at your leisure rather than read right through, though I don't discourage your doing that, either.

I was unable, of course, to include everything I wished to. Anthologies are costly to produce, and reprint rights can be prohibitive. Some of the writing, controversial in its own time, might seem tame by today's standards. As to be expected, there are essays on Mike Schmidt, Steve Carlton, and Dick Allen, though there isn't one on Pete Rose

---

1. Perhaps Smith was thinking of an 8–8 Phillies–Dodgers game in June in Shibe Park halted by the Sunday curfew.

(readers might want to turn to Michael Sokolove's insightful *Hustle: The Myth, Life, and Lies of Pete Rose* [1990, Simon and Schuster]). Why not Rose, or Bill Duggleby, Eppa Rixey, Gavvy Cravath, Claude Passeau, Flint Rhem, Curt Simmons, Del Ennis, Wes Covington, Jay Johnstone, Pope Owens, Greg "Bull" Luzinski, Lenny Dykstra? How I wish they could all be here. In a way, though, they are cavorting through one story or another like so many friendly ghosts. Admittedly, I have included more about the Phillies after 1950 than about Phillies from an earlier era, or even the Phils of today. But I think the writing speaks for itself.

There are several Phillies-related texts worth mentioning even though, for one reason or another, I have chosen not to use them. Certainly Lieb and Baumgartner's book (which, if you can find it, goes for $200 in good condition on the rare book market) has many worthwhile chapters. "It Took a War to Do It" from Tom Meany's *Baseball's Greatest Teams"* (1949, A. S. Barnes) concerns the 1915 National League champions; the war in the title refers to the Federal League wars, implying perhaps, as many believed, that if players hadn't jumped to the fledgling league that year (gone the next) the Phillies might not have made Meany's book. Meany begs to disagree, calling Pat Moran's Phillies one of the best, even if they did steal signs to help them win ball games. There are swell entries about the Phillies in both of Jim Brosnan's classic diaries, *The Long Season* (1960, Harper) and *Pennant Race* (1962, Harper). *Bo: Pitching and Wooing* (1973, Dial Press) by Maury Allen has a revealing chapter ("The Boo-Birds of Happiness") about Bo Belinsky's experiences with Gene Mauch and the 1965 Phillies. *Rowdy Richard* (1987, North Atlantic Books) by Dick Bartell with Norman Macht has plenty of insights about the Phillies of the early thirties by the late, fine second baseman, who became, in his own words, "the most hated man in the National League." In Michael Fedo's *One Shining Season* (1990, Pharos Books), there is a poignant chapter recalling Stan Lopata's one great year in 1956, as well as one on current general manager Lee Thomas's 1962 26–home run season with the Los Angeles Angels; *July 2, 1903* (1992, Macmillan) by Mike Sowell contains the best account of Phillies Hall of Famer Ed Delahanty as well as fascinating material on the great Napoleon Lajoie, who played with the team 1896–1900 before taking "French leave." A lot of interesting Phillies lore turns up in Bruce Kuklick's *To Everything a Season: Shibe Park and Urban Philadelphia, 1909–1976* (1991, Princeton University Press). Curt Smith has many appreciative words for former Phillies broadcaster Byrum Saam ("The Man of a Zillion Words") in his *Voices of the Game* (1987, Diamond Communications). Both Dave Anderson in *Pennant Races* (1995, Doubleday) and David Halberstam in *October 1964* (1994, Villard) have entertaining chapters on the Phillies' pennant collapse in 1964. *Crash: The Life and Times of Richie Allen* (1992, Ticknor and Fields) by Dick Allen and Tim Whitaker is a very underrated book. Mark Winegardner's compelling *Prophet of the Sandlots* (1990, Atlantic Monthly Press) recounts the author's year-long journey with the legendary but insecure septuagenarian Phillies scout Tony Lucadello (who signed Mike Schmidt, Fergie Jenkins, and forty-nine other major league ballplayers, including lastly Mickey Morandini and Tom Marsh). Lucadello, an old hand who in many ways was way ahead of his own time, became saddened by the awareness of his own obsolescence and later blew his brains out near the third-base line of a ballfield in his hometown of Fostoria, Ohio, thus unintentionally rewriting the end of Winegardner's book. There are, to be sure, some excellent Phillies stories to be found in the pages of old and current magazines and journals, mainstream and otherwise (*Phillies Report, Philly Sport, The Fan, The Sporting News,* and *The National Pastime,* just to name a few). Of course, there could be as many different Phillies Readers as there are Phillies fans. I stand by my selections, however, and welcome all criticisms, as well as suggestions for further inclusions. Bear in mind, though, that not all authors care to part with their copy these days, storing it up for volumes with their own names on them. I hope the selections I have made afford you the same pleasure these pieces, on several readings, have given me, too.

I would like to thank the following people who so graciously assisted me in one way or another with the preparation of this book: the late Ed "Dutch" Doyle, Joe McGillen, Frank Phelps, Harrington E. "Kit" Crissey, J. Douglas English, Rich Westcott, Bill Wood, Bill Hughes, Terence Malley, Dick Clark, Larry Lester, Harold Rosenthal, and most of all Barry Morrill, without whose support, guidance, and enthusiasm this book would not have been possible. Thanks also to David Updike for his meticulous and conscientious copyediting, even though he is not a baseball fan, and to my wife, Robyn, always at the top of the batting order.

Richard Orodenker

Early Years

Delahanty Hits Four Home Runs

from the *Chicago Tribune,* July 13, 1896

◆ ◆ ◆

Of the twelve players to hit four home runs in one game, three have been Phillies,
all of them Hall of Famers. The writer of this piece, more formal and restrained
than the author of the article on Chuck Klein's similar feat (see pp. 40–43), was
apparently unaware that Bobby Lowe of the Boston Nationals had been the first
major leaguer to hit four home runs in a single game, on May 30, 1894. Up
until the 1930s, writers were still spelling Delahanty's name with an "e." The
article is an example of the kind of baseball writing typified by Henry Chadwick
in the early days of the professional game.

Ed Delehanty made four home runs and a single in five times at
bat yesterday, placing a world's record opposite his name, but
still Chicago won. That was because only four other Philadelphians
could land on Terry's curves and drops with sufficient force to place
the ball in a safe place. The score at the end was 9 to 8, and Chicago
had at last won another game from the Quakers.

Delehanty's feat was never before equaled on a league ball field, and
when it was all over the thousand people who had been fortunate
enough to witness the game stood on their chairs and cheered the
smiling batter. Terry shook hands with him, and then the bleachers, to
a man, followed the hard-hitting Quaker to the omnibus and cheered
him again and again.

The first time he was up he put a fly that sailed over Ryan's head into
the right-field bleachers; the second time he singled to right, but the
third time he batted the ball over the scoreboard and out of the enclo-
sure—the longest hit of the year on the local grounds. It was thought
that he had reached his limit, but on the fourth attempt he caught the
ball fairly and sent it whizzing into deep center, completing the circuit

before Lange could throw the ball into the diamond, and Lange lost no time about it, either.

Chicago had a lead of two at the end of the eight and half the spectators arose to go, but some enthusiast who had figured it out that Delehanty would be the third man at bat shouted, "Wait till Del makes another homer," and everybody waited. The men ahead of him went out, and he bunted the first one over the foul line. "Line it out!" somebody yelled, and he did. Again the ball passed over Lange's head and this time it was lost beyond the clubhouse.

Counting his own, this wonderful hitter batted in seven runs—all but one made by his side.

Young Cy vs. the Phillies

Charles Dryden

◆ ◆ ◆

Like Napoleon Lajoie, sportswriter Charles Dryden was a major talent Phila-
delphia could not seem to hold for long. He covered home games of Connie
Mack's A's and "those Phillies" for the North American *from 1899 to 1905*
before becoming the highest paid sportswriter in America at the Chicago Tribune. *It would be difficult to find language as lively and original as Dryden's*
on today's sports pages, but in his time, wrote Stanley Walker, former city editor
of the New York Herald Tribune, *"Dryden's stuff was read as much for his*
comical treatment as for the news it contained." The following game account,
from the April 28, 1905, North American, *is of precious note because it intro-*
duces to the annals of baseball lore one Irving Melrose Young, a flash-in-the-pan
known as "Young Cy" or "Cy the Second." Though he went on to win 20 games
for the Boston Braves that season (and lose 21), Young Cy would win only 43
more in a six-year career, 448 fewer than his famous namesake. The gas com-
pany scandal alluded to in Dryden's P.S., by the way, was front-page news on
the day this story appeared.

Those depressing Phillies had lots of important things happen to
them. First they got paid off by Mr. Shettsline, who is presidenting
for the team this year. Then young Cy Young, a new sidewheel flinger
for Boston, fried our athletes 2 to 9. He did it in little more than an
hour, and three hits were among our important happenings.

When our President Bill waddled out to the ball yard toting checks
for services rendered up to the 30th ult., or inst., he little dreamed of
the sad returns in store. The game was swift and tobascoish; but the
locals couldn't hit the new-moon delivery of Young Cy. It was deceptive
and likewise provoking. But four men reached first base in nine
rounds, and they have somewhat hazy notions of how it happened.

For a left-hander, and a new one at that, Young Cy displayed remarkable control. He did nothing but put the ball over, and he refrained from soaking or passing a single athlete. His curve is a peach, much resembling the old No. 66 Round-House benders of Jocko Menefee. Were it not for the catcher and grand stand, Young Cy's curve would eventually come floating back and bump him in the solar plexus.

Like a Cannon Ball Tosser

A stocky youth is Cy; built like the gentleman who tosses cannon balls at the circus. Had he tossed up a few to those Phillies some more important things might have happened. Of the three swats, one was a rank scratch. Mr. Gleason bunted in the fourth. Cy forgot to look where he was going, and stepped on the bosom of the overworked Mr. Tenney, who was trying to field the ball near first base. Both athletes went up to grass, and Bill arrived. Very important.

Mr. B. Duggleby struggled madly against fearful odds. He caused seventeen Bostonese to pooh pooh on flies, and they made nine hits. Bill did the best he could with a hitless crew behind him. Mr. Abbott, our amateur pugilist, emerged from a brief sojourn in the swamps minus $50 on his check. Fred backstopped Bill to the limit, being glad to be among those present once more. He sawed off one of the three hits, which is pretty good for an exile.

Story of the Operation

Both runs were due to errors, which should be excused on account of the importance of the occasion. One gone in the seventh, Sharpe and Raymer singled. Needham hit to short. Sharpe, dodging the ball on the line, foozled Doolin for a moment and blighted his prospects for a double play. He didn't get anybody. Young skied to Courtney, and, with the bases filled, Cannel singled to centre. Sharpe tallied and Raymer was stopped at the plate on Roy's throw to Duggleby.

Two down in the ninth, Raymer and Needham singled. Young Cy

drove a safety to centre. Thomas and Gleason pushed the ball back in time to nag Raymer, but Abbott dropped the pill in the mix-up at the plate. Cannel forced Young.

Our only chance was in the fourth. One out, Gleason bunted. Courtney doubled. Magee hit to Wolverton, and he threw Gleason out at the plate. Mr. Titus lined to Mr. Raymer, the popular young dancing master from Medicine Bow, Neb. We don't know what county Medicine Bow is in.

Mr. Fraser was out in his store clothes attending to the financial end of the show for Mr. Tenney. To guard against any funny business, Mr. Fraser practiced bookkeeping with a lead pencil on the yellow bricks in the lobby. Just the same, President Bill held out 30 cents of the gross receipts, which sum, he said, Mr. Fraser so neatly resembled in the role of financial agent.

P. S. We cannot afford to waste much gas on those Phillies, owing to the imperiled state of the city's supply, which is being so ably defended in other parts of the paper. Hence this brief synapsis [*sic*] of many important happenings.

Notes of the Game

Magee had a B. D. in left.

Young Cy seemed to be well named.

Boston will exhibit at Utica, N. Y., on Sunday, just to keep Tenney from getting rusty.

Phillies were obliged to hustle in order to have a couple of athletes left on bases.

Messrs. Sparks and Caldwell practiced in new shoes. Both these athletes are pitchers.

Mr. David Wask has doused the lantern that looks like a pop bottle and installed a searchlight in the catacombs.

Duggleby's work was good enough had the Phillies been able to hit. In seven rounds they failed to reach first base.

How I Lost the 1915 World Series

Grover Cleveland Alexander

◆ ◆ ◆

Whether or not Grover Cleveland Alexander actually took pencil to paper for this piece for Baseball *magazine in 1915, the ideas must have been his own, and for a detailed game analysis it remains an extraordinary bit of writing. Why would Alexander, who won 31 games and pitched the Phillies to their only victory in the Series, feel that he lost it for them? Old Pete, who used to burn the candle at both ends regularly, didn't become a heavy drinker, according to his teammate Hans Lobert, until after World War I. "He was in his twenties and he had a wonderful constitution," recalls Lobert in* The Glory of Their Times *(1966, 1984, Morrow). But Lobert adds, "Funny thing, he never ran, like pitchers are supposed to. He'd get around third base and field some ground balls, and that would be that." Alexander blames his poor physical conditioning and regrets that he "didn't come through for" his team, a phrase often foreign to athletes of today.*

The World Series was a disappointment to me. It was not so much the result, which went against my team, Philadelphia, but my own individual showing, which was so far from what I hoped it might be. Everyone knows by now that the Boston Red Sox beat us with four victories to our one, but I feel it might have been considerably different if I had lived up to expectation.

I have never yet given alibis and I am not going to begin now. But I would like to explain to my fans and friends why I think I failed in the series.

Let me begin with a day during the last month of the pennant race. It was Labor Day. We opened a crucial series with Brooklyn. The club was right on our heels and our manager Pat Moran and his boys felt, with good reason, that we must come out on the winning side of this encounter. I believe no one on our team even considered that we might not win a single contest. That is, of course, exactly what happened.

I was picked to pitch the opener. Moran depended a great deal upon winning that game. If we won, we'd have that one on ice and we'd be confident besides. It is my own feeling that Moran did not exaggerate the importance of winning that first game. I always feel that a visiting team should put its best foot forward. The home team has obvious advantages, and it is important for a visiting manager to balance those advantages as soon as he possibly can.

Larry Cheney was on the mound for the Brooks. He was lately acquired from the Cubs, and I detected an unusual determination on his part to justify the move that had brought him from Chicago.

Brooklyn scored one run off me in the first inning. After that the game settled down into one of those contests where neither team will budge an inch and the pitcher must work his heart out. Cheney, while wild, as is natural with spitball pitchers, was invincible. We could not make a single hit off him for six innings. In the seventh, he strained himself and was obliged to leave the box. It was then that our boys fell on the opposition and drove in three runs.

We began the eighth with a two-run lead. Moran felt that the game was won. I hoped it was myself when Jake Daubert went out on the first ball pitched. But then something happened. I have never been able to understand it, but in some way I strained my shoulder and the muscles in my back. I have the misfortune of getting a blister on my middle finger from throwing the ball. I remember I had a blister on that finger Labor Day, and it bothered me considerably. The ball player doesn't pay much attention to minor injuries, but try as he will a twirler can hardly get normal results from his pitching hand when his fingers are sore. I know that I unconsciously tried to humor that blistered finger. In doing so I brought the muscles of my shoulder into play in an unusual manner. Pitching a fast ball to the next man up, I strained my shoulder. I immediately felt it, and I couldn't seem to control the ball so well. When I put forth all my strength and tried to get the ball over the plate, it would go outside. When I cut down a little on the stuff I was serving up, the Brooklyn batters would hit me.

I remember that I overheard a loud-voiced rooter in the stand when that inning began. The Brooklyn crowd seemed discouraged when we piled up those three runs. This particular rooter yelled out: "Never mind, boys. Go at Alexander. He's human like the rest of us."

He was certainly right. I felt human enough when they started to pound me around the lot. And I felt extremely human when at the end of that inning they had scored five runs off my delivery and snatched away a game that I had considered as good as won.

It was a bitter blow to Moran—and that Brooklyn series never got any better. We lost all three games. The third defeat ended in an accident to our first-string catcher, Reindeer Bill Killefer. My own thoughts as to the prospects for the pennant were gloomy. I worked my best with Killefer. He understood me and knew how to handle my peculiarities. However, on that score my pessimism was unnecessary. Ed Burns, Killefer's replacement, did a fine job through the closing laps of the pennant race.

I didn't tell Moran that I wrenched my shoulder during the Labor Day game. I knew he had enough on his mind without thinking about me. I was lucky enough to pitch a one-hit game against the Braves that clinched the pennant. That gave me, momentarily, the feeling that the shoulder might not disrupt me through the most important games of my career—the World Series.

It has never been my disposition to worry about things, but if there was one time in my whole life when I wanted to be in best pitching form it was for those World Series games. I would willingly have given my share of the receipts to have been able to pitch my team to a championship of the world. That is my answer to the oft-repeated suggestion that we ball players think only of the money that there is in the game.

The papers, unconsciously no doubt, added to the burden of my position. Many pitchers can work in great form when nothing in particular is at stake but crumple badly in a pinch. I do not believe I have ever faltered when I was asked to carry a heavy load, but it is human nature to feel responsibilities and to be weighted down by them. The papers spoke of Christy Mathewson and what he did in the famous series of 1905 (Matty pitched three shutouts). They said he won the series singlehanded. Some of my friends were good enough to predict equal success for me.

It is a fine thing to have friends who are confident in you, but I may say the responsibility of pitching in the World Series is enough in itself without the added consideration of living up to high expectations.

They said I was nervous in the first game. All right, I was. They hit me pretty hard, but that didn't worry me. There was a time when I used to burn up all my stuff on every ball pitched, but the pitcher grows wiser as he grows older. The fact that Boston was hitting me didn't worry me as long as I was able to keep the hits well scattered. What worried me most was the fact that our boys didn't seem to be able to hit Ernie Shore as much as the Red Sox were hitting me. At that, they only put their hits together in a single inning. They scored one run. However, I must admit in fairness that Shore had very hard luck and the breaks went badly against him. We won, 3–1.

The pitcher knows when he is not right It is a miserable experience to know you are not at your best when you are facing a pennant winner and the world's championship is at stake.

That thought came to me with overwhelming force in the first contest, and I had to fight against it all through the series. Perhaps I allowed too much for it. As I look back upon the series now, I can criticize myself because at times I was too careful, too exact, too conscious of myself. When I am at my best I can get the ball to break as I want it to, instinctively, with little effort. And I can get my fast ball to sweep across the plate just where I tell it to go. The pitcher can always work best when he has to use the least thought and care. The more he tries to supplement tired muscles or aching joints by mental effort, the more he loses the edge he may have had on the opposition. I tried to foresee every contingency, to guard against every accident, because I was not right. Had I been in my best form, I would have given those things scarcely a second thought. I would have pitched the best I could and trusted the ability of my fielders.

Again, the pitcher in a World Series game has none of the assurance that he may have during the season. In the short series he has to do whatever he is going to do then or never at all. If a slip occurs it is too late to change it. He has one or two, or at the most three chances to deliver, and if he fails it is too late. During the season if he loses a game or two successive games it doesn't matter so much. He feels that he will have time later on to redeem himself and comforts himself with the thought that the best of them can't win all the time.

In my second game, and the game that was destined to be my last, I had hoped I might feel in perfect shape. It was the third game of the series. Boston had taken the second game 2–1.

We got off to an early lead with a run in the third, but Boston came back with a score in the fourth. From the fourth until the ninth Dutch Leonard and I were knotted in a pitcher's duel. I think I was pitching better than I did in the first game, but as fate would have it Leonard was pitching even better.

The crucial point for me came in the last of the ninth. With the potential winning run on base I elected to pitch to Duffy Lewis. My critics contend that I should have elected to pass Lewis, a .291 hitter in the regular season, and pitched instead to Larry Gardner, who had a season's mark in the neighborhood of .250. That thought occurred to me, too, but I decided to pitch to Lewis for several reasons. In the first place, he had been going great guns in the series, and I figured the percentages were bound to catch up with him. Besides, I had faced him in twelve games in a previous All-Star tour, and he had made only two hits off me. On one occasion I had struck him out four straight times. Furthermore, I estimated Gardner as a far more dangerous man in a pinch.

All my reasons notwithstanding, I was wrong. It was Lewis' hit that won the game. However, had I passed Lewis and Gardner hit me safely, I'm sure these same critics would have leveled the same complaint. The ball player becomes accustomed to the second guess, in which the press writer seems to find a delight.

I have no desire to take anything away from the reputation of Duffy Lewis. He had a wonderful series. But regardless of the results, I still feel that I was right in pitching to him. It may have been the most disastrous decision of my career, but even in defeat my reason compels me to stick by it.

After my loss in the third game, I know our team felt down and out. That depression may very well have made the difference in the score of the fourth game, which Boston won, 2–1. It was Ernie Shore who won that one for Boston. It is an interesting note that he gave us seven hits in this game, which he won, compared to the five hits he gave us in the first game, which he lost.

Behind three games to one, our hopes were all but shattered. A great deal has been written about the fifth game. I was slated to pitch and, in fact, intended to pitch up till the last moment. I never wanted to pitch a game so much in my life. How I would have loved to beat Boston in that fifth game and put us back in the series!

But I knew when I started to warm up that I wasn't right. Once again I had to make a decision. I had to choose between my own instinctive desire to pitch and my knowledge that I was in no condition to properly represent my team. I decided to tell Moran how I felt. I must give him credit for taking this information without any great demonstration of disappointment.

"If you are not right, Alex," he said, "the rest of us will have to carry it."

Moran expressed a fine sentiment, but unfortunately it didn't work out so well. It was Mr. Lewis again who was our nemesis. He belted a lusty home run into the bleachers and Harry Hooper put the game on ice with his second home run of the contest. Again, it was a game decided in the ninth inning and Boston won, 5–4.

I do not wish to disparage the work of our pitchers, Jim Mayer and Jeptha Rixey. They did a fine job. Had the fates of the game been kinder in the ninth, they would have gained a deserved victory. But be that as it may, as long as I live I will always wonder how I might have fared had I pitched that fatal fifth game of the '15 series.

I shall always think of this series as a great personal disappointment. I was unable to live up to the expectations of my friends, and I didn't come through for my team. No matter what anyone else may say, I know the reason I lost the 1915 World Series was that I was not in the proper physical condition to give it my best.

When Casey Was a Phillie

Robert W. Creamer

◆ ◆ ◆

Casey Stengel came to the Phillies in 1920—reluctantly—on the heels of one of the many legends to accumulate around the equally legendary ballplayer. Finding a sparrow in the Brooklyn bullpen, which Stengel, then playing for the Pirates, stopped by to visit (as was the custom for visiting right fielders when they were unlikely to come to bat in the inning), Casey put the little creature under his hat. When he took his position the following inning, he responded to the usual catcalls that greeted him by lifting his cap, revealing the bird, which then flew off. Everyone—the fans, the home plate umpire, the press, even Dodger manager Wilbert Robinson ("Hell, he always did have birds in his garret")— loved the gesture. Everyone, that is, except Pirates owner Barney Dreyfuss. The punishment, as Bob Creamer, former Sports Illustrated *senior editor and author of* Stengel: His Life and Times *(1984, 1996, University of Nebraska Press), picks up the story, was banishment to Baker Bowl.*

The Pirates kept on losing after their weak performance in Brooklyn and fell well below .500. Stengel was playing well, leading the team in both hitting and runs batted in, but Dreyfuss longed for the gentlemanly Max Carey, his star center fielder, who had damaged his shoulder early in the year and hadn't played since. He had Carson Bigbee, a steady player, in the outfield, and Billy Southworth, who joined the Pirates in 1918 after Stengel left for the navy and led the league in hitting the rest of the year. Southworth, too, had been injured early in 1919, but he returned to the lineup the day before Casey let the sparrow out of his cap. When Carey returned at the begin-

From *Stengel: His Life and Times* by Robert W. Creamer (Lincoln: University of Nebraska Press, 1996). Reprinted by permission of the author.

ning of August, his shoulder better, Dreyfuss had a surfeit of first-string outfielders, and Stengel was still pestering him about raising his salary. Dreyfuss solved both problems on August 9 by trading Casey to the Philadelphia Phillies for Possum Whitted, an outfielder who could play the infield, whom the Pirates immediately stationed at first base. Whitted hit a splendid .389 the rest of the season for Pittsburgh, but Stengel didn't bat anything at all for Philadelphia. Irritated by the trade, he sent a wire to William Baker, the Phils' owner, demanding an increase in salary before he'd report. Baker, who had sold Grover Alexander to the Cubs after a salary dispute, replied that there wasn't much money in Philadelphia. Stengel said, well, in that case he could be found in Kansas City. He refused to report to the Phillies. He packed his bags and went home—in the middle of August.

In Kansas City he gathered a ragtag team of semipros and ex-minor-leaguers and under the guidance of a promoter named Logan Galbreath took them on a barnstorming tour through oilfield towns in Kansas, Oklahoma and Texas and then on through New Mexico and Arizona to California before returning to Kansas City. One stop was at Fort Huachuca, a military base near Douglas in southern Arizona just above the Mexican border, where they played a team of black soldiers that included a pitcher Stengel recalled as "Grogan" and whom he described as "next to Satchel Paige, the best colored pitcher I ever saw." "Grogan" was Joe (Bullet) Rogan, a hard-throwing right-hander who became one of the titans of Negro baseball in the 1920s and 1930s, when black players were barred from organized ball. Stengel also admired a black shortstop named Dobie Moore. "They were as good as any major-leaguers," Stengel said. (When he returned to Kansas City the following winter he mentioned the black stars he had seen to James L. Wilkinson, a white man who was organizing a team of black players to be called the Kansas City Monarchs. Wilkinson signed Rogan, Moore and three others.)

In California after the major-league season ended Casey added Emil Meusel and his kid brother Bob to the team. Emil, known as Irish, played left field for the Phillies (Bob was about to join the Yankees and would play for ten years in the same outfield with Babe Ruth), and he helped persuade Casey to work out his differences with Bill Baker. Sten-

gel had made good money on the barnstorming tour, but he knew that
no matter how talented and well known a player he was he couldn't
earn as decent a living playing exhibitions in tank towns as he could
playing outfield in the big leagues, even for a last-place team like the
Phillies.

During the winter he agreed to terms with Baker and in 1920 played
right field for Philadelphia. He and the good-natured Meusel became
fast friends, going out together, making jokes together about playing
ball in Philadelphia. The ball park the Phils used was called Baker
Bowl, and it was tiny, with a small outfield area that in right field was
bounded by a high fence faced with tin. "Playing right field there was
the softest job in baseball," Stengel said. "I had the wall behind me, the
second baseman in front of me, the foul line on my left and Cy Williams, the center fielder, on my right. The only time I had a chance to
catch the ball was when it was hit right at me."

Meusel had a chronic sore arm and hated to throw, although he led
the Philadelphia outfielders in assists in both 1919 and 1920. Stengel's
once fleet legs were creaking and his back was bothering him, and he
no longer felt the need to chase joyously after every fly ball hit anywhere near him. He and Meusel began to let Williams take all the flies
he could reach. They did it so routinely that later on, when Casey and
Irish were playing together on the Giants, they'd automatically shout,
"Take it, Cy!" on every ball hit to the outfield.

Baker, who did not appreciate the humor of it, called Stengel "just
plain plumb lazy" when he sat out games and let a splendidly named
substitute called DeWitt Wiley (Bevo) LeBourveau take over for him.
Baker's petulance was fueled by Stengel's loud, persistent criticism of
the tight-fisted owner.

Nevertheless, Casey was enjoying baseball again, despite the aches
and pains that had become chronic. One day that spring, as the Phils
barnstormed home after leaving their training site, the club played a
game in Fort Wayne, Indiana. Crowds gathered early before such exhibition games in order to watch the major-leaguers in practice, but one
loud-mouthed yokel sitting near the Phils' dugout kept up a noisy ha-
rangue, mocking the players' ability and disparaging every ball that was

batted. "You can't hit, you city loafers!" he'd cry. "You call that hitting? Anybody could hit better than that."

After a time the Philadelphia players began to answer him back. Finally one of them said, "You've got a pretty big mouth. You think you could do any better?"

"Dang right I could," said the fan, who was wearing overalls and a farmer's straw hat, with a red bandanna around his neck.

"Why don't you come out here and try?"

"All right, I will," said the farmer. He clumped his way onto the field, picked up a bat and went up to home plate. To the astonishment of the crowd he was good. He whacked out line drives and long flies and even put a couple of balls over the fence. Well, of course, it was Stengel, putting on a show for the crowd.

Another day that spring he put his uniform on backward and wore it that way all through batting practice. The Phils' manager was Gavvy Cravath, their once-great hitter, now in his last season in the majors. Cravath was a strong-jawed, impressive-looking man who later became a justice of the peace in California. He had a bad cold the day Stengel put the uniform on backward and wasn't terribly amused by the joke. "I'm not surprised, though," he told Stengel. "You've done everything else backward down here. You might as well wear your pants that way too."

Casey did a reprise of his sparrow trick in 1920. In Baker Bowl one afternoon before a sparse crowd of 500 or so he saw a bird in the outfield grass, popped his cap over it and put bird and cap on his head. A moment or so later a high fly came in his direction and, with everyone watching, he lifted his cap after he caught the ball and the bird flew away.

Some days he'd get the crowd laughing by catching easy fly balls behind his back. He enjoyed that kind of obvious fun, but he appreciated the hard, competitive aspects of baseball too. The Phils had a pitcher that season named Lee Meadows, a chunky right-hander who wore glasses and could throw hard, a combination that tended to make batters nervous at the plate. One day, with Meadows pitching, the Phils were leading the St. Louis Cardinals by one run in the ninth, with men on second and third, two out and Rogers Hornsby, the best hitter in the league, at bat. Cravath ordered Meadows to walk Hornsby intentionally and pitch to the next man. Stengel, out in right field, thought that was absolutely the right thing to do, even if there were two out. Hornsby was a devastating hitter.

Meadows thought different. With Hornsby waiting for a walk, Meadows slipped the first pitch over the plate for a strike. Hornsby got ready to swing at the next one, but Meadows threw the ball behind his head, and Hornsby had to hit the dirt. Meadows slipped the next pitch over for strike two, and then, with Hornsby angry and ready, knocked him down again. And then knocked him down a third time. With the count three and two, Meadows threw a hard curve, hoping for strike three, but Hornsby stepped into the pitch and hit what Stengel called "the damnedest line drive I ever saw." It went on a low flat line directly to Meusel in left field, who caught it for the final out. "That was the roughest I ever saw a man pitched to in the major leagues," Stengel recalled, "but the biggest thing was what Hornsby did, after all those fastballs thrown behind his head. Instead of falling away on that last curveball, he stepped in and hit a tremendous line drive."

That was the connoisseur of baseball talking, appreciating an example of rare skill and courage in the game he loved so much.

Casey batted .292 for the Phillies in 1920 but appeared in only 118 games in the outfield, the fewest he had ever played in a full season. Nonetheless, he hit nine home runs and only five players in the league hit more, two of them his fellow outfielders, Williams and Meusel. It had been a satisfactory season.

But 1921 was something else again. His legs were no better, and his back was worse. By the end of June he had been to bat only fifty-eight times. He was hitting over .300, but he wasn't much help to the team. He ached. The multiple injuries he had incurred during his career— the ankle, the knee, the shoulder, the pulled muscles, now the back— made him feel like an old man. He was going to be thirty-one in a month, and his best years were gone. The family back in Kansas City was getting by, but Casey knew they needed the money he sent them. His father's street-sprinkling business had petered out, and, past sixty now, he had a bad heart that kept him from working.

Casey had done the best he could, but the future seemed bleak.

Time had somehow passed him by when he wasn't looking. He wasn't "the fair-haired youth" anymore. He was in his eleventh season as a professional ballplayer, and while his major-league salary was nice it wasn't nearly as much as he might have been making. The distaste that Ebbets and Dreyfuss had felt for him, the exile to Pittsburgh and then to Philadelphia, the negative influence of the war—all those things had turned what should have been the peak of his career, the years from 1917 through 1921, into a kind of slow-motion seriocomic nightmare.

The 1921 season in Philadelphia was nightmarish enough in any case. Cravath had been dropped as manager, even though he had improved the team's won-lost record in 1919 after taking over as manager in mid-season and had improved it again in 1920, and Wild Bill Donovan had been named in his place. Wild Bill, so called because of the many bases on balls he had given up when he was a big-league pitcher, had had some remarkably successful seasons when he was a player (27–14 in 1901, 26–4 in 1907), but he had, literally, a fatal tendency to be in the wrong place at the wrong time. He had been made manager of the Yankees in 1915 after Jacob Ruppert and Cap Huston bought that once tatterdemalion team and started it on its road to glory. But Donovan had become the manager too early, before the team acquired its great players, and after three seasons he was dismissed.

If he was too early for the Yankees, he was too late for the Phils, who had finished first or second four times in five years, not long before Donovan took over from Cravath. Now they were a bad team getting worse, and Donovan didn't even last out the season. He was gone in August. In 1923, by then managing New Haven in the Eastern League, he was riding in a sleeping car through upstate New York on his way to the winter baseball meetings in Chicago with his boss, George Weiss. Weiss, a younger man, let Donovan have the lower berth in their compartment. That night there was a train wreck and Donovan was killed, while Weiss escaped without serious injury.

In June 1921 in Philadelphia, Donovan was not a happy man, and he let his players know it. He was quick to criticize, and his players chafed under his displeasure. The Phils had a portly red-faced catcher named Frank Bruggy, who owned a Stutz Bearcat. Donovan used to cadge rides home with Bruggy after games, which the catcher hated because Donovan would tell him on the way home what Bruggy had done wrong in that day's game. One day when Bruggy was catching, Donovan kept yelling at him from the bench to have the pitcher mix up his pitches. Bruggy had the pitcher throw his fastball, his curve, his change of pace, everything he could think of, but Donovan kept yelling, "Mix 'em up! Mix 'em up!" Bruggy finally called time, took off his mask, stood up, and turning his head so that Donovan could hear him, called out elegantly to the pitcher, "If you have anything else in your repertoire, please deliver it."

That amused the players but did little to cheer up Donovan, who continued to bawl people out. Stengel, whose locker was close to the manager's, finally moved his gear into a little closetlike space off the dressing room to get away from Donovan's post-game tirades, and possibly to gain a little privacy and a semblance of the dignity a man of his years and experience deserved. One rainy Thursday afternoon, the last day of June, after the game the Phillies were scheduled to play that day had been postponed, Jim Hagan, the club secretary, came into the clubhouse. Casey was in another room, having his leg worked on by a trainer. He heard Hagan ask, "Where's Stengel's locker?" Back there, someone said. "Back there?" said Hagan. "Well, he'll be dressing farther away than that pretty soon."

"Uh, oh," Stengel thought, "I'm gone. Donovan's gonna send me to Kalamazoo." Big-league careers ended abruptly in those years.

Hagan came into the trainer's room, saw Stengel, and said, "I've got something for you." He handed him a piece of paper. Casey glanced at it—and everything changed. It said the Phillies had traded Stengel and second baseman Johnny Rawlings to New York.

"Yee-ow!" Stengel yelled. He leaped off the table and began jumping around the room. The trainer stared at him.

"I thought your leg hurt," he said.

"Not anymore," Stengel shouted. "Not anymore. I've been traded to the Giants!"

All the things that had happened to Charley Stengel—the high school championship in Missouri, the batting title in Aurora, breaking in so spectacularly in Brooklyn, hitting that home run off Alexander, winning the pennant, batting .364 in the World Series, all the triumphs, all the fun, all the battles, all the injuries, all the failures—had been little more than a preamble. The most rewarding part of his life was about to begin.

The Pitchless Wonders

Jack Orr

◆ ◆ ◆

Lee Allen, former historian at the Hall of Fame's National Baseball Library in Cooperstown and Sporting News *columnist, once wrote, "Long before playing the National Anthem became standard procedure in ball parks, George E. Phair, a New York baseball writer and a man of astringent wit, customarily intoned 'My country 'tis a thee, Sweetland and Willoughby, of thee I sing' every time he entered the press coop at rickety old Baker Bowl in Philadelphia. He had invented the chant because it seemed to him that every game there began with either Lester (Sugar) Sweetland or Claude Willoughby pitching for the Phillies." Phair would also sum up the Futile Phillies in four short memorable lines of verse:*

"The Magic Number"
If the Giants win but two of four
And the Dodgers six of ten
The Phillies, as in days of yore,
Will finish last again.

Jack Orr, a Bristol, Pennsylvania, native who had the dubious distinction of having worked on the sports pages of three Philly papers at one time or another, recalled in a 1953 article for Sport *magazine the especially futile year of 1930, in which the aforementioned Sweetland and Willoughby won a combined 11 games and lost 32.*

This is the story of a big-league ball club which had eight men with averages of .313 or better (there were only three such hitters in the whole National League last year); a club which rattled out 1,783 hits (the Cubs led the league last year with 1,408); a club which had three men who drove in a total of 389 runs (the whole Dodger roster in

1952 drove in only 725 to lead the league)—and which, nevertheless, finished last, 40 games behind the pennant-winners.

The club is the almost legendary Philadelphia Phillies of 1930, an organization symbolic of an era of bloodthirsty hitting and of a ball so lively that pitchers used to hate to get up in the morning. Even fine pitchers such as Carl Hubbell, Burleigh Grimes, Wild Bill Hallahan and Dazzy Vance had their troubles. Not one of them managed to get 20 victories.

No, it was strictly a hitter's year and the Phillies had hitters, if nothing else. Chuck Klein led the team with a .386 average, including 40 homers and 170 runs driven in. Lefty O'Doul had to be consoled because he had a bad year, slipping from .398 in '29 to .383. Third baseman Pinky Whitney hit .342 and all-around-man Benny Friberg, .341. Don Hurst, at first, hit .327, outfielder Monk Sherlock, .324, and the two catchers, Harry McCurdy and Spud Davis, .331 and .313, respectively. Shortstop Tommy Thevenow was embarrassed by a .286 average, while second baseman Fresco Thompson, the captain of the team, had a lowly .282.

"I could have hit .300, though," Thompson complained recently. "I was going along fine, hitting around .320, but the other guys were so ashamed of my average that they wouldn't let me take batting practice. I wasn't allowed even to speak to O'Doul and Klein. Yeah, I was captain, but it was like being foreman of a WPA gang. Who'd pay attention to a hitter like me?"

Unfortunately for the Phillies and their manager, Burt Shotton, then a snappy 46, they had to take the field every now and then. Immediately there would be noises resembling artillery fire as the opposition raked Philly pitchers. The Phils played in old Baker Bowl with its famous right-field fence. Often, the story went, young infielders would pick up grounders and throw to Klein in right instead of Hurst at first. And though the Philly murderers were rocking the opposition pitching at a remarkable clip of 6.8 runs and 11.4 hits a game, Philly pitchers set a record which probably never will be broken: they gave up 1,199 runs, a breathtaking 7.7 a game.

"Those pitchers were really awful," Thompson said. "Once I took the lineup to home plate. I had written in the pitcher's spot, 'Willoughby—and others.' Bill Klem didn't think it was funny and made me cross it out. I was right, though, and in the first inning, when we were changing pitchers, I yelled, 'See, Bill, what'd I tell you?'"

That would have been Claude Willoughby, who won 4 and lost 17 that year. Some of the others were better. Les Sweetland won 7 and lost 15 and the ace, Fidgety Phil Collins, won 16 and lost 11. Then there were Ray Benge (11–15), Ace Elliott (6–11), Hap Collard (6–12), Roy Hansen (0–7), Bill Smythe (0–3) and 43-year-old Grover Cleveland Alexander (0–3).

There was no help from the fielders, either. The club made 236 errors, exactly 130 more than the Dodgers made last year in setting a new National League record. Opposing hitters smacked the right-field wall as if it were a gong and Klein, who had his work cut out for him, set a record that still stands, 44 assists by an outfielder.

"These Phillies," wrote the baseball expert of *The New York Times* before the season started, "are the dark horses. Here is a team which has been lifted . . . from nowhere to a position of considerable eminence." The eminence was hard to detect. By June 1 the club was seventh and sinking fast and it hit bottom that month and never got up, even though Klein, O'Doul, Whitney and the rest continued to endanger the lives of rival infielders. Of course, they weren't alone in the dynamiting department. That year 25 hitters in the league did better than .335.

Baseball men, sitting around in gab sessions, still talk about that 1930 Philly club. As they talk, you can almost hear the rattle of base hits off the tin wall at Baker Bowl.

Klein Hits Four Home Runs

from the *Philadelphia Inquirer/Public Ledger,* July 10, 1936

◆ ◆ ◆

The author of this piece on the day that Chuck Klein hit four home runs in a ten-inning game makes the Phillies Hall of Famer sound like Shoeless Joe Jackson and Babe Ruth rolled into one. The story demonstrates most of the excesses, and some of the virtues, of the ebullient "Gee Whiz" style of writing, which by the end of the 1930s had lapsed into self-parody. A running gag among sports writers of the 1930s was that there was a headline set in type for repeated use in Philadelphia: "Klein Hits Two as Phils Lose." Wrote Red Smith on the day Klein died in 1958, "Philadelphia readers didn't have to be told that the number 'two' referred to home runs, not singles. With Chuck Klein it was generally double or nothing, two or no-count. Curiously, he never hit three home runs in a game, though once he hit four. Chances are the Phillies lost that day, too." Actually, they won, 9–6, though victory didn't come easy for the Futile Phils. Some players believed that the left-handed hitting Klein would not have hit as many homers if he had played somewhere other than Baker Bowl; but, then again, he accomplished this extraordinary deed in Pittsburgh's Forbes Field, where a no-hitter never was thrown.

S tanding in the midst of immortal fame as one of the few players in the history of the game who hit four home runs in one ball game, Charles Herbert Klein, one of the greatest all-time hitters in baseball, this afternoon stood in right field in the tenth inning, mopped his perspiring brow, wiped the pelting rain off his face, twisted his cap in almost perceptible agony as he saw his masterpiece endangered—then joyfully ran to the clubhouse as the Phils staggered through to victory 9–6.

Joins Immortals

Four times "Chuck" had come to bat—and four times, twice off Jim Weaver, once off Mace Brown and once, the game winning wallop off Bill Swift in the tenth, he had rifled line drives in the far distant right field stands. Four times he hit balls more than 350 feet far beyond the playing field to place his name on baseball's honor list alongside Bobby Lowe, Ed Delehanty and Lou Gehrig as the only ones in the sixty-year life of baseball to hit four homers in one game.

The only flaw, if one would mention such a thing, came in the fact that his last one came in the tenth inning to win the game, while all the others had accomplished theirs in regulation time.

Lowe, then a member of the Boston Nationals, performed his stunt on May 30, 1894, eleven years before Klein first saw light of day at Indianapolis. Ed Delehanty, most famous of the famous Delehanty brothers, got his on July 13th, 1896, nine years before Klein was born. Gehrig entered the hall of baseball fame on June 3, 1932, when he blasted circuit blows in the first, fourth, fifth, and seventh innings.

Klein, driving six of the Phillies' nine runs, smashed his in the first, fifth, seventh and tenth, when he hit the first ball pitched to win the game, which three times in the late innings had been placed in jeopardy.

And—had it not been for the fleet Paul Waner, Klein might have shattered all existing records, as his line drive in the second, another rifle shot into right field, went afoul by about a foot and Waner raced over to pull it down. It was the only time in a long, dismal afternoon, which concluded with the lightning cracking, the thunder rolling and the rain pelting, that the Bucs had been able to get Chuck out.

Double Play Decides

A playwright able to read what was in Klein's mind as he stood out there in the tenth, seeing two Pirates on the bases and victory endangered, would have been able to pen a masterpiece. But then, just like an ending in the movies, came a double-play and a brilliant running catch to end the game which the veteran slugger had won single-handed.

A slight touch of baseball's injustice crept into the thing, too. Claude Passeau, braving the blistering heat, had toiled for eight and two-thirds innings, during which time he allowed eight hits and six runs. With two out in the ninth, he walked Cookie Lavagetto, who batted for Pep Young. Then Fred Schulte, batting for Brown, singled. Out came Passeau, wild went Klein, who had only three homers at that time. In came Bucky Walters to send cold chills, despite the heat, down Jimmy Wilson's spine.

Bucky walked Woody Jensen to fill the bases and then, before he could settle down, walked L. Waner to force in the tieing [*sic*] run and leave the bases still loaded. Jimmy Wilson was frantic on the bench. The whole Philly club was on the steps of the dugout as P. Waner came to bat.

A base-hit would ruin the Klein three-homer achievement, so far as a team victory. Walters toiled and toiled on the Pirate slugger. Finally Waner grounded out to Gomez and the game went into extra innings with the score tied.

Once again up came the mighty Klein. Everyone in the park had been wishing for just such a situation in the ninth when it looked as though Klein's best effort would be three. He would have been next at the bat had anyone of the Phils been able to get on in the ninth.

So—here was the situation—score tied, tenth inning. Klein the first hitter and Swift, the Pirates' third pitcher, on the mound. The storm, which had been brewing most of the afternoon, broke suddenly. Rain began to fall as "Chuck" came up. He took one look—Swift wound up—over came the pitch—and bang went the first ball, even farther than any of the other three.

Other Phils Add Pair

Four home runs—the game winning run and one of baseball's greatest individual days concluded. Then, to insure it, the Phils got two more to run their total to nine—six of which Klein was directly responsible for.

Camilli doubled and Atwood singled. As Vaughan threw wild Camilli scored and Atwood went to third, from where he scored when Norris rapped a base-hit to left. Gomez ended the day for the Phils by hitting into a double-play. Meanwhile, Arky Vaughan turned in a thriller when he ran deep into centre to take Chlozza's fly with his back to the plate.

Walters strode to the mound with the whole club slapping him on the back. But, in an instant he was in trouble. Vaughan singled and Suhr walked. Two on, none out, and three runs needed to tie. Brubaker came up swinging and bounced into an easy double-play to relieve the tension. Up came Lavagetto, still full of fight. He sent a looping Texas leaguers into left. J. Moore came running like a wild man— ran as far as he could—stretched his gloved hand as far as he could towards his knees—and plop—in went the ball—to end Klein's greatest day with victory and prove that the Phils, even though they stagger around plenty, can usually furnish the Bucs with enough excitement in one afternoon to do for a season.

Anything that happened before was ante-climax [*sic*]. Jim Weaver started for the Bucs and after a weird first inning, in which the Phils scored four runs, including Klein's first homer, straightened out unitl the sixth when he gave way to a pinch hitter. Brown came in and stayed until the tenth. Swift worked the tenth, but was charged with the defeat when Klein parked his first pitch in the far-away grandstand.

The Doormats of the Loop

Al Horwits

◆ ◆ ◆

Philadelphia-born Al Horwits covered the Phillies and A's for the Evening Ledger *from 1922 to 1942, the span of his entire newspaper career. There was
perhaps no more biting, cynical, and funny writer during the era of the Futile
Phillies than Horwits, who had every reason to be all three. "It was brutal because there was no interest," Horwits told Jerome Holtzman in* No Cheering in
the Press Box *(1976, 1995, Holt). "Our work suffered. We'd get to the ball
park just as the game was starting. Maybe twice a week we'd bother going down
to the field." The 1938 season, when this piece was written, did not turn out to
be the Phillies' worst after all. "But covering all those losers had its lighter side,
too," Horwits added, "especially in spring training. We never had to worry about
anything." This game account, in contrast to the preceding one, is a classic
example of the "Aw, Nuts!" style of sports prose.*

The conglomeration of ball players going through the motions at
Broad and Huntingdon Streets these warm afternoons may go
down in the books as the worst team to represent the Phillies since the
National League granted them a franchise.

Those with excellent memories and others who remember but refuse
to reminisce will admit that never before have the Quakers been so
weak and futile in every department of the game.

Down through the ages the Phils have been known as the doormats
of the loop, the farm team developing star talent to be sold for the
highest price to other members of the circuit. In past seasons, the
Quakers had weak teams, clubs that finished last, or somewhere in that
vicinity.

Miracle Needed

By virtue of yearly failures the fans became accustomed and resigned to the fate the Phils would never rear their heads above the second-division water line, but they were not convinced of the doom so early in the season as this year.

Not only that, the men of Wilson have a splendid chance of equaling or surpassing the 1935 record of the Boston Braves who won only thirty-eight games and lost 115. In defense of the Bostons, it must be pointed out one game was rained out and they did not have the opportunity of playing it.

At this point the Phils have won fourteen matches and lost thirty-five. At that rate of triumphs, they would finish the year under their log of 1928, the worst season in the thirty-eight years of recordings.

But this isn't based on technicalities. We present the facts on the performances exhibited for the edification of the customers here and abroad. And it isn't fair to place the responsibility entirely on the players.

Scharein, Martin O. K.

They are carrying out their duties, but what chance do they have when opposing big league ball clubs? Observers agree a great majority of them are not of big-time caliber. Many baseball men think Herschel Martin and George Scharein are the only ball players at the Band Box.

Chuck Klein is receding with years. Morrie Arnovich has not arrived. Phil Weintraub apparently is a good hitter in the local postage-stamp park. Del Young can field, but when it comes to batting, it is questionable whether he would hit .300 in the double A's.

Buck Jordan is a fair player and probably could hang around any major league team. The catching is fair and there are two good pitchers, Hugh Mulcahy and Claude Passeau.

Bad Shape

At present the Quakers are at low ebb. They have drained their resources, having sold all available material. Now only the cash—not much of that—and memories remain. The fate of the team seems sealed. It apparently has a good chance of winning the award as the worst team ever to represent this city.

There is a conspicuous absence of power. Sometimes four hits are required to manufacture a single run. When men are on the paths few, if any, deliver a telling wallop. They seem too tender against the pitching they are forced to face.

By the way, for the benefit of those who retired early last night, we bring you the results of the double-header played here yesterday. The Pirates grabbed the opener, 14–4, winning the battle in the very first inning. Many did not hear the returns of the nightcap. Pittsburgh took it by the slim margin of 16–3.

P. S.—In writing this piece we want it distinctly understood we were not influenced by the double-header. We've been watching the Phils a long time.

Nugent Shows Them, Instead

Red Smith

◆ ◆ ◆

The Rube Melton deal was one of those paradigmatic Phillies events that have become part of the team's rich lore. The affair developed gradually between 1941 and 1943 and has been told on several different occasions by different writers. No one put the deal into better perspective or written English than Red Smith, who was a young beat writer for the Philadelphia Record *in 1943, when this article was written. As Dick Bartell remembers, the Phillies under owner Gerry Nugent "became jobbers of players for the rest of the league. Somebody had to be sold to keep the operation going." Nugent sold Chuck Klein to the Cubs for sixty-five grand and then bought him back a few years later for fifty, plus a player. "Klein isn't the only star the Phillies have sold for a tidy sum," Harold C. Burr of the* Brooklyn Eagle *wrote in 1946. "The human chattels include Dolph Camilli, Rowdy Richard Bartell, Dave Bancroft, Kirby Higbe, Curt Davis and Claude Passeau, all of whom were bought originally for peanuts. Those were the days when the little red wagon went to market with its produce." The Melton deal turned out to be a swan song of sorts for both Nugent and the Futile Phils. His team riddled with debt and so many woeful ballplayers, Nugent was removed from his stewardship by the National League and replaced with William D. Cox, the George Steinbrenner of his day. Cox, for his part, lasted only one year before being banned from baseball for gambling (on the Phillies, of all things), after which the long reign of the Carpenter family began.*

Modern sensibilities will cringe at Smith's facetious remark about spousal abuse, although in fairness to Smith, such "jokes" about wife beating were even more common at the time than the criminal and cowardly act itself. The reference to pitcher Tommy Hughes's "soldier suit" relates to the player-depleted World War II years, when the Phillies, wrote Stan Baumgartner, resembled "the cat that was machine-gunned on the back fence."

This looks like as good a time as any to inquire who the misty-eyed dreamer was who thought the National League board of directors could tell Gerry Nugent anything about getting ahead in the baseball business.

For four long days out in Chicago a full staff of career geniuses sat and thought and talked and then talked and thought and sat some more in a seminar designed to teach the Phils' president the rudiments of taking a profit.

It ought to be clear by now that they'd have been a lot wiser just to sit, keeping a firm, protective clutch on their bank balances, and let Gerry do the talking.

Anybody who can pull off a horse-swap such as he engineered in the case of Pitcher Rube Melton doesn't need to be told how to count his change.

As far as is known, Brother Nugent is the only man in the world who ever induced Mahatma Branch Rickey to trade wallets in a dark room. Just review the Melton traffic:

On the eve of the 1940 World Series, the Phils didn't have any money. It is important to remember the date in order to avoid confusion with the eve of the 1939 World Series and the eve of the 1941 World Series, when the Phils didn't have any money, either.

Using a winning smile redeemable for a bowl of chicken gumbo at practically any soup kitchen in the land, Gerry went into the draft meeting and selected Melton from Columbus. Price: $7500.

In the same deft, fluid motion, Nugent wheeled and lateraled Melton to L. Stanford MacPhail, then presiding genius of the Dodgers, who was sprinting down the field with his arms full of $15,000. Net profit: A cool 100 per cent, without the inconvenience of paying Melton a single day's salary, the pain of seeing him pitch a single ball or the bother of bailing him out of a single jail.

That's the way the play looked from the pressbox but it soon developed that Gerry was tackled by Commissioner R. Eyebrows Landis just before he threw the lateral. In effect the ruling was:

"Collusion in the draft—that is, the selection of a player by one club for service with another—defeats the purpose of the draft, threatens the sanctity of the home and besmirches the dignity of motherhood. Signals over."

To MacPhail, Landis said sternly, "Burny, burny, papa spank," and rapped him smartly across the knuckles. The commissioner punished Nugent by making him keep Melton for two years, or until the pitcher's market value doubled.

Then Gerry peddled his right-handed bundle of joy to Mahatma Rickey, from whose minor league chain the Phils drafted in the first place. Price: $30,000 and Johnny Allen, who used to be known as a pitcher but has since cleared his name.

Net profit: 300 per cent, less the cost of a few headache powders.

From a financial point of view, it is a good deal for the Phils even if Allen never throws a pitch for them. Some might say it's a good deal for the Phils especially if Allen never throws a pitch for them.

Approval of a cash sale is a trifle off the party line. Viewing such transactions, it is customary for press and public to observe wittily that you can't put $30,000 out there on the mound and expect it to win you any ball games. But it isn't likely to lose you more than 20 ball games either, which was Melton's defeat quota for 1942.

Unless the money was spent some time last summer or the summer before, it will pay the Phils' spring training expenses and meet the first payroll or so. Thus it enables the club to put a team on the field, if that can be viewed as a desirable end.

And this time no one can protest that he didn't have fair warning. Nugent laid his cards on the table at the Chicago meeting.

"Find me a buyer," he offered, "and I'll sell out. Or show me some way I can operate without money."

When the league flunked on both questions, everybody realized there could be no other way out for the Phils than to sell players. The only questions were, who'd be sold and for how much?

Fans feared the guy to go would be Tommy Hughes, since he is the best ball player on the Phils' roster, one of the very best pitchers in baseball and, accordingly, the most readily marketable bit of merchandise in the Nugent Emporium.

Having thus prepared themselves for the worst, the fans will be grateful for this deal, just as a properly trained wife is grateful when you clout her with bare knuckles instead of a bung-starter.

Presumably, this financial reprieve will enable the Phils to preserve their title to Hughes. Which should be a great comfort to Gerry every time he sees a photo of Tommy in his nice new soldier suit.

Phillies in Black and White

The All-Black Phillies?

Bill Veeck as told to Ed Linn

◆ ◆ ◆

From the early 1940s to the early 1960s (and, some critics have argued, even after that), while most major league teams moved toward integration, the Phillies seemed to be going in the opposite direction. Bill Veeck's brainstorm to buy the flagging franchise and stock it with Negro League ballplayers during the war was an inspired idea, though Joe Bostic of the People's Voice *of Harlem in 1942 suggested "the admission of an entire Negro-owned, controlled and personalized team into one of the leagues if we just must play in their backyard. Then all of the money and jobs from there would come to us." Considered by many to be baseball's consummate showman, Veeck relates the particulars of the deal (though he is a little confused as to the year) in this excerpt from his classic autobiography* Veeck—As in Wreck *(1962, Putnam).*

I have always had a strong feeling for minority groups. The pat curbstone explanation would be that having lost a leg myself, I can very easily identify myself with the deprived. Right? Wrong. I had tried to buy the Philadelphia Phillies and stock it with Negro players well before I went into the service. I think we live in a time when we psychoanalyze everybody's motives too much and that it is entirely possible to look at something which is ugly and say "This is ugly" without regard to conditioning, environment or social status. My only personal experience with discrimination is that I am a left-hander in a right-handed world, a subject on which I can become violent.

Thinking about it, it seems to me that all my life I have been fighting against the status quo, against the tyranny of the fossilized majority

From *Veeck—As in Wreck* by Bill Veeck and Ed Linn (New York: Putnam, 1962). Reprinted by permission of Mary Frances Veeck and Ed Linn.

rule. I would suppose that whatever impels me to battle the old fossils of baseball also draws me to the side of the underdog. I would prefer to think of it as an essential decency. If someone wants to argue the point I won't object, although we'd have a better chance to be friends if he didn't.

Let me make it plain that my Philadelphia adventure was no idle dream. I had made my offer to Gerry Nugent, the president of the fast-sinking club, and he had expressed a willingness to accept it. As far as I knew I was the only bidder. The players were going to be assembled for me by Abe Saperstein and Doc Young, the sports editor of the Chicago *Defender*, two of the most knowledgeable men in the country on the subject of Negro baseball. With Satchel Paige, Roy Campanella, Luke Easter, Monte Irvin, and countless others in action and available, I had not the slightest doubt that in 1944, a war year, the Phils would have leaped from seventh place to the pennant.

I made one bad mistake. Out of my long respect for Judge Landis I felt he was entitled to prior notification of what I intended to do. I was aware of the risk I was taking although, to be honest, I could not see how he could stop me. The color line was a "gentleman's agreement" only. The only way the Commissioner could bar me from using Negroes would be to rule, officially and publicly, that they were "detrimental to baseball." With Negroes fighting in the war, such a ruling was unthinkable.

Judge Landis wasn't exactly shocked but he wasn't exactly overjoyed either. His first reaction, in fact, was that I was kidding him.

The next thing I knew I was informed that Nugent, being in bankruptcy, had turned the team back to the league and that I would therefore have to deal with the National League president, Ford Frick. Frick promptly informed me that the club had already been sold to William Cox, a lumber dealer, and that my agreement with Nugent was worthless. The Phillies were sold to Cox by Frick for about half what I had been willing to pay.

Word reached me soon enough that Frick was bragging all over the baseball world—strictly off the record, of course—about how he had stopped me from contaminating the league. That was my first direct encounter with Mr. Frick.

There is a suspicion, I suppose, that if I tried to buy the Phillies and stock it with Negro players, it was only because, showman that I am—promoter, con man, knave—I was grabbing for the quick and easy publicity and for the quick and easy way to rebuild a hopeless team. I am not going to suggest that I was innocent on either count.

On the other hand, I had no particular feeling about making it either an all-Negro team or not an all-Negro team. The one thing I did know was that I was not going to set up any quota system—a principle which cost me my original backer. As always, I was operating from a short bankroll. The most obvious backer, it seemed to me, was CIO, which had just begun a campaign to organize Negro workers in the South.

CIO was ready and eager to give me all the financing I needed. The money, in fact, was already escrowed when the CIO official I was dealing with asked for my assurance that there would always be a mixed team on the field. (I don't like to duck names, but there was a promise from the beginning of the negotiations that his name would not enter into any of the publicity.) The only assurance I am willing to give anybody, ever, is that I will try to put the best possible team on the field.

I had another potential—and logical—backer, Phillies Cigars, who had already indicated a willingness to bankroll me. Ford Frick lowered the boom.

What offends me about prejudice, I think, is that it assumes a totally unwarranted superiority. For as long as I can remember I have felt vaguely uneasy when anybody tells me an anti-Negro or anti-Semitic or anti-Catholic joke. It only takes one leg, you know, to walk away.

"We Doan Need No Niggers Here"

Roger Kahn

◆ ◆ ◆

By 1947, when Jackie Robinson broke the major league color barrier, the Phillies, led by manager Ben Chapman (from Alabama), greeted him early in the season during a Phillies–Dodgers series with such an ugly example of bench jockeying that, wrote Jules Tygiel in Baseball's Great Experiment *(1983, Oxford), it "exceeded even baseball's broadly defined sense of propriety." The facts of the incident, which came out just as St. Louis players were allegedly planning their own boycott against Robinson, have been surprisingly glossed over through the years. (The film* The Jackie Robinson Story *depicts rival players goading Robinson with a watermelon or shoeshine box, scenes that today come off like outtakes from an Ed Wood film.) Roger Kahn, in his book* The Era: 1947– 1957, When the Yankees, the Giants, and the Dodgers Ruled the World *(1993, Ticknor and Fields), wanted to write a subjective history of the 1947–57 seasons that would also attempt to set the record straight, rather than leave so many things off the record, as they were during the era. Here, then, is the Chapman–Robinson affair the way it actually happened and almost half a century later in retrospect.*

O n April 22, a clear, cold day—the temperature never rose above 45 degrees—the Philadelphia Phillies came to Ebbets Field to start a three-game series. Ben Chapman, born in Tennessee and raised in Alabama, was the manager of the Phillies, a thick-browed, volatile character with a tumultuous history. He played outfield for the Yankees during the early 1930s, batting as high as .316 and stealing sixty-one bases in a single season. Like anyone else, he made bad plays from time to time and when he did, the fans at Yankee Stadium sometimes jeered. Most ballplayers ignore hoots. Chapman took a different route. Jeered by Yankee fans in the Bronx one day in 1932, he turned to the grandstand and shouted: "Fucking Jew bastards."

His intemperance persisted. Fans complained to the Yankee management, and at length, in 1936, the Yankees traded Chapman to Washington for another outfielder, Alvin "Jake" Powell.* Chapman went from Washington to the Red Sox to the Indians to the White Sox, before dropping out of the major leagues. Late in World War II, when the military had claimed the best ballplayers—Greenberg, DiMaggio, Musial, Williams—Chapman signed with a weak Dodger team as a backup outfielder and sometime pitcher. The Phillies hired him to manage in 1945.

If Chapman disliked Jews, and he did dislike Jews, he *hated* "nigras." As the Dodger–Phillies game began, Chapman's strong, carrying drawl rose from the visiting dugout.

"Hey you, there. Snowflake. Yeah, you. You heah me. When did they let you outa the jungle . . .

"Hey, we doan need no niggers here . . .

"Hey, black boy. You like white poontang, black boy? You like white pussy? Which one o' the white boys' wives are you fucking tonight?"

Usually in baseball, even crude assaults give rise to back and forth banter. None was forthcoming in Ebbets Field that chilly April day. The Dodgers, southern and northern Dodgers, Dixie Walker and Carl Furillo, Pee Wee Reese and Spider Jorgensen, were shocked. Like Robinson, they sat in silence.

Lee Handley, Ben Chapman's third baseman, later made it a point to seek out Robinson. He said quietly, "I'm sorry. I want you to know that stuff doesn't go for me." Handley was the first opposing major leaguer to treat Robinson as a man.

Robinson remembered Lee Handley, out of Clarion, Iowa, for the rest of his life But he could no more respond to Handley at the time

*Powell himself was no peony. Off season, he told reporters at his first Yankee press conference, he worked as a cop in Toledo, Ohio. When asked specifically what he did on the Toledo police force, Powell told the New York press "I hit niggers over the head with my nightstick."

than he could respond to Ben Chapman. He thought of the many times he had been told that he *had* to turn the other cheek. But, Robinson asked himself, do I really have to live a sermon?

Years later, when we were working up a story on bigotry for *Our Sports*, a magazine in which he had invested, Robinson recalled his reactions to Ben Chapman in the Golgotha of that clear, cold April day.

"I don't remember everything they shouted. Probably just as well. My wife, Rae, she's into psychology. She says that some things that are too upsetting, you make yourself forget."

Although Robinson could not or would not recount all that he heard, he vividly remembered his emotions. "All my life I've been a proud guy. I won't sit in the back of a bus. If you call me nigger or boy, I want to tear your throat out. I'm a proud guy.

"So there I am in Brooklyn, which is supposed to be the Promised Land, and I'm hearing the worst garbage I ever heard in my whole life, counting the streets, counting the army, but I've sworn to Mr. Rickey that I won't fight back.

"It's Chapman and some of the Phillies ballplayers, and I set my face and I say goddamn, I'm supposed to ignore 'em and just play ball.

"So I play ball, but they don't stop. Jungle bunny. Snowflake. I start breathing hard. I'm just playing ball. I'm doing my job. I'm a good ballplayer. Deep down, I've been thinking, people will see I'm a good ballplayer and they'll see I'm black and they'll put that together. A black guy's a good ballplayer. A black guy can be a good guy.

"But that's not happening. What do the Phillies want from me? What did I ever do to them? What does Mr. Rickey want? I'm in great shape. I'm playing hard. I'm not sassing anybody. What the hell does everybody want from me?

"All of a sudden I thought, the hell with this. This isn't me. They're making me be some crazy pacifist black freak. Hell, no. Hell, no. I'm going back to being myself. Right now. I'm going into the Phillie dugout and grab one of those white sons of bitches and smash his fucking teeth and walk away. Walk away from this ballpark. Walk away from baseball.

"I thought some more. This didn't take as long in my head as it takes to tell you, Rog. I thought of Mr. Rickey and Rae and my baby son.

Standing on that ballfield in Brooklyn, standing still, I had come to a crossroads.

"For a second I felt, this is it. I'm cracking up.

"But wait, wait, wait. Am I gonna give Ben Chapman that satisfaction . . ."

In the eighth inning Robinson singled up the middle. Then he stole second base. When Andy Seminick's throw bounced into center field, Robinson ran on to third. Gene Hermanski singled to right. That was the run. There weren't any more. The Dodgers defeated the Phillies, 1 to 0, on Robinson's run.

Robinson took the subway back to the McAlpin Hotel on 34th Street in Manhattan, where he lived while looking for an apartment. Rachel cooked dinner on an electric hotplate. The baby, Jack Roosevelt Robinson, Jr., had a cold and the couple stayed up much of the night trying to help their child sleep.

At Ebbets Field the next day, Robinson walked up to bat in the first inning feeling better than he had the day before.

"Hey, Jungle Bunny," Ben Chapman shouted. "You go out and get yo-sef some white pussy last night?"

Stanky and a few other ballplayers told newspapermen what was going on. Branch Rickey, informed by his new manager, Burt Shotton, telephoned the commissioner, Happy Chandler. Something had to be done, Rickey said, in the name of decency.

Chandler had suspended Leo Durocher for a year, ostensibly for living loosely. What punishment, then, would be appropriate for William Benjamin Chapman, Klansman without a hood?

Chandler considered at length. Then he ordered Chapman to grant an interview to Wendell Smith, a congenial black sportswriter for the black newspaper the *Pittsburgh Courier.*

No suspension. Not even a fine. Just a suggestion that Chapman ease up and an order that he spend one hour in civil conversation with a Negro.

Dan Parker wrote a column in the *Daily Mirror* criticizing Chapman's "guttersnipe" language. But generally the press persisted in its belligerent neutrality. This account, from *The Sporting News* of May 7, 1947, is characteristic:

Jackie Robinson's position in the major leagues and the manner in which he will be treated by the Philadelphia Phillies was clarified in a straight from the shoulder interview from Ben Chapman. . . .

"We treat Robinson the same as we do Hank Greenberg of the Pirates, Clint Hartung of the Giants, Connie Ryan of the Braves," Chapman said.

"When I came into the big leagues, pitchers threw at me, dusted me off, pegged at my head, my legs. I was dangerous.

"Robinson can run. He can bunt. He's dangerous.

"When I came into the league, they wanted to see if I would lose my temper and forget to play ball. They tried to break my morale. They played baseball for keeps. That's the way we're going to play with Robinson.

"If Robinson has the stuff, he'll be accepted in baseball, the same as the Sullivans and the Grodzickis. All I expect him to do is prove it. Let's get the chips off our shoulders and play ball."

I mean to suggest that at this point, early in the 1947 season, the issue of Robinson's success—the question of integrated baseball—was seriously in doubt. (So, indeed, was Robinson's mental health.) Oddly, his most vociferous ballfield supporter at that time was Eddie Stanky, the second baseman from Philadelphia who had moved to Mobile and who years later himself needled Robinson in unpleasant ways. But in May 1947 something deep and good was touched within Eddie Stanky, a combative, thin-lipped, verbal ballplayer with limited physical skills and limitless fire. "Those guys [the Phillies] are a disgrace," Stanky told the New York newspapermen. "They know Robinson can't fight back. There isn't one of them who has the guts of a louse." After Chapman's behavior moved Stanky to Jackie Robinson's side, other Dodgers, notably Pee Wee Reese, quickly followed. Some—Bobby Bragan, Hugh Casey, Cookie Lavagetto, and Dixie Walker—did not.

The issue still was in doubt. Herb Pennock, the general manager of the Phillies, had been the leading left-handed pitcher on the 1927 New York Yankees, a team that remains the benchmark of baseball excellence. Tall, lean, dignified, Pennock was nicknamed "The Squire of Kennett Square," after the Pennsylvania town where he was born.

The Dodgers were scheduled to begin a series in Philadelphia on

May 9 and Pennock telephoned Branch Rickey to impose conditions. "You just can't bring the nigger here with the rest of your team, Branch," Pennock said. "We're not ready for that sort of thing yet in Philadelphia. We won't be able to take the field [at Shibe Park] against your Brooklyn team, if that boy is in uniform."

Major league rules require that both sides field a team for every scheduled game. Should one side fail to appear, the other team is awarded victory by forfeit. The score of a forfeit is recorded as 9 to 0.

"Very well, Herbert," Rickey said, "if you don't field a team and we must claim the game, 9 to 0, we will do just that, I assure you."

Rickey hung up. Pennock was not through making mischief. When the Dodgers arrived at the 30th Street Station in Philadelphia and took taxis to the Benjamin Franklin Hotel on the morning of May 9, they were turned away in the lobby. Pennock and his employers had spoken to the hotel owners. The hotel would take "no ballclub nigras." Harold Parrott, the Dodgers' toothy traveling secretary, had to shuttle about Philadelphia for hours before he found a hotel—the Warwick—willing to accommodate the team. Until then, the Dodgers were considering commuting for the series. Recalling that Philadelphia story, Parrott summed up: "Talk about brotherly love."

Rickey, not satisfied with Ben Chapman's feathery reprimand, continued to press Commissioner Chandler for significant action. Chandler responded by hiring Jack Demoise, a former FBI agent, to travel the National League "and look for troublemakers." Then, finally, the commissioner telephoned Pennock. "If you move in on Robinson," Chandler said, "I'll move in on you."

Chapman himself was slow recognizing the new thrust of things. Gene Hermanski, a Dodger outfielder for seven seasons, is white-haired now, but so vigorous and feisty in his seventies that someone describes him as a "walking advertisement *against* Grecian Formula" (a popular over-the-counter product that turns white hair dark). Hermanski, who was born in Pittsfield, Massachusetts, and resides in central New Jersey, says, as so many old Dodgers do, "Jackie Robinson was a great man."

"Philadelphia, Gene," I say. "Do you remember Philadelphia, 1947?"

Hermanski's eyes light. "That bastard Chapman." Hermanski moves backwards on wings of memory. His eyes are burning now.

In Philadelphia, first game there, during pregame warm-ups, Chapman started shouting again. But not at Robinson this time. "Hey, Pee Wee," Chapman yelled. "Yeah, you. Reese. How ya like playin' with a fuckin' nigger?"

Reese ignored Chapman, who shouted the question again. And yet a third time.

Reese stopped picking up ground balls and jogged over to Robinson at first base. Then, staring into the Philadelphia dugout, Reese put an arm around Jackie Robinson's shoulders.

"Pee Wee didn't say a word," Gene Hermanski remembers. "But Chapman had his answer."

Later that day or early the next, someone prominent in baseball placed a long-distance telephone call to Chapman. (Commissioner Chandler took credit for the call three or four decades later, but Chandler was a frightfully unreliable source.) The telephone call to Chapman probably came from Ford Frick, the president of the National League, or from one of Frick's assistants.

The sense of the call was this: Chapman's behavior was out of line. It had to stop. On moral grounds and on *practical* grounds as well.

Walter Winchell, the famous gossip columnist, had picked up reports on Chapman's conduct. He was telling flunkies at the Stork Club in New York that he was going to "use the column to get Chapman out of baseball. I'll nail him on my radio show, too. I'm gonna make a *big hit* on that *bigot*."

The caller told Ben Chapman that organized baseball would not tolerate syndicated embarrassment. If Chapman intended to keep his job, he had better curb his tongue immediately. An apology would not be out of line.

Cornered, Chapman sent word to Robinson before the next day's ballgame. He would like to start fresh. Maybe he *had* been kinda loud. Would Robinson pose with him for newspaper photographers?

In a remarkably forgiving mood, Robinson agreed. The surviving prints show each man looking as though he'd like to be ten thousand miles away, but after that Chapman never again dared to bait Jackie Robinson or Pee Wee Reese or any others among the athletes Branch Rickey proudly called in subsequent years "my ferocious gentlemen."

Phillies Warned on "Riding" Jackie

Wendell Smith

◆ ◆ ◆

The Chapman affair caused a stir throughout the baseball world, not the least of which occurred in the pages of the black newspapers. Hall-of-Fame sportswriter Wendell Smith, sports editor of the Pittsburgh Courier *(and a leading player in baseball integration), remained on top of the story. In addition to being a model news story, the piece included here is infused with Smith's crusading spirit and his sense that the issues involved here far transcend the ballfield. Like Jackie Robinson, Smith did not want to do anything that would jeopardize Branch Rickey's "experiment." As for the Philadelphia bench jockeys, no longer allowed to use racial epithets, they aimed bats at Robinson's head and made gunlike sounds.*

Big league teams can "ride" Jackie Robinson if they want to . . . but not on the basis of his race!

That is the substance of an order Commissioner A. B. (Happy) Chandler handed down to the Philadelphia Phillies last week after he had received a report that Manager Ben Chapman and his players had been hurling "profane and derogatory" remarks at the Brooklyn Dodger's first baseman from the bench.

The Commissioner handed down the ultimatum soon after The Pittsburgh Courier had exposed the conduct of the Phillies during their recent series with the Dodgers in Brooklyn. Jack Saunders of The Courier's Philadelphia office brought the "issue" to a head last Tuesday during an exclusive interview with Chapman and revealed that the Philadelphia pilot, who hails from Alabama, had instructed the Phillies to "ride Robinson unmercifully."

Chapman's Instructions

Saunders interviewed Chapman last week in Philadelphia and the big league manager admitted that he had instructed his "bench-jockeys" to "give it to" Robinson without restraint. He said he told his players to call Robinson everything and anything they wanted to. He assured them that they had his unswerving support.

The Pittsburgh Courier learned Monday morning, however, that soon after the story was published, Commissioner Chandler cracked down on the fiery Phillies and issued an order restraining them from using "vicious un-American racial remarks" in their efforts to "upset" Jackie.

During an interview by long-distance telephone Monday evening, Walter Mulbry, secretary-treasurer of the commissioner's office, told The Pittsburgh Courier that the Commissioner had instructed the Phillies to stop slurring the Negro first baseman on the basis of his color.

Chandler Was Firm

Commissioner Chandler was away from his office on a routine check-up of minor league operations and was not available when the Courier called his Cincinatti office. Mr. Mulbry, however, explained that he could talk for the Commissioner and then revealed that orders had already been passed down to the Phillies.

"As soon as Commissioner Chandler heard of the Phillies' alleged name-calling," Mr. Mulbry said, "he contacted Herb Pennock, general manager of the Philadelphia club, and told him that his office would not tolerate that kind of "bench-riding."

"The Commissioner was very emphatic about it, too," he assured The

Courier. "He told Mr. Pennock that he had received a number of reports to the effect that the Philadelphia team had not stopped at merely riding Robinson, but that they had been insulting him on the basis of his race. Mr. Chandler said that such riding was contrary to the concepts of big league baseball, and Americanism as well."

Mr. Mulbry further stated that the Commissioner instructed Pennock just how far he "expected the team to go in their 'riding' campaigns."

Expects No Favors

"Mr. Chandler said that no favors should be granted Robinson from the bench," Mr. Mulbry stated, "but there is a limit to everything and he thought that hurling racial epithets was beyond that limit. The Commissioner also said that if the Phillies continued their 'tirade,' he'd be forced to take more drastic action."

Chandler's action marks the first time in the history of organized baseball that the commissioner has taken action in matters of a racial nature. During the reign of the late Commissioner Landis it was not necessary, of course, because there were no Negroes in the majors. However, Landis was confronted many times with the problem of breaking down the barrier against Negro players and in most instances was evasive.

Chandler, however, seems to have taken the bull by the horns and apparently will not let other players and managers try to get Robinson's 'goat' by calling him names reflecting on his race. It is one of the most momentous steps he has taken since he took over the stormy office of commissioner.

In commenting on Chandler's action, Mr. Mulbry said: "I suppose some people will think that this action was taken because of Walter Winchell's bristling remarks about the Phillies' treatment of Robinson during his Sunday night radio braodcast. But I assure you that he contacted the Phillies at least three days before that. He just didn't make the matter a public affair, that's all."

No Protest

Mr. Mulbry said that the commissioner did not take action because a formal protest had not been filed in his office.

"The Commissioner heard that the Phillies had been riding Robinson on the basis of his race. One fan, for instance, wrote him and alleged that the Phillies were insulting Robinson. He did not receive a protest from the Dodgers or anyone else officially connected with the game. He simply took it upon himself to jump into the matter on his own."

Chandler's surprising and welcomed action means that the Phillies and all other clubs will have to 'tone down' their remarks to Robinson and definitely cannot make uncomplimentary remarks about his race when 'riding' him from the bench.

Major League "Dozens" Playing

Dan Burley

◆ ◆ ◆

In the pages of the Amsterdam News, *another black newspaper, sports editor Dan Burley offered a contrary point of view on the Chapman–Robinson affair. In today's era of political correctness and hate-speech codes on college campuses, it might be difficult for Burley to sell his point that "the word has no power of itself to hurt." But he made the compelling argument that Robinson's own actions on the ballfield would ultimately determine his true value and character and those of whoever might come after him. In that respect Burley has not been proven wrong.*

I'll throw this one out and then duck. It's about the Ben Chapman—Jackie Robinson yow-yow. You know the situation in which Chapman, the Phillies manager, told his charges to "ride" Jackie from the bench every chance they got and to do it with no holds barred. Ben, incidentally, is from Alabama, and wanted it laid on Jackie good and heavy, the explosive results of which brought words of wisdom from Commissioner Happy Chandler's office. Happy, you might recall, is a Kentuckian. Well, it seems that Chapman tried to explain to Dan Parker and the other scriveners who discovered the dastardly plot, that it was a prerogative of baseball big leaguers to "ride" everybody on an opposing team, and to "ride" them in any manner possible, including those that are legitimate.

Prior to 1947, such riding was confined to the racial distinctions whites were making among themselves. Thus, Italian players got it in the neck as did Irish and the few Jews who are in the majors. In other words, ballplayers played the "dozens" and made an art of it. The

From the *Amsterdam News*, June 25, 1947. Reprinted by permission.

dozens, if you don't know what is meant by the term, can be played anywhere and heard anywhere, but Uptown and in the Harlems throughout the land, the "dozens" is an art and the practitioners are many and varied. The "dozens" then, is a manner of serious and derogatory discussion of ancestry with all the florid word extravaganzas of which one can conceive.

With Jackie Robinson in the majors, the complexion changed, and Ben Chapman was the first to publicly and openly decide that Robinson was suited for a baptism in the "dozens" as played by the major leaguers. Of course, "dozens" playing will get your head whipped in most circles, since few like disparaging remarks made about their parents by people they don't know. Now, the idea of putting Jackie in the major league "dozens" revolved mainly about his color, and it was there that Chapman hit on a splendid method of "riding" the Brooklyn Dodger first sacker. For a less handy person than Robinson, such "dozens" playing would be highly likely to be upsetting and might even bring about a clash if the equilibrium of the player in question is shaky. And Robinson's mental balance was supposed to be at the snapping point, what with all the responsibility shoved onto his shoulders. The Phillies opened on Jackie with all guns blazing and the logical response would have been for Jackie to run over to the Phillies' dugout and hit somebody in the jaw. He didn't, however, and Parker and others took up the matter and urged a stop before it got too far.

So widespread was public reaction to Chapman's program that Ben called it off, what with the front office hollering and the fans booing. Now, Chapman speaks up again, declaring that Robinson has not only made the major league grade, but was the principal figure in the Brooklyn drive toward a pennant. Said Ben: "He is a major leaguer in every respect. He can run, he can hit, he is fast, he is quick with the ball—and his fine base-running keeps the other team in an uproar."

You can write your own opinion about these remarks by Chapman. It might be pointed out that Ben is trying to get some of the publicity so richly given big Hank Greenberg, when he encouraged Jackie by identifying the Robinson attempt to make good with what he, Greenberg, had to take before he was accepted as a ballplayer. Chapman's opinion might be accepted tongue-in-the-cheek in light of what Ben had to say when he was busy siccing his players on Jackie and letting them put him in the "dozens" with impunity. However, in talking about the major league "dozens," it could be said that the emphasis laid on race and color and not ancestry, as might be the case where all Negro players were involved. The reason I'm pitching this up and getting set to duck, is that Chapman might be right after all. If they make fun of Greenberg, razzed the late Tony Lazzeri and made life holy hell for all racial stocks, why does Jackie have to be exempted? Robinson is up there purely on his own.

The whole idea from the beginning was to divorce him from racial responsibilities and to allow him to sail on baseball's unchartered-for-a-Negro sea without strings attached. In such a condition, Robinson would necessarily run into a lot of anti-black shoals. He ran into 'em in Florida when the Dodgers trained there. He encounters them in many places, and expects to run into many, many more.

I hold that one of the biggest obstacles to full participation by us in what benefits there may be under democracy, will be removed or reduced when we learn not to flinch at the word we all hate so thoroughly that others use to describe us and embarrass us. Yep, I mean the word, "nigger." Now, I'm the first to smack somebody in the kisser if they had the effrontery to call me one. So would you. But, that doesn't take away from the fact that the word has no power of itself to hurt. If we stopped letting it make us feel so badly or inferior, we would overcome a major barrier toward our advancement. Perhaps this isn't as clear as it should be. I'll try it from this angle: If a guy hits you, shoots you, refuses to let you in out of the rain or gets you put in jail, he's doing something tangible to hurt you. If he calls you out of name, as all of us frequently call one another, nothing is expended but the air used to form the words. If we worry too much over the air thus used, we can't play the game as in the case of Jackie.

Suppose Jack Johnson, when he was climbing toward the world heavyweight championship, had been deterred by what the fans, those in the boxing world and the newspapers, called him? And don't worry. They called him a thousand different kinds of you-know-what. But, Jack learned early what they called him didn't count. All that mattered was what happened once he got into the ring with 'em. And also, according to Jack, is how they paid off—a whole lot or a whole little. Sam Langford was called "The Boston Tarbaby," as a lot of old timers will recall, but that didn't keep him from being the terror of his day. Fritz Pollard was called a lot of you-know-what I'm talking about: So were Paul Robeson, Duke Slater, Rube Foster, Eddie Tolan, Sol Butler, Harry Wills, Charley West and others who were out there on the racial firing line in the early days of Negro participation in organized sports. While none of 'em liked being called you-know-what and while none would condone such descriptions, none have come up with scars to prove the word left them injured.

Unwittingly, Ben Chapman might have brought the problem out into the open, and to have centered the spotlight on a condition that should be attacked from another angle. Maybe, by his ordering of the Phillies to call Jackie Robinson such names, the proof has come out all the stronger that a mere word or term can't hurt, and also that the payoff is whether Robinson can run, field, hit, use his head and play ball like a major leaguer. The boys who are sure to follow Robinson in the big show will have to be big enough to shake off the discomfort at being called something they don't like, and to take such terms in stride, and to concentrate on being a great player, as in Robinson, and as are Greenberg, the Italians, the Poles, the Irish, the Germans, the Hungarians, the Czechs, the French, the Swedes, the Bohemians and others who have made baseball a racial polyglot of personalities, religion, race and background.

Johnny Kennedy

Claude E. Harrison, Jr.

◆ ◆ ◆

Contrary to popular belief, John Kennedy was not the first African American to be signed by the Phillies. (That distinction, as Ed Linn notes [see p. 109], belongs to Teddy Washington, who was signed in 1952, and two more black players were inked to contracts before Kennedy.) But Kennedy, signed in 1956, was the first black to make the squad heading north from spring training in Clearwater, Florida. Kennedy was a small-ticket item in the mainstream newspapers, but big news in the local black press. Philadelphia Tribune *sports columnist Claude Harrison was overly optimistic about Kennedy's chances and about the recent signings of local black ballplayers, including Eddie Logan, better known as a high school football star. Logan never made the team, and Kennedy played in a total of five games before being sent back down, never to be heard from again. Chico Fernandez, a light-skinned Cuban acquired from the Dodgers (for a small chunk of a minor league franchise), became the first black to play in a regular-season game for the Phillies, but he, too, never panned out. Not until Dick Allen surfaced in 1964 would the Phillies have a black player of the caliber of a Lou Brock, Frank Robinson, or Henry Aaron. But, then again, perhaps none of those men before him, like the black Philadelphia Stars of old, really ever had much of a chance.*

Bill Yancey, the Phillie baseball scout who came up with John Kennedy, is more than pleased with the reports coming out of Clearwater, Fla., the Phils' spring training base, about young Kennedy. Bill never talks too much about Kennedy's future, because as he puts it, "all I know is what I read in the papers." But on the other hand he did have something to say about Eddie Logan, the former Ridley Township

From the *Philadelphia Tribune*, April 13, 1957. Reprinted by permission.

High football and track star, who topped all of the Phillies' farm hands with a .384 average at Class D level in 1956. Logan, along with Kennedy, was given the once over at the Phillies' rookie training school during March. However, the school teachers sent Logan back to the minors and as you know held Kennedy over to train with the parent club.

Eddie, now listed on Schenectady's roster, has been shifted from the outfield to first base, where he shouldn't be in the position of making too many throws. It is said that Logan's "bad" arm is the governing factor keeping him out of the majors. On this subject Yancy had this to say, "Logan could win more games with his bat than he would lose with his arm." So, if and when Eddie can master first base he may be able to speed up his trip to the big league.

Back to Kennedy again. What we would like to know is what does he have to do in order to prove he's major league material. At the beginning of the season word came out of Clearwater that he couldn't field. Yet he has made only one blunder. While on the other hand the player they paid $75,000 for makes two in one day. John's batting of .333 is second highest for the club.

What more can the Phils ask? Maybe he should pull some of Ozark Ike's stunts. At one time a Phillie official said "If and when we do make a trade for a shortstop he will have to take the job away from Kennedy." But as of now John hasn't been in a position to defend his claim to the job.

If I were a betting man I would take all comers that Kennedy will have the job in his hip pocket by mid-July if not sooner. What's more if things don't go right at the plate with the bat swingers and first base, Eddie Logan may be called up.

Eddie Waitkus

Ira Berkow

◆ ◆ ◆

No single Phillies incident has become as much a part of baseball lore as the Eddie Waitkus shooting in 1949. No incident, except for the Black Sox scandal, has gone as quickly from front page news to baseball myth. The pathology of the assailant, Ruth Ann Steinhagen, became known to baseball fans with the publication of "A Report to Felony Court" by the chief of the county behavior clinic in Charles Einstein's first Fireside Book of Baseball *(1956, Simon and Schuster). Waitkus recovered to play in the 1950 World Series but, as Ira Berkow notes, was never the same person afterward. Steinhagen was out on the streets by the time Einstein's book was published. Berkow not only describes the Waitkus shooting but also explains what it meant to him personally as "a boy growing up in Chicago," where it happened.*

I don't remember what I did or even what I thought when I heard about the shooting, but I know I have never forgotten it.

The bullet that tore through the chest of Eddie Waitkus, the first baseman for the Philadelphia Phillies, ripped a hole through my idea—a nine-year-old boy's fantasy notion—that sports was not a part of the real world, and that athletes were greater than mere mortals.

The rifle shot that exploded in that hotel room that night in Chicago exploded the following day on the front pages of newspapers all across the country.

The shooting remains with us even though it happened so many years ago, on that warm, quiet night of June 14, 1949. The incident is now a part not only of our national history, but it provided a scene in our literature, and our print and celluloid mythology. In one of the most dramatic moments in the *The Natural*, a novel by Bernard Malamud, published in 1952, and which years later was made into a Hollywood motion picture starring Robert Redford, an unsuspecting major league baseball player is shot in a hotel room by a woman wearing a dark veil.

I believe I felt closer to it than many, and closer, oddly, to Waitkus, though, of course, I didn't know him personally.

I was a boy growing up in Chicago, living several miles away from Wrigley Field, and from the Edgewater Beach Hotel, that sprawling, pink, castlelike building on Lake Shore Drive, where Waitkus was shot.

I went to the Cub games regularly with my friends, having only about a year before discovered baseball, and like so many American boys, having the game and its players and the legends swiftly sinking deep into my consciousness, and my heart.

I also played first base in sandlot games. In my neighborhood, it seemed that first base was less than a glamorous position. It wasn't pitcher, say, or shortstop or center field. And being younger than most of the guys I played with—but tall for my age—I gravitated, or possibly was shunted, to first.

In 1948, the Cubs had an excellent first baseman named Eddie Waitkus, who would be traded that winter to the Phillies. The Cubs were always trading some of their best players, which is how they managed to remain such a miserable team for so long, and why, after all these years, they continue to cause their passionate fans so much grief.

Waitkus, meanwhile, had a cool and buttery style around the bag. He was left-handed and I was a righty, but I still tried to imitate his wonderful and yet almost comical little midair jitterbug of stretching, catching the ball, and toeing the base all in one smooth motion. He was six feet tall, lean, with sharp Slavic features, and as I recall from waiting with my friends after games at Wrigley Field for the players to emerge from the clubhouse, with warm, rather slanted eyes.

The players came out all slicked-back hair and deific. They signed autographs, or didn't, hurrying and pushing through the crowd. I remember Waitkus being fairly patient. I admired him, but I was hardly alone. l found out later that a Chicago teenager, someone I assume stood in some of those crowds with me waiting for the players after games, was also very fond of him but in a totally different way. Her name was Ruth Ann Steinhagen.

She talked about Waitkus constantly, dreamed about him, even built a little shrine in her bedroom with newspaper photos of him. In a report later prepared by the chief of the Cook County behavioral clinic in response to an order from the felony court, which found her deranged, she admitted:

"As time went on I just became nuttier and nuttier about the guy, and I knew I would never get to know him in a normal way . . . and if I can't have him, nobody else can. And I then decided I would kill him."

Steinhagen, age nineteen, purchased a secondhand rifle, checked into a room at the Edgewater Beach, where Waitkus was staying with the Phillies during a series against the Cubs, and sent a message to the front desk for Waitkus.

The message said that a woman named Ruth Ann Burns wished to see him in her room—Room 1297-A. Steinhagen had decided to use a pseudonym, but typically strange, only for her last name. The message added that it was about "something important." The time was close to midnight. Waitkus, a bachelor, decided to go up to her room to see what this mystery was all about.

Decades later, when writing about the incident, I received a letter from Edward (Ted) Waitkus, Jr., a lawyer in Boulder, Colorado, and we subsequently spoke on the phone.

"My dad was an easy-going, trusting guy at the time, and kind of flippant with women," recalled Ted Waitkus. "He walked into her room and said something like, 'Well, babe, what's happening?' He didn't know anything about her, that she was so crazy about him she even learned Lithuanian, which was Dad's heritage. I guess she was a fanatic in the way the guy who shot John Lennon was. Then she went into a closet, took out the .22, and shot him. The first thing he said was, 'Why'd you do that?' "

His father told him that it was hard to believe that "a little bullet could make you feel as though six men had slammed you against the wall."

Waitkus, Jr., added that his father's recovery from the shooting was "miraculous." Eddie Waitkus returned the next season, played the entire 154-game schedule for the Phillies, the team nicknamed "The Whiz Kids" that year, won Comeback-of-the-Year honors, and played in the World Series. In the Series, Waitkus batted a respectable .267, slightly down from the .284 average during the regular season, and the .306 he was hitting—and incidentally, leading in the all-star-game balloting at the time—when he was shot, some sixteen months earlier. The Phillies lost to the Yankees in four straight games, but Waitkus told his son that "the World Series was the high point of my career."

"The shooting changed my father a great deal, as you might imagine," said Ted Waitkus. "Before, he was a very outgoing person. Then he became paranoid about meeting new people, and pretty much even stopped going out drinking with his teammates, which is what I guess they did in those days.

"When she was about to be released from the mental hospital after only a few years—they said she had fully recovered—my father and my family fought to keep her in. My father feared for his life."

Despite the pleas, Ruth Ann Steinhagen was released; Waitkus never heard from her again.

Waitkus was sold by the Phillies to the Orioles in 1954, then sent back to the Phillies midway through the 1955 season. He retired as an active player after that season, having compiled a .285 batting average during his eleven-year major league career.

He had got married and had two children, a daughter and a son. Born and raised in the Boston area himself, Waitkus now remained there, working summers as an instructor at Ted Williams's baseball camp. Waitkus made banquet talks, collected his baseball pension, and, his sister, Stella Kasperwicz, would recall, "pretty much took it easy."

"After baseball," said Ted Waitkus, "Dad had some trouble finding himself."

On the morning of September 16, 1972—a little more than twenty-three years after the shooting—I opened the *New York Times* and happened to run across a modest-sized obituary notice on Edward Stephen Waitkus, former major league baseball player. He was dead at age fifty-three.

"Different doctors through the years have expressed the theory that the stress of the shooting, combined with the four operations, allowed the cancer to take hold," said Ted Waitkus. "Cancer of the lung or esophagus can take up to twenty years or more to be fatal. My dad was never diagnosed as having cancer. It wasn't until after the autopsy that this came out. So I think Ruth Steinhagen was more successful than she thought."

I remember reading the Waitkus obituary and thinking how the shooting was the beginning of a heightened awareness for me of senseless violence and tragedy. Many more times would I experience that terrible feeling in the pit of my stomach of helplessness and rage. It was there after the murders of John Kennedy and Robert Kennedy and Martin Luther King, and when I learned of the sniper Whitman, the malevolent Manson, and the terrible slaughter in Vietnam. And again, only weeks before the death of Waitkus. I had recently returned from Munich, from covering the 1972 Olympics, where the eleven Israelis had only recently been killed in the most grotesque fashion.

In the *Times* obituary on Waitkus it noted that he died in the Veterans Administration Hospital in Boston (Waitkus had served four years in the military during World War II). Through the hospital I was able to reach Waitkus's sister.

Mrs. Kasperwicz told me that Eddie had retained an interest in sports and had watched the Olympics and talked about the Arab terrorists who had shot the Israelis.

"Eddie thought it was awful," she recalled. "He said that none of us will ever be the same because of it."

I understood, I told her. I said I also had felt that way about a similar incident that had occurred many years before, when I was a boy growing up in Chicago.

The Whiz Kids Come of Age

Bob Stevens

◆ ◆ ◆

The Carpenter regime finally hit pay dirt in 1950 when the Phillies won their first pennant in thirty-five years. It would take thirty years to win another, but the early 1950s spelled hope for a resurgent franchise. The story of Dick Sisler's home run, Richie Ashburn's throw, and Robin Roberts's gutsy pitching in the game that clinched the pennant has been told and retold in many different ways, but Bob Stevens of the San Francisco Chronicle *wrote what many of his peers thought was the best account of the game at the time—and also one of the funniest. The reference to Seals Stadium might escape modern readers; Joe Di-Maggio played minor league ball there for the San Francisco Seals, a venerable Pacific Coast League franchise, and the Giants occupied it in 1957 while Candlestick Park was being built.*

The agonizing growing pains that were felt round the world were finally ended here today, and the patient is delirious. The Philadelphia Phillies, the incredible Whiz Kids, today became of age.

After a tortuous, pain-wracked, blood-letting final two weeks of a National League stretch run that will never, no never, be forgotten, the beardless wonders of Eddie Sawyer tacked the Phillies' first pennant to the mast in 35 years by prevailing over the Brooklyn Dodgers, 4–1, in ten innings.

It wasn't an ordinary game of baseball. It was terrific. Heart hurting and indescribably dramatic. It was youth, kid stuff, against a tooled, especially selected group of veterans from the Nation's greatest farming system that came out on top in a grim, last-game struggle for the pennant.

It left 35,073 people, jam-packed in this house of heroics, blunders and histrionics, limp with emotions, some sad, some maniacal as the loved and sentimentally favored Whiz Kids grew up.

And, it was done in manly fashion, muscularly, dramatically, conclusively.

With one away, runners on first and second, and the count against him, two and one, Dick Sisler, whose pappy, George, was the greatest first baseman of his day, became, at least for a fleeting, monumental moment, his equal by smashing his 13th home run into the left-field bleachers. It wound up 35 years of desperate building, 35 years of being ridiculed throughout the National League as the setups of all time, 35 years of fanciful dreaming.

They're toasting Sisler and the cherubic-faced Robin Roberts, one day into his 25th year, tonight throughout a Nation that takes its baseball more seriously than its politics.

Sisler delivered the coup de grace, a fancy way of saying the blow that killed father and stilled the waters of the Gowanus and ended one of the most courageous uphill struggles in baseball history. From nine games off the pace on September 12, the doughty, unbelievably audacious Dodgers cut steadily into the lead of the faltering, choking, stumbling Phils to come within one game, one pitch, actually, of forcing a play-off.

They didn't get it. Sisler and Roberts saw to that.

The drama, and it dripped, was crowded into the last of the ninth, when a colossal blunder wiped the Bums out of contention as surely as though they refused to take the field, and the top of the tenth, the pay-off panel.

But, let's crown the kids with the laurels of conquest, before hacking away at the disconsolate Dodgers who lost behind their 19-game winner, massive Don Newcombe.

Roberts, who becomes a 20-gamer today, opened the tenth with a single through the box and into center. Newcombe furiously pounded his glove in vexation, and Ralph Branca continued his frantic warming-up in the Bums' bull pen. Then, Eddie Waitkus, the narrow survivor of a love sick babe's bullet, looped a single to the feet of the diving Duke Snider and the kids started filing for scoring privileges.

Ritchie [*sic*] Ashburn, who had his moment in this great hour of Philadelphia triumph, tried to bunt the boys along, but Newcombe swallowed his grounder and fired to Billy Cox at third to nail Roberts, who came in on a wing, a prayer and a cloud of dust.

Newcombe, momentarily reprieved, breezed two strikes past the eager Sisler and the few Phil partisans who dared open their yaps in this land of Bum lovers, groaned audibly, and miserably. A ball, high, which Sisler started out after, then reconsidered, thudded into Catcher Roy Campanella's moist glove.

Six thousand dollars' worth of pitch was delivered then by the sweat-drenched Newcombe. It was a little high, a little on the faraway corner, and Sisler lashed out. The ball was met squarely, and the crowd hushed as it started its epic flight into left field. Cal Abrams backed into the wall, groping, clutching, jumping, impatiently, pitifully. Into the stands it disappeared, and Ebbets Field exploded. So did Philadelphia. And, so did Sisler.

Losing his dignity, Dick pogo-sticked down the line from first to second, waving his arms and screaming.

He rounded third base to cheers he'd never before heard, fell into the arms of his teammates at the plate, and went toward the dugout, there to shake hands and wink mischievously at his father, the great George of yesteryear.

Pappy didn't know whether to laugh or to cry. His son was a hero, but he got that way by beating Pappy's ball club, the Dodgers, for whom the elder Sisler works as a scout.

It was ironical, too, in another way. Accepted as the greatest first-baseman the game has ever known, George Sisler never made a World Series. Dick, the most successful son of an immortal in the business today, enters his second fall classic Wednesday when the New York Yankees rumble into Shibe Park. Dick first made it with the victorious St. Louis Cardinals in 1946.

After that blow the rest was anti-climactic. Roberts, now assured, poured the coal to Campanella and Pinch-hitters Jim Russell and Tommy Brown, and the growing pains were over. Win or lose to the Yankees, the Whiz kids are men!

Brooklyn could have forced the issue into a three-game play-off except for an ill-advised play by third-base Coach Milt Stock in the ninth, Roberts' worst, and near fatal frame. After Abrams walked, Pee Wee Reese, who collected three of the five hits off Roberts, including a home run for the Bums' only score, singled. Snider then slashed a scorcher into center, and Abrams was off and running.

Instead of holding at third Cal was waved on in and a perfect throw from Ashburn to Catcher Stan Lopata cut down Abrams without a slide. It would have been the winning tally. Had Stock held Abrams at third, the bases would have been loaded, none out, and all the Dodgers needed then was a fly to the outfield to clinch their eleventh consecutive victory in a breath-taking stretch drive.

As it was, it left first base open, and Jackie Robinson was deliberately walked, rejamming the paths. Carl Furillo fouled out limply to Waitkus close to the box seats back of first, and Gil Hodges lofted a routine fly to Del Ennis in right to close out the inning.

It closed out the Dodgers, 1950 vintage, too. And ended in failure a comeback that would have rivaled the incredible move from last to first by the Boston Braves of 1914 after July 4.

Both the Phils' and the Dodgers' only runs were tinged with cheapness. In the sixth, the kids broke out into a 1–0 lead when, after two were down, Sisler singled, and Ennis dittoed. Del's blow was a broken back liner into short center that fell in a human puddle formed by Snider, Robinson and Furillo. Puddin'-head Jones then slashed a nifty through the box past Newcombe to tally Sisler.

In the bottom of the sixth, the Bums came back. Reese leaned into an outside curve and swept it high into right field. The ball thudded against the screen, bounced down onto the signboards, teetered precariously on the ledge, and finally lodged there while Ennis insanely jumped up and down waiting for it to come down.

Ordinarily it would have rolled off and been nothing more damaging than a double. But, in Ebbets Field, they don't do things in routine fashion. That I know from past experiences in this madhouse of bat and ball.

The Phils offered a mild protest, but were overruled and that freak blow, poorly hit, but expertly placed, loomed larger and larger as this pennant battle progressed. In finale, it meant nothing more than the run that deprived Roberts, truly a great pitcher with courage to spare, of a shutout.

For those who see their baseball in the dimensions of Seals Stadium back home, Joe Grace would have had to come in to latch on to Reese's homer, and Sisler's would have landed just about where Brooks Holder tends bar every right.

There was a difference, however. Sisler's clout meant $6000 to his mates. Which is an important piece of meaning.

Though a tense duel, it had its comedy, too. It happened in the seventh, and helped to momentarily relieve the tension that was mounting with each pitch. Hodges fouled back of the plate and down toward first base where Andy Seminick and Waitkus gave chase. Both tumbled into the laps of spectators, Waitkus' glove hitting in the middle of a beer cup and spraying everybody with wet suds, the greatest bath New York has seen since Anna Held jumped into a milk tub for Flo Ziegfeld to astonish, as well as tease, Broadway. Eddie wiped the foam off his kisser, thrust a finger into his mouth, smacked his lips, winked, and went back to work.

The kids, now the men, hustle back to Philly tonight while the Yankees, who will probably eat them alive, return to New York from Boston, where they will work out tomorrow in The House That Ruth Built.

Game Two, 1950

Joe Williams

◆ ◆ ◆

*The 1950 World Series was anything but a washout: three close games, includ-
ing the 1–0 opening heartbreaker pitched by Jim Konstanty, the MVP relief
pitcher pressed into service as a starter. Game Two, however, was the watershed.
The New York press was unrelenting when it came to the Phillies. Joe Williams of
the* New York World Telegram and Sun *was one of the most respected baseball writers in the country. He wrote this column from his hospital bed, where he
watched the game on television: a few days earlier he had narrowly escaped
death in a plane crash.*

*Game Two, as he admits, somewhat reluctantly, was all Robin Roberts; but it
eventually came down to DiMaggio. In* Baseball Between the Lines *(1976,
1993, University of Nebraska Press) by Donald Honig, Roberts recalls the game
going into the tenth inning, tied at 1–1: "DiMaggio came up. He had popped
out four straight times. When he came up in the tenth it was the only time that
day that I wasn't leery of him. I assumed after getting him out four straight
times that I was handling him all right. I think I might have been just a little
bit overconfident with him that last time. The moment I saw the pitch going in I
knew it didn't have the drive it should have had and I saw DiMaggio's whole
body moving into it, and he hit it upstairs. That was the ball game."*

Trouble with precocious kids—and they can be as cute, cunning
and cuddly as all get out—is that sooner or later the brat in them
shows. Like this Robin Roberts and the shocking lack of respect he had
for the old Yankees over in Philly yesterday.

It had been sickening enough the afternoon before when Jim Kon-

From the *New York World Telegram and Sun*, October 6, 1950. Reprinted by permission of
J. Peter Williams.

stanty had DiMag and Mize falling on their kissers trying to get a piece of his custard pudding pitch but at least he was mannerly and matured about it. An old guy himself, he was properly sympathetic.

Besides the Yankees had got one run in the fourth and behind the strong-arm pitching of Vic Raschi were making it look like a million, so the Whiz Kids, as the fuzz-cheeked members of Bob Carpenter's scout troop are heroically called, had small chance to get fresh with their elderly visitors.

It was somewhat different in the second game of the World Series. The children were getting on bases more often and some of them were making real grown-up noises with their bats. In the second inning Granny Hamner, the shortstop who didn't start playing pro baseball until he was 17—just wouldn't eat his spinach!—hit one of Allie Reynolds' pitches all the way to the fence in left and didn't stop running until he pulled up at third.

Those of us in the TV audience could only imagine the great wave of boyish joy which must have swept over the Philly bench and the happy shrieks of "Oh, you Superman!" . . . "Just like Capt Marvel." . . . "Wait till Hopalong hears about this." All against a staccato background of bubble gum explosions and a shower of torn comic books.

No Respect for Gray Hairs

After nine innings the score was tied and the children had not only held the old people even on the board but were becoming increasingly brash and assertive. Once Master Hamner, who must be no less than an Eagle Scout, and who was particularly obnoxious all afternoon, stole second so easily and with such gay abandon it was impossible to make a play on him.

But this was simply a manifestation of animal energy and youthful spirit, a quality to be admired and encouraged, though as Mr. Shaw has observed—or was it Connie Mack?—'tis a pity to waste it on the young. There was not, however, in this incident any suggestion of impudence or disrespect for gray hairs.

Unfortunately it appears that Master Roberts has not been as well disciplined as most of Prof. Carpenter's eager little beavers. Possibly he is just naturally incorrigible, a confirmed problem child. It has been clinically established that most children have a curious capacity for cruelty. Very likely a psychologist would find Master Roberts' background a revealing and perhaps a horrifying study.

It was significant that he made no effort to torture the younger Yankees. Woodling got two hits. So did Brown. And Coleman's pass with two down in the second became the Yankees' first run. It was against the venerable antiques that Master Roberts threw the full force of his disdain. There was something fiendish, even fanatical about the way he slashed at the royal robes of greatness and mocked the enduring tablets of time.

The TV voice which helps us understand the pictures became a monotone of misery. . . . "DiMaggio pops to Goliat . . . Mize goes down swinging . . . DiMaggio pops to Jones . . . Waitkus camps under Mize's infield fly . . . DiMaggio is easy." . . . etc., etc., etc.

They Learn the Hard Way

Rizzuto, who is getting along, too, hadn't got a hit all day either. Mize was taken out in the eighth, his record for the series showing one demure single. Coming up to the tenth, DiMag hadn't got the ball past the infield in two full games. By now the malevolent moppets in the Philly nursery pen no doubt were laughing like crazy at the big bad man's feeble efforts to solve Master Roberts' magic. It was funnier than Howdy Doody or Lucky Pup.

To others it was more like tragedy. None of us could remember a series in which the Clipper had started so poorly or looked more pathetic at the plate. Time, of course, was catching up with him. Conceivably, he could be making his bow out as a series stalwart. It was no sure bet he'd be strong enough to play regularly another year. Was this then to be his role at the finish, one of dismal fumbling frustration?

. . . "It's going, it's going and it's in there for a home run and the Yankees are back in front, 2 to 1!"

That's how the voice with rapturous suddenness told us DiMag had snapped out of it in the tenth with a thunderous wallop which was not only to win the ball game but teach Master Roberts and the rest of the small fry a lesson most of us old-fashioned people learned years ago. Never laugh at an old man. Might be your own pop.

First Robin of Fling

Edgar Williams

◆ ◆ ◆

Edgar Williams, veteran columnist and feature writer for the Philadelphia Inquirer, *wrote sports in the 1950s. In this "conversation" piece, written for* Baseball Digest *in January 1953, Williams caught the young Robin Roberts as the pitcher entered his prime, having just come off a 28–7 season—Roberts's third straight twenty-game season and the best of his career. The essay's cutesy title was typical of* Baseball Digest*'s editors in the fifties, and Williams, who couldn't possibly think up anything that bad, hated it. So did Roberts, who said to him, "Don't you have any more imagination than that!" A postscript by Williams to the story asked, "Can Roberts Win 30 in '53?" He didn't, but he did win 23 games his next three seasons in a row. In 1956 a similar piece on Roberts would become* Time *magazine's cover story for May 28. The author, Dick Seamon, titled it "The Whole Story of Pitching" and noted that Roberts "never bothers with the fancy stuff but makes do with what he has: a dinky curve, a sneaky but unspectacular fast ball, and a frustrating change of pace. . . . Robin Roberts can put the ball where he wants. There is one precious-diamond word for him—control."*

O n the night of last September 17, the Phillies' clubhouse in Shibe Park, Philadelphia, took on the aura of Times Square on New Year's Eve. Robin Roberts had just beaten the Cincinnati Reds, 4–2, for his 25th victory of the season, and it seemed that most of baseball's elder statesmen had jammed into the steam-shrouded room to join in the hooraying.

"Roberts is the best pitcher in baseball today," proclaimed Bullet Joe

Bush, the old A's and Yankees' pitching star. "He would have been great in any era."

Hans Lobert, once a teammate of Grover Cleveland Alexander's, agreed. So did Cy Perkins, the whilom A's catcher, now a coach with the Phillies.

Another old catcher—Manager Steve O'Neill, of the Phillies—summed it all up.

"Robbie," he said, "compares with any pitcher who ever lived."

And what was Roberts doing while the talk was at its height? He was sitting in front of his locker, wearing an expression of perplexity and very little else.

"Hey, Robbie," someone said, "why so sad?" The big six-foot, 190-pound, right-hander looked up and grinned.

"I'm not sad," he replied. "I'm just trying to figure how I can get to a television set right after tomorrow night's game. I want to watch Chuck Davey lick Rocky Graziano in Chicago. Chuck's my boy."

Ask Robin Evan Roberts about his 1952 record of 28 victories and seven defeats, and he gives you a "what's-so-wonderful-about-it" answer. But mention Chuck Davey, and Robbie talks like a press agent.

Five years ago Davey and Roberts were classmates at Michigan State College. Chuck was the big wheel of the boxing team, and Robbie was an equally outstanding baseball and basketball player. Yet, to hear Roberts tell it now, Davey was the undisputed big man on campus and his climb to the position of challenger for a world boxing championship is much more noteworthy than the development of another ex-Spartan into one of the best pitchers major league baseball has known in years.

Which is typical of the young man. At 26, Robbie has won 20 or more games in each of three consecutive seasons; he is the first National League pitcher to win 28 games in one season since Dizzy Dean did it in 1935, and he is being hailed in many quarters as the modern Grover Cleveland Alexander. But Roberts appears eminently unimpressed by Roberts. A highly articulate fellow, he has a light, deprecating way of talking about himself.

"So I'm supposed to be another Alexander?" he says. "Why, Alexander won 28 games in his first year in the majors. I didn't do that until my fourth full season."

Or on the possibility of his winning 30 games in 1953: "Look, I got as many breaks last season as I could hope to get. So how can I say whether or not I'll be able to win 30 in any year? What a lot of people forget is that I got rocked pretty hard in a lot of games last season, but usually the boys got me enough runs to win."

Which does not imply that Roberts doesn't believe he ever will be a 30-game winner. As Eddie Sawyer, his former boss on the Phillies, once put it: "The thought of failure never occurs to Robbie." It's just that Roberts is a realist. "You simply keep going, taking one game at a time," he says. "You can't be thinking of whether you're going to win 20 or 25 or even 30 games in a season. You try to win today's game, and not look ahead. Certainly, I'd like to win 30 some season. But I know very well that I'll have to have a lot of luck running for me to do it."

Off the statistical evidence adduced from his 1952 performances, it would seem that Roberts gives too much credit to good luck and not enough to his good right arm. In notching his 28 victories, Robbie started 37 games and went the route in 30 of them, including a 19-inning job in which he outlasted the Boston Braves. He had an earned run average of 2.62, and in 330 innings allowed 104 runs, 292 hits, fanned 148 and—get this—walked only 45.

"And the most amazing thing about the guy," says Benny Bengough, the one-time Yankee catcher who now is a Phillies' coach, "is that he wins big without knocking anybody down. He simply won't brush those hitters back from the plate. So they dig in on him and look for that good fast ball. But even then they can't hit it."

When he first came up to the Phillies in midseason of 1948, Robbie pitched as though he considered it cowardly to throw a curve. His fast ball whistles like the wolf of Company A, and virtually the only condescension Roberts made to the niceties of pitching in those days was to come in with a change-up now and then. Now he throws a good curve, the development of which he credits largely to Ken Johnson, a scatter-shot southpaw who failed to stick with the Phils because, ironically, he couldn't control his own curve.

"Last season," Roberts says, "I threw a lot more curves than ever before. I wanted to break the hitters of the habit of always looking for the fast ball. But whenever I got into a jam, I gave them the fast one."

92 ◆ *Edgar Williams*

Probably nothing is so illustrative of the quiet confidence Robbie has in himself as is an incident that took place in the training camp of the Wilmington Blue Rocks, of the Class B Inter-State League, one afternoon in late March, 1948.

Robbie, fresh out of Michigan State with the degree of Bachelor of Science in Education in his pocket, had gone south with the Phillies, and during the first portion of the Grapefruit League season had done nothing to make any member of the organization regret the $25,000 bonus paid Roberts for signing. In fact, he had been the most impressive pitcher in camp. Therefore, there were expressions of astonishment by sports writers traveling with the club when the then manager, Ben Chapman, announced that Roberts was being farmed out to Wilmington. Chapman explained that Roberts would derive more benefit from taking a regular turn with the Blue Rocks than from sitting around in Shibe Park, awaiting a relief job now and then.

So Roberts reported to the Blue Rocks at their camp in Sumter, S.C. On his first day there, Robbie pitched in batting practice, then set out to jog around the field. Sunning himself in left field was one Al Cartwright, sports editor of a Wilmington newspaper, who gave the youngster a big hello.

"Glad to have you with us," Cartwright said. "By the way, what's this story about your being disappointed at being sent down by the Phillies?"

"I am—a little," Roberts replied.

"Well, look at it this way," Cartwright said. "Would you rather be pitching regularly in Wilmington, or sitting on the bench in Philly?"

"I'd rather be pitching regularly in Philadelphia," Roberts said with a shy grin. "I know I can win up there."

He got to Philadelphia sooner than he expected. He won nine of his first ten starts with the Blue Rocks, prompting one rival manager to suggest the Phillies were trying to break up the Inter-State League by stationing Robbie at Wilmington. On June 18, however, the Phils recalled him, and he made his first major league start the following night, losing to Pittsburgh, 2–0, although he pitched a five-hitter. On June 23, he beat Cincinnati, 3–2, and was on his way.

Roberts won seven and lost nine that first year. In 1949 he had a 15–

15 record, and in 1950, when the Phillies won the pennant, he made his first entry into the 20-game circle, winning 20 and losing 11. In 1951 he won 21 and lost 15.

It would appear that some strange fate has decreed that Robbie be more or less overlooked in times of his greatest achievements. Take his 4–1 victory over Brooklyn on the final day of the 1950 season that enabled the Phillies to clinch the pennant. Making his fourth start in eight days, he pitched masterfully, and would have won, 1–0, had not Pee Wee Reese hit a freak homer in the sixth inning; the ball lodged on a ledge at the base of the screen in right field at Ebbets Field, instead of falling back for a single or double, and the score was tied.

Then, in the top half of the tenth inning, Dick Sisler walloped a three-run homer for the Phils, and that was the ball game. Sisler was the talk of baseball, and Robbie, who had pitched out of a bases-loaded jam in the ninth to carry the game into overtime, was a sort of secondary hero.

"But I didn't mind," he says. "We won, didn't we? That game was the greatest experience of my life."

Last season it wasn't until the final weeks that baseball fandom came to the realization that Roberts was pitching as no National Leaguer had pitched since the days of Dizzy Dean, Paul Derringer and Bucky Walters.

For Bobby Shantz, the A's great little left-hander, had captured the public's fancy, in Philadelphia as elsewhere. So Robbie went along winning game after game—he won 20 of his last 22 outings—and not until his victory total topped Bobby's was there much fuss made about him.

"I don't blame anyone for going overboard for Bobby," Roberts says. "He's a great pitcher, and if I were a sports writer, I'd have given him a big play myself. It's a spectacular thing to watch a fellow of Bobby's stature beat big men. It's not so spectacular to watch a big guy like me work against other big guys. So I give Shantz all the credit due him, and I hope he goes on winning for many years."

Roberts hands out credit lines like a photography editor; coming from many other big name athletes, this would sound like the tall, tall corn, but when you listen to Robbie you get the feeling he means it.

He credits his parents, Thomas and Sarah Roberts, of Springfield, Ill., with having given him and his three brothers and two sisters a desire to do their best in whatever they undertake. Thomas Roberts, a Welshman, and his wife, a Briton, emigrated to this country in 1921, became citizens and reared their family. It wasn't always easy for them, and young Robin was aware of this. So when he received the first half of his bonus from the Phillies in the autumn of 1947 (he got $12,500 that year, the other $12,500 in 1948, for tax purposes), a major portion of the money went toward building his parents a new home.

Robbie credits C. B. Lindsay, who taught him in grammar school in Springfield, with having first aroused his interest in baseball. He gives credit to John Kobs, his baseball coach at Michigan State, for having insisted he be a pitcher instead of the first baseman he aspired to be when he entered Michigan State under the Army Specialized Training Program in 1944, after having starred in football, basketball and baseball at Springfield's Lanphier High School.

And he credits Ray Fisher, the University of Michigan baseball coach, who was his manager for two summers at Montpelier, Vt., in the independent Northern League, with polishing his pitching style. "I guess Ray must have thought me ungrateful," Robbie says, "because the spring following my first season with him in Vermont, I beat his Michigan team twice."

In the autumn of 1948, Robbie went back to Springfield to prepare for his first full season with the Phillies. One evening he went out on a blind date with Mary Ann Kalnes, from McFarland, Wis., who taught history in one of the Springfield junior high schools. Mary didn't know a bunt from a Buick, but was willing to learn. She's still learning, but she is certain of at least one thing; her husband is the best pitcher in baseball. Robbie and Mary were married Dec. 27, 1949.

There is a young Robbie now—Robin Evan Roberts, Jr., who was born Oct. 20, 1950, just after his daddy had pitched in the World Series, losing his only start against the Yankees, 2–1, in ten innings. Not long ago the Roberts family moved into a new ranch home in one of the Philadelphia suburbs. Aptly enough, the house is located on Robin Hood Lane. In the house next door live Curt Simmons, the Phillies' southpaw, and his wife.

During the season, Robbie has a definite routine for days when he is scheduled to pitch. He rises early, putters around the house and yard, and if it is a day game, eats a steak "dinner" at about 10 A.M. If the game is to be played at night, he downs the steak at about 2 P.M., takes a nap and goes to the ball park two hours before game-time. He dresses leisurely, participates in batting practice, then retires to the clubhouse to read a newspaper. With 20 minutes to go before the start of the game, he goes on the field to warm up.

During the off-season, Robbie is employed as a salesman by a manufacturer of corrugated boxes in Philadelphia. He works as hard at selling as he does at pitching, and his employer says he would be a successful salesman even if he didn't have his name going for him. Nearly every afternoon he goes to a midcity gymnasium for a two-hour workout.

Roberts isn't much of a hobbyist. He describes himself as an unusual ball player, because he doesn't care for hunting or fishing. He is an eager, if not accomplished, gardener. He enjoys reading light fiction, but he merely scans the sports pages. He makes numerous unpublicized visits to hospitals, and has been known to go to considerable inconvenience to visit shut-ins.

He goes to the movies only when the team is on the road. He and Mary spend most of their evenings at home watching television. On nights when a Chuck Davey fight is televised, visitors are warned not to approach Robbie, lest they get themselves conked by one of the haymakers he throws by way of helping Chuck—vicariously, of course.

And when the fight ends and Davey is announced as the winner, Robbie settles back in his chair, grins broadly and says:

"What a fighter. There's a Michigan State boy who really made good."

The Nebraska Comet

Mike Gaven

◆ ◆ ◆

The late Mike Gaven of the New York Journal-American *told baseball readers in 1955 what many Phillies fans already knew about Richie Ashburn, who finally became a Hall of Famer in 1995. Focusing on Ashburn's fielding and some primitive sabermetrics, Gaven made a case for Ashburn that it took baseball thirty years to acknowledge. And he reminds readers of the most glowing moment of Ashburn's career—the throw to home plate in the final game of the 1950 regular season—with a few related anecdotes tossed in. Ashburn didn't have to prove anything to anyone with either his bat or his speed. As Stan Musial told long-time* Philadelphia Bulletin *columnist Frank Yeutter during a spring training game in 1951, "Ashburn's going to surprise everyone. He's learned how to hit. He won't knock down any fences maybe, but he'll hit where's he's pitched. Look at the way he hit that outside pitch to left field, then turned right around and pulled one to right. And with that speed of his he'll beat out most of the infield shots and bunts he tries. Take my word for it, he'll be up among the leaders." He was, indeed, one of baseball's finest all-around players, no matter how many home runs he didn't hit.*

It isn't exactly true that Willie Mays led the National League in everything except stolen towels. For example, Willie didn't even lead in his own specialty, which is catching fly balls.

The National League leader in putouts for the sixth consecutive season was Richie Ashburn, the woefully underrated center fielder of the Phillies.

So what, you might ask. Didn't Willie catch everything he got his hands on? Perhaps true, but when a man leads his league in putouts for six straight seasons, it's high time his name was at least mentioned with the best.

Because no one in baseball history had ever done it before. Max

Carey, one of the greatest, led the National League in putouts nine times, but over a period of 13 seasons. The immortal Tris Speaker was tops seven times from 1909 to 1919, inclusive.

The book also tells that Carey was the only outfielder to make 400 or more putouts for six seasons. Ashburn has now bettered 400 putouts for six years in a row, going over the 500 mark twice.

Taylor Douthit, of the 1928 Cardinals, set the record with 547 in 1938. The American League all-time high is 503 by Dom DiMaggio in 1948. Ashburn's high was 538 in 1951. Last season he caught 483 flies to 448 by Mays, 360 by Duke Snider, and 327 by Mickey Mantle.

Mind you, I make no reference to fielding percentages. Those figures are for the birds. Groundkeepers should be charged with most errors tabbed against outfielders.

But, in my book, the fielder who handles the most chances over a season is the leader at his position. In so far as outfielders go, that spells Ashburn, difficult as that could be for admirers of Mays, Snider and Mantle to believe.

The blond Phillie isn't as spectacular as Mays and Snider, to be sure, but he catches the balls. The figures also tend to prove he catches many the Say Hey Kid and the Duke don't reach.

Definitely, he plays the hitters better and pays more attention to where the pitcher is trying to make the batter hit the ball. Therein may lie one advantage because Robin Roberts is one pitcher who has some idea where he is throwing the ball.

However, Whitey plays every day, regardless of who pitches. Mays also played behind some good pitchers last year and in the most spacious center field in baseball. Like the Dodger hurlers, the Giant flingers try to prevent the batters from pulling and make them hit to center.

Snider had a disadvantage there. The Brooklyn pitchers are woefully lacking in ideas, but hardly to the extent indicated in the putout totals, what with the Duke making 123 fewer than Ashburn.

More astounding figures are these: over the last six seasons, Ashburn has made 2,864 putouts to 2,234 for Snider. This is not intended to be a rap at the Duke, certainly one of the best, but brought up to prove that Ashburn belongs with the greatest. Not only with the current greats, but the all-time immortals.

You might say he doesn't hit with the big boys in center field. Well, there again, I have news for you. Ashburn's .312 lifetime batting average is bettered only by Stan Musial and Jackie Robinson among still active players. Snider is fourth with .307. Mays has played too few games for comparison here. Ashburn hasn't missed a game since 1950.

So he can't throw? Twice leading the league in assists, Whitey has had 103 major league assists to 72 by the Duke of Flatbush for the same length of service.

O. K., they run on him, but respect Snider's arm. Partly true, but most times when they run he gets 'em. The Dodgers know that.

Going into the final day of the 1950 season when the Phillies had to win at Brooklyn to beat the Dodgers in the pennant race, Ashburn had only seven assists, by far his poorest year. He hadn't thrown out a Brooklyn runner all season.

So it was only natural that Coach Milt Stock would send Cal Abrams home from second when Snider singled through the middle with none out and the score tied. Much to the surprise of everyone except Ashburn, he threw out Abrams at the plate with yards to spare, and the Dodgers did not tie for the pennant.

There were two stories behind that story which cost both Stock and Barney Shotton their jobs. Number one, it was the first time all season Shotton didn't order a bunt with runners on first and second and none out in the late innings of a close game.

Ashburn knew that, of course, and was running in to cover second in case of a pop bunt or pickoff when Snider hit the ball right at him about 15 yards behind the infield grass. His alertness led him into one of the most telling plays of all time.

Story number two was written the following spring in an intrasquad game at Vero Beach. Pee Wee Reese, the manager of one team, was coaching at third when somone hit a clean single with Abrams on second. Abie broke back toward the bag and as a result, started so late that Reese held him up at third.

"I think you cost me $5,000 last fall," said Reese, as Abrams pulled up alongside of him.

Baseball Eye

John Lardner

◆ ◆ ◆

There was no better sportswriter in the late 1940s and 1950s than Ring Lardner's eldest, John Lardner. He wrote a consistently excellent regular column for Newsweek *("John Lardner's Week"), in addition to contributing literary essays to just about every major magazine in the country. He, and nearly every other sportswriter in America, got a royal kick out of the story that Phillies owner Bob Carpenter had hired a private detective (not an unusual practice among baseball owners, it turned out) to trail certain members of the Phillies squad. True to Phillies' form, however, the private eye Carpenter hired proved to be totally inept. What's more remarkable about the piece is how much fact Lardner manages to get in while maintaining the satirical tone. Lardner, on another occasion, wrote of the Philadelphia baseball crowd: "In adversity, it sounds like feeding time in the lion house at the zoo; in success (if any) it sounds like the French Revolution."*

Case 1

I'm Jack Larkin, a private eye. You name it, I'll do it. Right now, I'm on a trick in Philly, tailing ballplayers.

You think I'm a lucky guy? Well, I've got to admit it looks that way. I'm 6.2. I'm hard as nails. I'm beautiful. Dames follow me, and I follow ballplayers. If they don't get home by midnight (or 2 A.M. after night games), they're dead. I've sent many a left-handed hitter to the hot squat. That doesn't bother me. I see it this way: If a ballplayer gets in at 12:01 (or 2:01, after night games), he's not fit to live. He's a mad dog. In this game, society calls the shots.

From *Newsweek*, May 31, 1954. Reprinted by permission of Susan Lardner.

But the assignment is not all steak and eggs. It's mean. It's murder. You probably read in the papers the other day where a private op, name of Charles Leland, was picked up by the cops while tailing Hamner, the Phillie infielder. What happened? This Hamner pulled a hidden-ball gimmick on him. He spotted the tail and phoned police headquarters.

Before the shamus knew what had happened, he was in the can, under $500 bail. He had to pretend he'd got Hamner mixed up with a divorce case, driving the same make and color heap.

Bob Carpenter, the Phillie president, finally took him off the hook. He said that all ball clubs put tails on their players. He said it's for the good of the game. Suppose Hamner got in at 2:02 some night? Suppose he took a beer? What do we want here, Russia?

Well, Mr. Carpenter was right. But that didn't do the dick any good. For him, it was tough. It was embarrassing. These ballplayers are mean as foxes.

I had a trick the same night. The Old Man said: "They want you to tail Robin Roberts. If you lose him, don't come back." I looked right at him. I figured I could do one of three things: Punch him, borrow $10, or do what he said. So I sneered, "OK," and drove to Philly.

I took a plant at the ball park. Pretty soon, out came Roberts, looking innocent. He climbed into his boiler, and drove away. I followed, keeping two blocks between us all the way. Don't ask me which two blocks. Probably Walnut and Chestnut.

Suddenly, at the corner of Third and Peanut, crash! Bam! Another bucket, a blue-gray sedan, hit me from the side. The driver came out with his gun in his hand. I came out the same way.

But it was only Charlie Schultz, another op from our office. I recognized him before we'd exchanged more than half a dozen shots. I said: "What's the matter with you?" He said: "I'm tailing Richie Ashburn. He can fly." I told him to get lost, and we went back to work.

For a few blocks, I still thought I had Roberts in front of me. But then he scratched his nose with his left hand, and I knew it was Simmons. Well, I thought, what's the difference? These pitchers are all alike. One of them is just as liable to get drunk, or sell our secrets to Hawaii, as the next one. And just then, sure enough, he parked his car across a sidewalk at Fifth and Coconut and went into a gin mill.

I followed, and took a plant behind a cuspidor. I watched him drink six fast bourbon-and-waters in a row. I was ready to turn to the next page in my notebook—we average six drinks a page—when he took the glass away from his face for a split second, and I saw it wasn't Simmons. It was Charlie Gratz, another private eye.

"What's up?" I snapped at him. He said: "I was tailing Willie Jones. I had him in a rundown between Fourth and Betel-nut, but he got away." "Kicked the ball out of your hands, I suppose?" I sneered—and I meant it to hurt. But he wouldn't tell me any more. He was low—mighty low.

We left the joint together. There, walking down the street right in front of us, was Jim Konstanty. At least, it looked like him. We were on him like a couple of wildcats. I socked him in the pit of the stomach. Charlie kicked him in the knee. Then the guy socked, kicked, gouged and butted us, tied us up, and threw us into the meat wagon. He turned out to be Sergeant Delehanty, the light heavyweight champion of the riot squad.

As Mr. Carpenter says, if the players aren't watched, what will become of the game?

Case 2

You remember me. Jack Larkin, private eye. They had me tailing the Philadelphia Phillies some weeks back, to see where they went. I found out. They went into the second division.

Back at the office, the Old Man told me: "New orders just came in. You're the Phillies' manager. That puts you on the inside, where you can look around."

It surprised me. But I kept my face dead, lit a cigarette, and said: "That means I replace Big Fred Fitzsimmons." The Old Man knocked the cigarette out of my mouth. He hates my insides. I appeal to dames; he doesn't. He said: "Who're you voting for this year, Garfield? They fired Fitzsimmons. Then they fired Big Ed Sawyer. Then they fired Big Steve O'Neill. You're next. You'll work under the name of Terry Moore."

I said: "I get it. Nice casting. Moore could catch anything." The Old Man said: "You couldn't catch a spoon in a cup of coffee. But you're the only op I got available. Now get out of here. Grab a train West, and pick up your ball club."

I caught the team in Cincinnati, and we lost four straight. Then we hit St. Louis. You could cook your dinner on the sidewalk. There was a doubleheader Sunday. We won the first one, 11 to 10, according to the scoreboard, which I cased all the way. This Stanky was handling the other club. I could see he wasn't feeling good. Every now and then he shot a dirty look across at me. I ignored him. When you're a guy women go for, you get used to dirty looks from your own sex. Besides, if I had the kind of pitching this fellow has, I'd be sore, too.

In the second game, we were leading 8 to 1 in the fifth inning when they dusted Torgeson, my first baseman. He hollered like a moose. Then he started an argument with Yvars, the Cardinal catcher. It sounded like the kind of stuff I was after, so I beat it out there with my notebook and took a plant behind the umpire.

Yvars looked my man right in the kisser. He said: "You slugged me in June 1952. Now it is July 1954, and I am going to slug you." I could see the case had a lot of background.

The next thing I knew, Stanky came at me. He said: "Are you Moore, the guy that said I was temperamentally unsuited to manage a ball club?" Hell, I thought, here's more background. In my grift, you learn to think fast. I stalled him. I said: "Well, I'm not G. David Doubleday." Stanky said: "I think you're the guy that said I was temperamentally unsuited to manage a ball club." Then he knocked me down.

I didn't go for my gun. In a stranger's town, you have to play it easy. But I promised myself that the first time I met him in my own yard, I would look down his throat and tell him that I thought he was temperamentally unsuited to manage a ball club.

By the time they ran us off the field, it was nearly dark. I kept an eye on Stanky, over the way. I thought he might try a shot from the hip. Pretty soon, I got a feeling that he was up to something else: Delaying the game. It was hard to put your finger on; just a shadow of a hunch. He sent the bases out to be dry-cleaned. He recited the Gettysburg

Address at the plate. He called in new pitchers. Then he waved at the distance and yelled: "Corcoran!"

Pinelli, the umpire, said: "Who?" Stanky said: "Corcoran. He's a pitcher in Rochester. He ought to be able to catch the next train."

Pinelli threw us all out of the park. He told me: "It's a forfeit. You win, 9 to 0." I gave him a wink, to show him the rib wasn't getting across. I knew the score. I'd seen them make a run in the second inning. I said to Pinelli: "Don't forget, kid, I'm Terry Moore. I know the score." Pinelli said: "If you're Terry Moore, I'm Chief Justice Warren."

Maybe he was, at that. The next thing I knew, I was back in Philadelphia, and Moore had the job. The Old Man put me on a stolen-dog call. A blonde had lost a chihuahua. He told me to remember which was which. Then he knocked the cigarette out of my mouth. But it didn't scare me. I had another, and he knew it.

The Tragedy of the Phillies

Ed Linn

◆ ◆ ◆

By the late 1950s the Whiz Kids were falling apart. Veteran writer Ed Linn attempted to figure out what the problem could possibly be. His essay, published in Sport *in March 1955, shows clearly that the Phillies were on their way to squandering the talented franchise they had worked so hard to build, and he comes to several important conclusions: first, that the Phillies might have done more harm than good by winning the pennant in 1950, several years too soon; and second, that their failure to recruit black players (especially Roy Campanella, in their own backyard) had hurt the team, perhaps irreparably. Hank Mason, mentioned in the article, became the first black pitcher for the Phils, and Fran Huerra was none other than Pancho Herrera, the black Cuban who played first base for the Phils 1958–61.*

"**A**ll I want these guys to do," Terry Moore was explaining, "is to act like major-leaguers. If major-leaguers miss curfews, I say, 'All right, let them miss curfews'; if major-leaguers get drunk, I say, 'All right, let them get drunk'; if major-leaguers carouse around, I say, 'All right, let them carouse around.'

"But," he said, his soft Alabama drawl tightening in angry disbelief, "is that the way major-leaguers act?"

As a member of the old Gas-House Gang, Terry Moore was scarcely as easy to shock as the little old lady next door, but the Phillies' general manager, Roy Hamey, apparently decided he needed a manager with a stronger stomach and a tighter mouth. Moore is now tending his bowling alleys in St. Louis, sadder, perhaps a little wiser but, according to Hamey, no more experienced. Terry may feel differently about that last point.

From *Sport*, March 1955. Reprinted by permission of Ed Linn.

Hamey himself had come fresh to the Philadelphia scene during the first week of the season, and it was he who had hired Moore to replace Steve O'Neill. (Any man who, like O'Neill, was popularly described as "genial," was obviously not well-suited to handle the steadily aging Whiz Kids.) But Moore had his troubles, too. Before the season was over, Terry, 44, was to tell his players: "I know why they hired a young man for this job. An old man couldn't keep up with you guys."

When club president Bob Carpenter hired Hamey, it was a reluctant, and belated, admission that he himself needed help. After five years of operating as his own general manager, Carpenter took himself upstairs to the business office and let more experienced heads run the store.

In making the move, Carpenter wasn't accepting full blame for the tragedy of the Phillies—and if tragedy sounds like too strong a term, consider the testimony that follows. But one reason why, since the pennant-winning season of 1950, the Phillies have finished fifth, fourth, third and fourth, and have never seriously menaced the Dodgers or Giants in the last four years, is that too many members of the team grew to maturity as a rich man's spoiled brats.

Carpenter is an almost perfect example of the old grad who never quite outgrows the cheering section. (He is a Duke alumnus.) A man who can afford to indulge his hobbies, Carpenter gets a big kick out of sitting around in the clubhouse talking the game over with the boys. Wealthy though he is (we will make every effort not to refer to him anywhere herein as the scion of the DuPonts but we shall probably fail), Carpenter is not insensitive to such simple pleasures of life as being called 'Bob' by major-league ballplayers. Even ballplayers whose salaries he is paying.

During spring training, he has always liked to get out in the sunshine and work out with his players. Since he was once a semi-pro pitcher of some ability, he has never been too proud to pass on a few tips to the rookies.

Friendship is a quality never to be frowned upon in print; still, in the relationship between a club owner and his employees, it is bound to become a complicating factor. During his tenure as the entire front office (1948–1953), Carpenter handled the unpleasant business about his over-exuberant ballplayers by calling them into his private office and lecturing them at length on the harm they were doing themselves, their team and the loyal fans of Philadelphia. It was all on a very personal, man-to-man basis.

Carpenter, without question, meant well, but if there is a more effective way of undermining a manager's authority, it has not yet been discovered.

To add to his woes, Bob is inclined to look upon himself as a practical psychologist. Before last year's contracts went out, for instance, he announced that Robin Roberts had disappointed him cruelly by winning only 23 games, a season of malingering that would cost him a $3,500 cut in salary. (If this is brute psychology, then the beast had two heads. Carpenter was obviously talking beyond Roberts to the team as a whole. For if Robin could expect a cut, then the rest of them could quail in their storm cellars until the contracts arrived.)

Now, Roberts is a quiet, earnest professional, but, like many another outwardly phlegmatic man, he harbors an ulcer in his stomach. If you or I had the best pitcher in baseball, and the best pitcher in baseball had an ulcer, we might be reluctant to go out of our way to irritate him. But then, you and I are not psychologists. Roberts let it be known that Carpenter had hurt him—right here. In the end, to the surprise of no one, he got a small raise instead of a small cut, and went on to another disgraceful 23-game season. The wonderful part of practicing your psychology on Roberts is that he is going to win his 20 games no matter what you do to him.

To give the Phils' president his due, he is personally popular with almost every man who has ever played for him. "You have to like the guy," one of them says. "The only thing you can say against him is that he's a baseball *fan*, not a baseball *man*. He couldn't see that he was out of his depth trying to run a major-league team by himself. Contract talks, for instance. To me they're bread and butter, to him they're a game. If he could cut you down a thousand dollars, it was as if he had beaten you at checkers or something.

"Not that he cared about the money. A little while later—during the winter even—he might hear that somebody in your family was sick, and he'd have a specialist flown in, the best money could buy. He was always doing things like that and never letting anybody know about it. How can you knock a guy like that?"

It would be rank misrepresentation, in any case—and any baseball fan knows it—to imply that the Phillies deteriorated from pennant winners in 1950 to their present bedraggled state solely because some of the Whiz Kids were not held in tighter tether. If a ball team has enough good players, it can win a pennant between drinks. The Yankees of the 1920 proved that. No team ever shattered more training rules or wore out more private detectives than Babe Ruth and his playmates, but no team ever shattered more records, either.

The real tragedy of the Phils may well be not that they have been flying too high, but that they have been flying under false colors. Carpenter deliberately went into the bonus-baby business, rather than the used-star business, because his master plan called for an organization that would feed the top team year by year. A few years ago, when the debate was hot, the Phils were pointed to as baseball's prize proof that a winning team could be built upon this foundation. It seems now, against all logic, that the Phils' experience shows that while a bonus-baby program may produce quick results—of the few who make the grade almost immediately—it may be the worst possible way to build for the future.

It may be that a big bonus, with its attendant flood of publicity, leaves a boy psychologically unfit to start at the bottom of the bus-and-sandwiches leagues (as he was allowed to do before 1947) and learn and persevere at his trade like any kid picked up at a tryout camp. For those who have to learn from a big-league bench—running for somebody about twice a month, getting into only the hopelessly lost games—it may be, as the Dodgers' Fresco Thompson believes, that they tend after a while to accept their status as benchwarmers. Once they do that, the end is near.

No law of nature can be drawn from the history of one team, but one thing is sure. The Phils, who had set themselves to the task of building for the long haul, became one-year wonders. We asked some of the members of that 1950 team what they thought had contributed most to the collapse with the understanding that they would not be directly quoted. Two of the answers pretty well sum up the points raised by all of them:

"The trouble," one of them said, "was that we had a bunch of young kids from small towns, and everything came too quick and went to their heads. Sawyer was a good manager, but he was too nice a guy to handle them the way they should have been handled. O'Neill? He'd already lost three jobs for being too soft, anybody who reads the sports pages knows that. Maybe I'm prejudiced about it, though. I figured I was on a real contender for five years, and instead we dropped right out of it. It has been the biggest disappointment of my life."

Another player, since traded away, said: "That Whiz Kid stuff was just so much newspaper talk. There were some young guys—Roberts, Simmons, Hamner, Jones, Ashburn—but look at the rest of the guys. Ennis was no kid. Konstanty, Waitkus, Meyer, Sisler, Seminick, that was solid experience.

"The man who made that team was Sawyer. He has never been given the credit he deserves. He developed most of the young guys at Utica and Toronto and he made the trades that got him Waitkus and Meyer. Then he took a chance on a 32-year-old relief pitcher, made an outfielder out of Sisler, squeezed that one good year out of half-a-dozen guys, and stole a pennant. He had imagination, that Sawyer. How they let him get out of baseball, I'll never know."

Sawyer himself, now a representative for a Pennsylvania golf ball manufacturer, says only: "We built the club to win in 1951 or 1952. If it is possible to say that you can win a pennant a year too early— and I doubt if it is, really—then we did win it too early. That's no explanation, though. Looking back, I think the real reason we never came on again was that Simmons never became the 20-game winner we thought he'd be and we got no help at all from the farms."

No help? *Since 1950 not one player has come off the farm to win a solid position in the lineup.* Mel Clark has looked the part of a hitter at times, but he has been hobbled by a bad knee. Ted Kazanski, a $50,000 bonus boy, was presented the shortstop position last year, although nobody except O'Neill and Carpenter thought he was ready. Of course, they didn't have much choice. Behind Kazanski, Hamner and a sore-legged Jones, the Phils had only two kids out of the Class B Three-I League,

Ben Tompkins and Mickey Micelotta. To plug up the infield, Carpenter had to pay $75,000 for Bobby Morgan, an expendable Dodger. While the Phils were riffling through their rosters and finding nothing but Class-B ballplayers, the Dodgers had infielders they didn't know what to do with. Morgan, a journeyman infielder, eventually had to take over at shortstop when it became evident that Kazanski was not going to hit National League pitching.

The outfield situation has been no better. Since Sisler departed in 1952, the Phils have scoured their system for a left-fielder. Eight men were taken south to fight for the job last year, and the Phils ended up with Clark (.240) against left-handers and Danny Schell (.283) against right-handers.

Not only was the farm system unable to staff the Phils with young ballplayers, it couldn't even help the AAA farm. The Phils had a working agreement with Baltimore from 1950 to 1953, and in that time the Orioles' lineup was sprayed with such ex-major-leaguers as Roy Weatherly, Al Lakeman, Blix Donnelly, Buddy Kerr, Dick Starr, Nippy Jones, Damon Phillips, Ken Trinkle, Marv Rackley, Tom Herrin, Jack Lohrke, Jack Graham, Howie Fox, Marv Rickert and Ferrell Anderson.

The agreement worked out pretty evenly, though. If the Orioles got nothing from the Phils, then the Phils got nothing from the Orioles. Only Karl Drews, no kid himself, was any help to them.

To be perfectly fair, it should be admitted right away that in these days of the military draft, any farm system is vulnerable to a certain amount of depletion. A promising player can be drafted—as most promising players are—and come back out with his skills and reflexes damaged beyond repair. By the same token, though, none of the other clubs have been free of this worry. The Phils have had 144 of their players drafted since the end of World War II; the Dodgers have had 355 taken.

The Phils have been criticized extensively for ignoring the one new source of players opened up since the war, the source that was uncovered in 1946 when Branch Rickey signed Jackie Robinson. Far from rushing out to mine that vein, Carpenter was able to restrain himself from signing a Negro player until 1952. And then the Phils signed shortstop Teddy Washington, who was about to go into the Army. While

Carpenter was general manager, no Negro wore a Philadelphia uniform.

During this period, the Phils' farm system was failing so completely that after the death of general manger Herb Pennock in January, 1948, not one player was signed who was able to come on and help the team—unless you want to count Kazanski. This from a system which supports nine teams and costs $500,000 a year.

It is hardly surprising that Bob Carpenter should have an affinity for bonus babies, for he was one of the greatest bonus babies of them all. Robert Ruliph Morgan Carpenter, Jr. got $5,000,000 just for being born. His mother was Margaretta DuPont, and his father, Robert R. M. Carpenter, Sr., was a DuPont vice-president. In the ordinary course of events the young man would have been expected to go through school, enter the executive offices at DuPont, and end up with his name gracing half-a-dozen Board of Director lists. Instead, this being a land of unlimited opportunities, he grew up to become a sports buff. He backed a pro basketball team, owned a couple of fighters, angeled Delaware University's football teams, and started a Class B ball club in Wilmington—a club which is now a part of the Phils' farm system

The purchase of the Phils came about almost by accident. William Cox, a New York lumber dealer who had owned the club for only a year, admitted at the end of the 1943 season that he had been betting on his team, a practice which Commissioner Kenesaw Mountain Landis looked upon with cold and unrelenting disapproval. Landis ordered Cox to pick up his lumber and his bookmaker and go. The franchise was up for sale for $200,000—less than Tom Yawkey paid for Joe Cronin.

The elder Carpenter put up the money, and at the age of 28, Bob Carpenter became the owner and president of a major-league baseball club.

For his money, Carpenter had in his possession the scrawniest franchise in baseball. In 21 of the previous 25 years, the Phils had finished either last or next to last. The only players who were to be of any use to him were Andy Seminick, the third-string catcher, and Del Ennis, a young outfielder who'd had a big year at Trenton and was just about to go into the Army.

Carpenter's first move was his best one. He got in touch with an old family friend, Herb Pennock, who had been a great left-hander with the Yankees in the 1920s and was then serving as head of the Red Sox farm system. Carpenter was lucky enough to get Pennock for his general manager and wise enough to put him in complete charge.

Pennock, who had seen Tom Yawkey try to buy a quick pennant with established stars, convinced Carpenter that the place to start buying was at the beginning of the talent ladder, not at the end. In his first year, Carpenter put out $211,000 in bonuses, almost all on kids who were either still in high school or just about to come out of school and go into the Army. Even after the majors limited the minor-league training of bonus boys to one year and prohibited the clubs from tampering with boys still in high school, Carpenter's scouts turned up at graduation exercises with money in their hands.

By the time the pennant was won, $850,000 had been paid out in bonuses.

There were some who made it. Roberts ($25,000); Simmons ($65,000); Jones ($20,000); Hamner ($9,500); Lopata ($25,000). There were plenty who didn't, notably Hugh Radcliffe, who got $40,000 and never won a game in the National League.

The Phillies ate their losses and built their team. The tragedy was that just before the boys were ready, Herb Pennock died of a cerebral hemorrhage.

In 1946, Ennis came back from the wars and stepped right into the lineup, but it wasn't until 1948 that the rest of the team began to piece itself together. Curt Simmons, having served the year's apprenticeship to which he was limited, was on the squad. Granny Hamner, whom Phillie fans had booed into tears as a 17-year-old out of high school, came back to stay. Richie Ashburn was a training-camp sensation. Dick Sisler was acquired from the Cards at the end of spring training. In June, Robin Roberts, having pitched 11 games for Wilmington and proved he was something special, was brought up. Willie Jones came up at the end of the season. Russ Meyer came over from the Cubs right after the World Series, and Waitkus came along in a trade a few months later.

It was in 1948, too, that Eddie Sawyer became the Phils' manager.

Pennock had lured Sawyer from the Yankee system with the under-standing that he would work with the Phils' kids in the minors and eventually come up and manage them in the majors. Sawyer had won two out of three pennants with Utica in the Eastern League, then had moved on to the International League in 1948 when the Phils signed a working agreement with Toronto. In July, Carpenter decided that the time had come to bring him up to Philadelphia.

Brief as Sawyer's stay in Toronto had been, it turned out to be most fruitful. As the season was coming to an end, he called up Jim Kon-stanty, a nothing-ball pitcher who had had two unsuccessful shots in the majors and not very much success in the minors (48–69 over seven years). Somehow, Konstanty had impressed Eddie as the type of pitcher who might go well in relief.

In 1949, Sawyer's boys got both experience and third place, the high-est a Philadelphia National League team had finished since 1917. Russ Meyer and old Kenny Heintzelman were the pitching stars. Konstanty appeared in 53 games and turned in some great relief work. Roberts, with a 15–15 record, established himself. Simmons (4–10) was learning how to pitch.

In 1950, the Phils picked up a second-baseman, Mike Goliat. They also came up with a couple of second-line pitchers, Bob Miller and Bubba Church, who were to pick up 19 big games between them.

Whatever the Phils' timetable was, it was just as well that they won the pennant in 1950; they were not going to win it any other year. Simmons and Miller had by far the best seasons they've ever had. Sisler, Seminick, Jones and Goliat had the best years of their lives. Ennis, the power man, had his best year. And most of all, Konstanty, shattering all records, appeared in 74 games, winning 16 and saving 30 more. Just as important, the starting line-up remained remarkably healthy through-out the year. It wasn't until Andy Seminick had to limp through the World Series with a broken bone in his ankle, and Sisler had to stay in there with a sprained wrist, that the utter worthlessness of the Phils' bench was exposed.

The kindest thing to do about the World Series is to skip over it quickly. That's what the Phils did. Although they had won the pennant, they had won it dying. After Simmons (17–8) went into the Army early in September, they seemed to lose confidence in themselves. With only 13 games to play they had a seven and a half game lead over Brooklyn; on the last day of the season it had dwindled to one lone game. They won that game, of course, on Roberts' pitching (his 20th victory) and Sisler's well-remembered tenth-inning homer, but they played through the Series as if they were apologizing for being there. When the Phils needed a hit, there was no hit. When they needed a fly, there was no fly. When they had to make an error to give the Yanks the third game, they labored and produced the error. When a routine fly ball had to fall in left-center to give the Yanks the sweep, the ball fell.

There is an adage, quoted anew whenever the Series ends in a sweep, that no poor team ever gets into the Series. Adage or no, the Series showed that the Phils were as poor a ball club as ever won a pennant in a peacetime year.

There are some historians of the game who date the general collapse of the Phillies back to the beating they took from the Yanks. Actually, the club's disciplinary troubles, which seemed to break around the head of Granny Hamner during the 1954 season, go back much further than that.

The trouble first became evident on August 15, 1949, when the Phils, having been belted by the Giants, were staying over at the Commodore Hotel in New York for a three-game series with the Dodgers. The Phillies had got off to a great start, inspiring a case of spring fever in their fans, but had gone into a miserable slump that had knocked them clear out of the first division.

Sawyer, at the end of his almost inexhaustible patience, called his players into his suite and chewed them out for playing harder off the field than on. He told them that thereafter they would live rigidly by the curfew, and that their wives would not be allowed to accompany them on road trips or even come up from Philadelphia to meet them in New York. Unless things improved, he warned them, he was not even going to permit their wives and families to accompany them to spring training.

As a final disciplinary measure, he put an end to the system whereby the players were allowed to sign for their meals. In the future, he told them, they would pick up a $6 meal allowance from trainer Frank

Wiechec, and they would pick it up by 8:30 in the morning. Anyone not able to get there in time—for reasons best known to himself—would starve for the day or, worse, pay for his own meals.

The Phils' performance picked up at once. They swept the series from Brooklyn, then ran their streak to six straight by sweeping the Giants back in Philly. Where they had been two games under .500 when Sawyer decided to shake them up, they played 27–17 ball on to the finish and came up to get third place.

Far from being grateful to Sawyer for the psychological kick in the pants, there was a clique that forever after referred to him contemptuously as "the Boy Scout."

Sawyer did not enforce the no-wife rule at Clearwater in the spring of 1950, and since the Phils went on to win the pennant, he held a light rein in 1951.

That was a mistake. In 1951, baseball was a chore for the champions. Even for champions who had been trampled and left for dead by the Yankees. Training, they seemed to feel, was strictly for the poor people. A few of the boys came out only when they were in the mood for a little baseball. At other times they would call in sick, then go out for a quiet day's fishing away from the hustle and bustle of the workaday world.

The team got away from Sawyer, as he admits, and he never quite caught up with it again. The Phils not only failed to defend their title, they dropped right out of the first division. It didn't seem possible that they had gone back that much, though. It was generally agreed that they had had an unusual run of bad luck and that when Simmons came out of the Army they would be right back up there again.

In the spring of 1952, Sawyer put his no-family, no-car rule into effect. The players' attitude, if we may stoop to historical reference, paraphrased Jefferson's reaction to a Supreme Court decision. *Sawyer has announced his rule,* they said in effect, *now let us see him enforce it.*

A couple of the boys, with fine, legal minds, installed their wives in rented homes and insisted that Clearwater was their legal residence. It was only after Sawyer threatened to move the training quarters that they sent their wives home.

Another player rented a cottage for his wife outside of town, while he himself lived at the hotel with the team. Sawyer told him to stay away from the park until she went home.

By this time, the discipline was too much and too late. The resentment against Sawyer (who could have said, like Terry Moore, "All I want these guys to do is behave like major-leaguers") was so great that his authority was gone.

It finally got so bad that at the end of May, with the Phils in the second division, Sawyer had to pull Cy Perkins out of the bullpen to act as liaison man between him and his team. He even had Perkins sit on the bench while he himself went out to the third-base coaching line to try to assume an active, visible control of his team. The only visible result, though, was a remarkable run of missed signals.

Carpenter joined the team in Cincinnati to lend Sawyer his support, and accompanied them into St. Louis. When the Phils lost their sixth straight game and dropped to sixth place, Sawyer threw up his hands and asked Carpenter to see if he could talk any sense into them.

Carpenter met the team captain, Granny Hamner, in private, in what could not have been a particularly successful parlay, since Hamner was almost immediately demoted back to the ranks.

At 3 a. m., Carpenter had all the other regulars, starting pitchers included, called to his suite at the Chase Hotel. For the first time, he ate out the team collectively and publicly. He went from player to player, telling each one exactly what he was doing wrong, both on the field and in his private life. Some of his information could only have come from private detective reports, so it was no great surprise to many of the players when the Hamner incident brought that practice to light two years later.

With a few of the players, tempers flared and Carpenter's censures brought indignant demands to be traded. "I'd love to," Carpenter said, in one case, "but who'd have you?"

With others, there was little more than Carpenter's expression of disappointment. To Roberts, who had a 7–4 record, Carpenter complained: "Robbie, you're being paid to win 20 games."

Roberts, who seemed on schedule, answered quietly, "And when the season's over, I'll have them." He did, too.

The meeting, whatever else it might have accomplished, could hardly have been expected to clear the air between Sawyer and the players. When Sawyer called in the club president, he was admitting—to the players, as well as to Carpenter—that he could no longer control his team. It meant, although Sawyer did not seem to realize it, that he was through.

Carpenter, who was personally attached to Sawyer, put off the execution for two weeks. Meanwhile he tried to decide what kind of a manager to bring in, one who would rule his team with firmness, or one who would win it with kindness. He decided to try to end the bickering by hiring Steve O'Neill, a man known to operate on the precept that major-league ballplayers are big boys now and should be treated as responsible professionals.

O'Neill didn't meet the exacting standards set up by the Phillies, either. Perhaps the sport went out of the game when there was nobody to care whether they observed training rules or not; at any rate, the players began to complain that O'Neill was indifferent to the ball game, that he might as well have been asleep on the bench for all the attention he paid to what they were doing.

By the spring of 1954, Carpenter, nearing 40 and about ready to put aside childish things, came to the conclusion that he would be well advised to turn the general manager's job over to a wage slave. The week the season opened, he hired Roy Hamey, a man of wide and responsible experience.

Hamey had entered the game as business manager for Springfield in the Three-Eye League in 1925, joined the Yankee farm system in 1933 and remained there except for a shot as president of the American Association in 1946 and a three-year tour of duty as general manager of the Pittsburgh Pirates from 1947 to 1950. He was working as George Weiss' assistant when Carpenter hired him.

In all those years, Hamey had learned a few things about the importance of the chain of command. In almost his first public statement, he let the players know that he would be available to them only after their visit had first been cleared through the manager. The unmistakable extension to that was that Carpenter's office was not open to them until it had also been cleared through channels.

The farm system could not be overhauled in a day or a week or a year, but there was one thing that could be done at once. Hamey immediately ordered an extensive scouting of the Negro Leagues. By the end of the year, 19 games had been scouted and, in October, two Negro players, Jim Mason, a pitcher, and Fran Huerra, a six-foot-five-inch first-baseman, were bought from the Kansas City Monarchs. A few weeks later, Negro scout Bill Yancey was signed. Mason and Huerra will join Teddy Washington at Clearwater this spring.

It took Hamey only one month to find himself in an incident, just about par for Philadelphia. The case of Hamner and the private eye has been pretty well chewed over by now, but to refresh any flagging memories, Granny was driving home with a friend after a night game with Milwaukee, when he spotted a car driving almost bumper to bumper with him. After Hamner got home, the car circled the block a couple of times, then parked across the street. Granny called the police, who, upon investigation, arrested private detective Charles Leland, of the aptly named Brandywine Investigation Agency. Beside him were a loaded .38 revolver and a blonde (his wife). In the rear seat, the cops found another revolver (presumably a right-handed gun used for tailing left-handed hitters).

Leland's explanation was that he had been tailing an airman on a divorce case, that the airman had a two-tone gray Cadillac with Florida license plates much like Hamner's, and that he had somehow got the two cars mixed up. Considering the stories that were to come later, Leland's was a literary gem.

It might have ended right there if Carpenter had not rushed down to the station to post bail and proclaim: "This is no case of mistaken identity. It was a case of my employing a detective agency to check on some of my players. . . . Most major-league clubs follow the same policy."

Carpenter hastened to add that he had "no suspicions of the behavior of my players, nor do I doubt their sincerity. I merely want a baseball team that will be physically and mentally prepared to play in a pennant race."

Hamner, who may have been a physical and mental wreck, but was batting .365, was furious. Never slow to take offense—he once bawled out a batboy for being slow in bringing him his bat—he accused Carpenter of "Gestapo tactics which could wreck the ball club."

Carpenter, all apologies, called a press conference at which he accepted full blame, "I made the mistake," he said, "of hiring the wrong fellow." The implication was that Private Eye Leland would be sent down to Utica for further seasoning.

Carpenter tried to make it as clear as possible that the detective had been following the wrong player (the club apparently being heavy with two-tone gray Caddies with Florida plates). Eulogizing Hamner as "one of the finest men on the club," he announced in rapid order:

1) Hamner was "entirely justified" at being burned up.

2) He intended to continue to "keep a close watch on" his players.

To a reasonable man, it could only seem as if Carpenter was saying that he was absolutely wrong in carrying out the dirty business of spying on his employees (why else would Hamner have a right to be sore?) but that he intended to keep right on doing it.

The private-detective incident seemed happily forgotten when Terry Moore came in to take over from O'Neill after the All-Star game. Although Moore was signed only for the remainder of the year, Hamey went to some lengths to emphasize that this was merely following club policy. In no manner, he insisted, was it to be considered an interim appointment. Nevertheless, the impression got out among the players that Moore was a fill-in manager. After a month, Moore called the boys together and told them that despite what they might have heard, he was set for 1955. He had let them go on thinking otherwise, he said, in order to find out which players put out all the time and which players put out only as much—or as little—as they thought they had to. What he had seen both on the field and off, he let them know, had not made him the jolliest man in Philadelphia. In the future, he warned them, there would be a $100 fine waiting for anybody extending the curfew once, and a $300 fine, publicly posted, for anybody slipping a second time.

A few days later, when Moore passed a much milder version of this lecture on to the newspapermen, Hamner reacted as if he had never heard it before. "I just can't understand it," he said. "I never saw so many silly and unfounded statements from one club as has been issued by the Phillies. When are they going to stop treating us like high-school kids?"

The Phils were in fourth place, Hamner went on to say, not because the players didn't want to finish higher, but because the top three clubs had better ballplayers.

At first glance, Hamner's remarks do not seem quite so inflammatory as, say, the Communist Manifesto. In rapid order, nevertheless, the following things happened:

1) Terry Moore announced that he was going to fine Hamner for promoting dissension.

2) Roy Hamey said that a terrible situation was being brought to light. He had heard, he said, that some of the players had been boasting: "We got Sawyer, we got O'Neill, and now we'll get this guy."

3) The players met in solemn conclave and issued a statement, which every member of the team except Hamner signed. It read: "The statements made in the press recently about our ball club were strictly the personal opinion of one player and do not represent the feelings of the rest of our squad. We have too much respect for our manager, Terry Moore, to let this go unanswered. We hope the future results on the field will bear out our feelings."

It was, of course, a direct slap at Hamner, who had to sit through the meeting, then fill the air with "no comments" afterwards.

Terry Moore revoked his fine when Hamner apologized and the manager would have been happy to let the whole thing die there. But Hamey, who perhaps looked upon the incident as a lever to break open a bad situation, continued to brief the press on the contempt—or at least indifference—the players had shown toward Moore, not only by breaking training rules, but by breaking them within sight, sound and smell of him. Whatever else you might say about the Phils, furtiveness was not one of their vices.

When the reporters went to Moore for verification, there was nothing he could do but back up his general manager. To his amazement, he kept picking up the morning papers and finding Hamey's original words attributed to him. If Moore began to have certain misgivings that he was being fattened for the hatchet, it was perhaps understandable. Although Hamey and Carpenter were pledging their swift and terrible support in any disciplinary measures he might see fit to inflict, Hamey was also going to some pains to make it clear that whatever Moore might have told the ballplayers in that historic meeting, he had *not* been signed for 1955.

As the season was coming to an end, Moore could only say wistfully: "I want to come back now, I'll admit that. This is a tough job, and I've never run out on a tough job yet."

The fury with which the front office and the players fell upon Hamner for what was, after all, a minor sort of offense at most, seems to indicate that this day of reckoning had been building for Granny ever since the private-eye caper. In both instances, Granny's outbursts, while perhaps soothing to his outraged soul, had brought the Phillies' family problems out of the clubhouse where they belonged and into the open for all the world to gaze upon. The players had even less desire than Moore to see their troubles splashed all over the newspapers.

If the players were surprised that Hamner had reacted so indignantly toward a statement he had already heard, with embellishments, in the clubhouse, they had, frankly, been just as surprised that he had been so innocent of the Phillies' policy of hiring detectives. Since that meeting at the Chase Hotel in St. Louis—and even before that, as a result of some of their private talks with Carpenter—most of the players had been both aware of and reconciled to the fact that they were being watched. None of them had thought it necessary to appeal to the American Civil Liberties Union.

Some of the boys—perhaps unfairly—even thought that Hamner had spotted Leland immediately for what he was, a detective hired to report on him, and had, on angry impulse, decided to blow the whistle on the whole deal.

With Robin Roberts, their player representative, acting as spokesman, the players insisted that both the meeting and the statement of censure had been their own idea from beginning to end. Maybe so.

To accept that explanation, though, you have to accept certain basic premises. The players didn't gather in the clubhouse to discuss it out of some common impulse; somebody had to call them there. You have to start with two or more players getting together and saying: "Look, Granny shouldn't have shot his mouth off like that about our fine manager, Terry Moore. Let's all get together and issue a statement that this does not represent the feeling of the rest of us."

Maybe that's the way it happened. On the other hand, it is possible that Roy Hamey told Carpenter exactly what he wanted out of the players *and no kidding about it;* and Carpenter called in Roberts and told him to get that statement *and no kidding about it.* As we say, it is possible that the players wrote it out themselves, but frankly, it has the smell of a lawyer's hand all over it.

Terry Moore got the support of the president of his ball club, he got the support of the general manager, he got the support of all his players, he got into the first division on the final day of the season—and then he got the gate.

By that time, however, Hamey had clearly established that the decision to dispense with Moore was his own, not the players'. With Hamey calling the signals, and Moore running a perhaps unenthusiastic interference, Mayo Smith, the Great Unknown from Birmingham, comes into Philadelphia with his control over his ball club already established.

Smith will even get a couple of boys from the farm system. From Syracuse, now owned for all practical purposes by the Phils, he will get two great pitching prospects, Jack Meyer and Jim Owens. Meyer, 23, holds the strikeout record for the Eastern League (226 in 218 innings) and he led the International League last year with 173 strikeouts in 209 innings. Owens, 21, owns a strikeout record only slightly less imposing than Meyer's, and his over-all record has been even better.

After Meyer and Owens, it's the same old story. Of the others, the best prospect seems to be Marv Blaylock, a left-handed-hitting first-baseman, whom the Phils got with the Syracuse franchise. Blaylock, who had a shot with the Giants as an outfielder in 1950, batted .303 and hit 22 home runs. Since the Phils need some power to go with Ennis—who blows very hot and very cold—Blaylock has to get a good look.

The obvious man to trade for the power the Phils need so badly would seem to be Hamner—except that Hamner, in addition to being the team's best clutch hitter, is the guts of the infield. It seems far more likely that Hamey would go all out for a second-baseman so that Hamner can go back to shortstop where he belongs. This would enable manager Smith to move Morgan over to third.

Maybe the tragedy of the Phillies will have a happy ending yet.

The
Mauch
Years

The Many Moods of Mauch

Furman Bisher

◆ ◆ ◆

Not many folks in Philadelphia had ever heard of Gene Mauch when he was hired to manage the Phillies after the first game of the 1960 season. The Atlanta Journal and Constitution *'s ageless sports editor Furman Bisher, who got one of the last interviews with Shoeless Joe Jackson nearly fifty years ago, knew the man who would come to be called the Little General. Bisher wrote one of the first pieces to appear on the young manager at the outset of what would be a long and frustrating major league career. The conventional wisdom about Mauch has been that he was the classic overmanaging type; his supporters argue that he often got better-than-average clubs just close enough to Valhalla before failing in some dramatic fashion ('64, '82, '86). But as far as the character of the man himself was concerned, Gene Mauch hasn't changed since the day in 1960 that Bisher wrote this pungent profile.*

There was a strikingly familiar photograph of Gene Mauch in the sports section of the Cincinnati *Enquirer* Sunday morning. He had Bill Jackowski, a National League umpire by the ear and was filling it full of complaint after his pitcher, Jack Meyer, had been called out on an interference play.

It was a pose that Mauch struck so frequently in the year 1953, while employed as manager, second baseman and umpire baiter by the Atlanta Crackers.

This bit of Saturday negotiation, however, was merely a rehearsal for what was to follow Sunday afternoon at Crosley Field. Under the management of Mauch, the Philadelphia Phillies and the Cincinnati Reds were concluding a four-game series with a double-header.

Reprinted with permission from *The Atlanta Journal* and *The Atlanta Constitution*.

On Saturday, the Phillies had broken a nine-game winning streak for the Reds, and on Sunday they were rubbing their noses in the dirt. As the eighth inning of the first game arrived, Philadelphia was leading Cincinnati, 9–1.

Raul Sanchez, a Cuban as thin as a soda straw, was pitching in relief for the Reds. He walked Tony Taylor, John Callison and Ken Walters singled. A run had scored and Ted Lepcio came to bat.

Sanchez, who is a sidearm pitcher, was wild with a curve and hit Lepcio on the rump. This loaded the bases. Cal Neeman, the catcher, was next and Sanchez hit him on the rump, too. Sanchez missed Joe Koppe, the shortstop, four times and walked him.

Gene Conley, pitcher by summer, rebounder for the Boston Celtics by winter, was the next batter. He is long and lank and does not offer an inviting target, but Sanchez hit him, also on his inconspicuous rump.

Conley started slowly toward first base, and as he did, this figure wearing No. 32 on the back burst out of the Phillies' dugout and charged the mound. Then, sirs and mams, the damnedest baseball brawl you ever saw broke out.

No. 32 was Gene Mauch, who had had a craw full, and who had gone to the aid of his defenseless six-foot-eight-inch pitcher. Fist fights broke out all over Crosley field and turned into wrestling matches. Ball players, coaches and umpires were wallowing all about the place in rare and sometimes ludicrous forms of combat, and it was at least 10 minutes before the riot subsided.

Before it was over Billy Martin, former welterweight champion of the American League, was led off the field bloody and torn. Robin Roberts, customarily a disciple of peace, and Frank Robinson, the Cincinnati first baseman, had squared off like Peter Jackson and Bob Fitzsimmons.

It was purely coincidental that before this game, Mauch had explained in deliberate and forthright manner his new devotion to patience, mildness and all forms of temperance.

"The best thing that ever happened to me was that year of managing in Atlanta," he said. "It took that to teach me how much I didn't know about baseball. Then I went back to playing for five more years to learn.

"I found out, for one thing, that you can't chew out a bunch of Double A Ball players because they don't play like big leaguers. I learned to sit back and watch some before I made a move."

Now in the Phillies' clubhouse, a somewhat sheepish and a somewhat serious Mauch met a rather amused press with a dour countenance.

"Well, what would you do?" he asked. "They knock down three out of four of your guys and the umpires say nothing to the pitcher. The next time they throw at the head and they hurt somebody bad. How much you gonna take of this?"

In his short time as a major league manager, Mauch has gradually won respect complimentary to a man of his position. "It wasn't sudden and easy," Sandy Grady, the Philadelphia columnist said. "For the first two or three days he didn't say much. He'd just look at you every time you asked a question, like you were a subversive agent."

Of course the conditions under which Mauch became manager of the Phillies were rather ripe with involvement. Eddie Sawyer developed a deep-seated grouch against the Phillies and gave in to a violent urge to get out the day after the season opened.

That night, in a motel room in Pompano Beach, Fla., Mauch's telephone rang him out of a deep sleep. He had the Minneapolis ball club there for an exhibition series with Dallas.

"It was John Quinn," Gene said. "He said, 'A friend of mine wants to know if you're interested in managing a major league club.'

"He said, 'Are you interested; I want to know that first.'

"I said, 'Who is it, the Phillies?'

"That's the way it happened. I took the job right there."

There was a story the other day that Mauch had called on his athletes, who have a reputation for playboyism, and laid down the law. That varies a bit from the official version.

"I didn't want to walk in here new and start off with a set of rules that might be needed," Mauch said. "I wanted to see for myself what was necessary and what wasn't, see what kind of fellows these guys were.

"I found out and then I made up my rules and I posted them, that's what took place. Now they know what I expect of them."

Patient, temperate, reserved, mild, objective, humanitarian, all of these virtues possessed our young man until Sunday afternoon in the eighth inning of the first game. Then the hell with all that. He wasn't going to take nothing off nobody no more.

He is still learning and this was one of those lessons.

The Dalton Gang Rides Again

Walter Bingham

◆ ◆ ◆

It's hard to believe that this piece by Walter Bingham nearly caused him and
Sports Illustrated *legal problems. This story of the Phillies' bullpen crew laid
the groundwork for later writers (like Jim Bouton) willing to test libelous waters,
and for the tell-all exposés and biographies that have saturated the market since.
This piece might put some readers in mind of the 1993 Phillies; but, as
Bingham notes, throwbacks to an earlier age of hard-living ballplayers or not,
the Dalton Gang just wasn't good enough to be so bad.*

The old days in baseball, seen through the prim prism of the present, are remembered by many nostalgic fans as a glorious, untamed era of roughhouse and riot. There were Ty Cobb and his flying
spikes, the rowdy Gashouse Gang, the terrible-tempered John McGraw;
there was Grover Cleveland Alexander, a mighty man on the mound or
at the bar; most of all, there was Babe Ruth, carousing his way through
the frightened West with bat and bottle.

Nowadays baseball seems much milder. Wally Moon has a master's
degree, Stan Musial is vice-president of a bank, Vernon Law is a deacon
of the Mormon Church. The typical ballplayer is an exemplary citizen,
a conservative businessman whose business just happens to be swinging
a bat.

But last week a splash of headlines served to remind the fan—who
took the news not entirely with regret—that a few throwbacks to the
raucous old days still exist. The most successful upholders of the old
tradition are a group of wild-living, fun-loving, hell-raising players on

the last-place Philadelphia Phillies who are known as The Dalton Gang. Whenever one of their nocturnal escapades lands them in trouble and makes the papers, someone around the National League invariably says: "I see where the Dalton Boys were out riding again last night."

Currently there are three members of the gang, all pitchers, Dick Farrell, 26, alias The Turk, and Jim Owens, 26, alias The Bear, are charter members, dating back to early last year, when Tom Ferrick, then the Phillies' pitching coach, gave the group its name. Jack Meyer, 28, called The Bird, is new to The Dalton Gang this year. ("He was a fringe member last season," says one sportswriter. "You might say he rode shotgun.") Seth Morehead, a fourth pitcher, was also a member last year, but he was traded to Chicago.

Two weeks ago in Pittsburgh, on a Saturday night, Jack (The Bird) Meyer went out on what may prove to be his last ride for the Daltons. It sent him to the hospital with a herniated disk and it also cost him $1,200, the amount of the fine slapped on him by Philadelphia General Manager John Quinn. It was, in proportion to salary, the largest fine ever levied on a ballplayer. Babe Ruth and Ted Williams were each hit with a $5,000 fine during their careers, but Ruth was making $80,000 at the time and Williams $125,000. Meyer is making about $14,000, so the fine represents roughly 9% of his 1960 salary.

The Bird's trouble began in a night spot just up the street from the hotel in Pittsburgh where the Phillies were staying. Meyer, who had been drinking, and his roommate, Harry Anderson, were at a table near two sportswriters, Allen Lewis and Ray Kelly, and broadcaster Byrum Saam. Meyer was talking loudly on the subject of race horses. Lewis tried to quiet him down. Meyer became furious, wanted to punch Lewis and had to be led back to the hotel by his roommate. After Meyer had been put to bed, Turk Farrell decided it would be amusing to pour ice water on him. Again Meyer came up fighting, and again the patient Anderson, with the help of a teammate, John Buzhardt, had to calm Meyer and get him to bed. Then Meyer received a phone call, which for some reason upset him once more. He stormed about the room, ripping the Venetian blinds, smashing the radio and trying to fight his teammates. At some point during the battle, Meyer hurt his back. The next day he told Manager Gene Mauch what had happened. Mauch bundled Meyer off to Philadelphia to a hospital, his name was placed on the team's disabled list and he was fined.

When he learned the amount of the fine, Meyer was incensed. "What do they think I am, a millionaire?" he demanded. "I've got four kids to support." In rapid order Meyer threatened to hire a lawyer and fight the fine, announced he would quit baseball, and asked Phillie Owner Bob Carpenter for his unconditional release so he could sign with another club. Hearing all this, Manager Gene Mauch said, "Meyer is a problem. Do you think any manager wants to take a problem off my hands?"

Mauch's statement made Philadelphia sportswriters smile. One of the first questions they asked the new manager when he took over the Phillies two months ago was how he planned to handle the team's problem players.

"No problems as far as I'm concerned," Mauch said at the time. Later on he hedged. "If problems do arise," he conceded, "I'll try something to solve them. If that doesn't work out, I'll try something else." Not long after that Mauch said grimly: "Some of these guys are taking liberties."

More Trouble

The Dalton Gang has taken a lot of liberties since its formation. Last year Farrell was fined after he smashed a barroom mirror. Owens' after-game behavior was bad enough to warrant a special lecture on the subject by General Manager Quinn when the two discussed Owens' 1960 contract. Owens was promised a $500 bonus if his conduct this year met the club's approval. The Bear didn't even make it through spring training. He got involved in a barroom brawl in Florida, lost the bonus and was fined an extra hundred to boot. For one day he quit baseball, during which time he explained to reporters that he was that rare kind of pitcher who could stay up all night drinking and then go out and throw a shutout.

Despite their common love of the fast, loose life—hard drinking, frequent fighting, late hours and casual friendships—the members of

The Dalton Gang have widely different backgrounds. Meyer comes from a well-to-do New Jersey family and went to school at Philadelphia's Penn Charter School and Duke University. He is blond, good looking and he dresses well. "He can be pleasant one moment, mean the next," says a sportswriter. "He has a great need to be wanted and applauded."

Farrell is from a quiet, middle-class family that lives near Boston. He had polio as a boy, managed to overcome it, but still walks with a slight limp. He is big and tough, occasionally unfriendly, occasionally abusive.

Owens comes from a broken home. "His father used to come down to breakfast and put a bottle on the table," says a man who knows him. "Jim started drinking early."

"They're a wild bunch," one National League player said recently. "I don't believe there's anything they wouldn't try."

Mauch and Quinn cracked down heavily on Jack Meyer because the Phillies, while they are going nowhere this season, have many young and talented rookies. "It is up to the older players to set an example," Mauch has said. He knows that while barroom brawls may be fun, they don't win pennants.

Unlike some of the storied hellraisers of old, the members of The Dalton Gang aren't really good enough to be so bad. Perhaps the fine Jack Meyer must pay will shock him and his friends into a more moderate way of life. If not, members of The Dalton Gang probably will find themselves riding elsewhere, and separately.

What It Feels Like
to Lose 23 in a Row

Si Burick

◆ ◆ ◆

Si Burick, the Ohio sportswriter who never failed to make the Dutton Best
Sports Stories *year after year, was a master of the interview piece, a veteran
author who knew how to quote at length and what to ask (see his books on
Walter Alston and Sparky Anderson, if you can find them). In this brief clip
from the* Dayton Daily News, *which in some ways foreshadows the heartbreak-
ing '64 season, Burick makes his point, quotes Gene Mauch on the 1961 experience, and sums it all up in a few choice words. If brevity is the soul of wit, this
piece does the same for the soul of futility. The headline of Sandy Grady's column in the* Evening Bulletin *on the day after the 7–4 victory against the
Milwaukee Braves ended the Phillies 23-game losing streak asked, "Now the Big
Question Is: Can Phils Win 2 in Row?"*

There was a time last summer when the Philadelphia Phils
stumbled onto a seemingly bottomless slide that did not end until
they had lost 23 straight games.

Gene Mauch, ambitious, boyish-looking Philly manager, hates to
think that he will be remembered for surviving this experience, one of
the most miserable in baseball history.

"What did you think, Gene, when it began to look as if the Phils
would never win another game?"

"I'll never be able to describe it," Mauch said. "I doubt if anyone can
describe it for me. But, as you can imagine, it was awful.

"The first seven or eight games of the streak weren't tough to take.

Reprinted by permission of the *Dayton Daily News*.

We had a young club. We were building for the future. We knew those kids would lose a lot.

"When the streak got into double figures, I kept telling myself it would have to end today. But it didn't. I'd go home and tell myself, 'I'm gonna quit; I've gotta quit.' But I didn't. I'd show up the next day and something would go wrong and we'd lose again. I'd say, 'I wish they'd fire me. Why don't they fire me?' But they didn't fire me.

"We got into a stretch where we'd be leading and then something would happen in the late innings—usually, a mistake—and we'd lose again. So I'd tell myself the boys are too tense. They want to win too much. They're too tight. I'll play it loose. We'll kid around on the bench. We'd play it that way and lose again.

"Then I told myself that wasn't the system. We'd have to play it tighter. We'd go down fighting to the last out. We lost again. Nothing went right. I had terrible nights and days. Then there came a day—after 23 beatings in a row—when we won one. Finally, I had a good night's sleep. The whole thing was over.

"You don't get any compensation out of another guy's misery, but when the Dodgers blew their chance at the pennant by losing ten straight late in the season, I said to myself, 'Suppose this was you instead of Smokey Alston. Suppose you had a pitching staff of four arms like the Dodgers and you went around that staff two-and-a-half times before you picked up a win. How would you feel about that?'

"All I can say is that I don't wish it on my worst enemy. You think it's going to kill you but the human body and mind can take punishment. That's what I found out when we were losing those 23 in a row," Gene Mauch concluded and he shuddered at the memory.

Something Special

Larry Merchant

◆ ◆ ◆

Richie Allen was my boyhood hero. I remember getting letters from my mother at summer camp that began "Dear Richy," which I abruptly corrected by signing my letters home, "Love, Richie," though Allen preferred to be called Dick. I was further thrilled by the fact that my sister taught Allen's son at the private school he attended in Mt. Airy. Though I never met him, I will never forget watching Allen at the plate, swinging the bat so effortlessly it seemed and hitting the ball so far.

Despite the troubles that would follow him around, Allen remained one of my all-time favorites, both times he played in Philadelphia. There are stories enough to fill a book concerning Allen's alleged dissention on the five teams he played for during his career, but just about all of his managers have said that if they had to do it all over again, they would still want him on their teams. Though he did not play in Philadelphia until nearly ten years after Johnny Kennedy, Allen, in the racially volatile year of 1963, was responsible for breaking the color barrier at the Phillies minor league franchise in Little Rock, Arkansas, where, writes Tim Whitaker, many people "believe that things first began to go awry for the powerful slugger." A lot of people complain about what Allen might have *done (if only, if only), but a quick study of his lifetime stats will show that he accomplished more in fifteen years than most major leaguers could ever dream to.*

This short profile, written by one of Philadelphia's and the nation's most celebrated sportswriters in the middle of Allen's rookie year in 1964, captures Dick Allen as we would like to remember him: so young and raw, full of potential, and happy to be here. Merchant may have been one of the few writers to understand what Allen had gone through to get to the majors and what, given his ability, he could achieve.

From the *Philadelphia Daily News*, July 13, 1964. Reprinted by permission.

It is fairly obvious by now that the Phillies have something more substantial at third base than noise, tape, a glover and a prayer, which has been the formula since Willie Jones and his chiropodist retired. They have Richie Allen. He is something special.

As the Phils come to the halfway point in the schedule tonight, Richie Allen is on his way to one of the great rookie seasons in the history of the game. If he isn't a superstar in the making, Haley's Comet won't come back in 1975.

The figures on Allen show this: at his present pace he will hit around .300, drive in and score 100 runs, get 190 to 200 base hits with 30–35 homers, 35–40 doubles and 10 triples: and he'll strike out 160 times. It won't work out just that way, of course. His average and home run production may sag. But there is no way he can have anything but a big, big, year.

Allen already is a strong favorite to become Rookie of the Year and he has a shot at a much gaudier prize if the Phillies win the pennant: Most Valuable Player. The odds on such a parley are astronomical; it has never been done before. But no one has ever had a better chance than Allen.

He Defies Generalities

Putting it in another perspective, among active players only Vada Pinson, Frank Robinson, Orlando Cepeda and Mickey Mantle have had major league debuts as impressive as Allen is having. You could add Tony Oliva, the Minnesota phenom, to the list. He, for goodness sakes, is outhitting Allen.

"When you talk about Allen," says Gene Mauch, "you can't make generalities.

He is one of those players who defies the generalities."

He is one of those players who defies even his own generalities. A slow starter in the minors, he got off to a fast start here. Occasionally a streaky hitter in the minors, he has been a model of consistency here— he hasn't gone more than two games in a row without a hit.

"There's no telling what he'll do when he gets to know the League," says Mauch. "You can see signs of it now. A pitcher he hasn't seen before may get him out three times in a row, but the fourth time he's rough."

Richie Allen is laconic and he walks and talks softly and he smokes a pipe. He looked back at the first half of the season after yesterday's two losses to Milwaukee through curls of smoke. He saw it clearly.

Not Surprised, He Feels Happier

"I'm not surprised by anything," he said. "It's a game up here, just like anywhere else. It's a game I love to play. Somehow I feel happier."

A month and a half after he joined the Phillies' farm system, Allen was hitting nothing. He went through turmoil of one kind or another through much of his minor league career, some of it self-inflicted, some of it not. Perhaps this explains what he meant by his happiness remark. He wouldn't elaborate on it.

"I was hitting .154," he said. "Usually I don't pay any attention to my average until the end of the season, but I knew it because the manager, Jack Phillips, told me he was going to bench me. He wanted to change me. He told me I'd never make the majors unless I changed. I told him I didn't want to change. Then I went 11-for-12 in a series in Billings and 9-for-12 in Idaho Falls."

They leave him alone and let him play ball now, Richie Allen seemed to be saying. They credit him with enough intelligence to figure things out for himself.

"The book on me at the start of the season was throw me fast balls high and tight," he said. "That's why I was pulling the ball more than usual. Then, abruptly, they switched. It happened when we went from Milwaukee to St. Louis. They started to pitch me outside. I had a little trouble because I was still trying to pull, but I adapted. You have to adapt in this game."

If Allen has absorbed more than a handful of impressions in his brief tour he is keeping them to himself. Bob Gibson has showed him the No. 1 fast ball. Hank Aaron and Ernie Banks have showed him the best attitude—loose, even-tempered, business-like. Brooks Robinson, who he hasn't seen much of, has shown him the best glove at third base.

"That's what I want to be, the best," Richie Allen said. "Not one of the best. The best."

Jim Bunning: Daddy's-Day Pitcher

Ray Robinson

◆ ◆ ◆

This crisply written account of Jim Bunning's perfect game against the Mets on Fathers' Day, 1964, arguably the defining moment of that season, originally appeared in Baseball Stars of 1965, *Ray Robinson's yearly review for Pyramid Books. I remember June 21, 1964, vividly and, in fact, wrote about it myself in a piece for* Nine: A Journal of Baseball History and Social Policy Perspectives *(Vol. 4, no. 2). Bunning got some unintentional help for his perfect game from catcher Gus Triandos by shaking him off about 10 percent of the time. As John Steadman wrote in the* Baltimore News-American, *Triandos might have been "the only man in the history of baseball who didn't know he was catching a perfect game . . . although from the fifth inning on he realized it was a no-hitter." Ray Robinson is also the author of* Iron Horse: Lou Gehrig in His Time *(1991, Harper Perennial) and* Matty: An American Hero *(1994, Oxford University Press). Kentuckyian Bunning is a member of the U.S. House of Representatives and the Baseball Hall of Fame.*

It has become popular to assume that anything can and will happen at Shea Stadium, the home of the New York Mets. The assumption is based part on persistent press agentry and part on performance.

On Father's Day, June 21, 1964, a very hot Sunday in New York, when anyone with a bathing suit and the price of a trip to the beach was lolling at the seashore—that is, anyone who wasn't a Mets fan—something unusual *did* occur in Casey Stengel's solarium. A tall, right-handed pitcher named Jim Bunning, with a keen eye for the shifting fortunes of the stock market and an even keener eye for the dimen-

From *Baseball Stars of 1965* by Ray Robinson (New York: Pyramid Books, 1965). Reprinted by permission of Ray Robinson.

sions of home plate, threw a total of 90 pitches in nine innings. Only 21 of them were balls. The rest were strikes, fouls or were hit for outs.

The result: the first perfect game in the National League since someone named John Ward licked Buffalo back in June, 1880. Someone else named Don Larsen, more likely to be remembered by the current crop of ball fans, spun his perfectionist magic in 1956, for the Yanks against the Brooklyn Dodgers in the World Series. Until Jim Bunning consumed less than two-and-a-half hours anesthetizing the Mets, in behalf of the Philadelphia Phillies, nobody in either league had bothered equalling Larsen's perfect game. And before Larsen had done it, you had to go all the way back to Charley Robertson's 1922 game against the Detroit Tigers, to find a no-hit, no-run, no-man-on ball game.

In other words, Jim Bunning really made Shea Stadium live up to its press notices. Yet, despite the fact that Bunning pitched the most talked-about, most publicized single game of the 1964 season, he would probably have turned the whole thing in for a routine 20th victory.

The reason is quite simple and has nothing to do with Bunning's aversion to perfection or the ultimate in pitching prowess. His team lost the National League flag to the Cards by a single game. In the last two weeks of the season, when the Phillies melted away like snowballs in the late summer sun, Jim, working sometimes with only two days rest, couldn't produce a victory. Then, on the final day of the campaign he shut out the Cincinnati Reds for his 19th win. Perfect games, shutouts, schmutouts—he would have settled for a mediocre 12–11 triumph, if it could have meant the pennant for his club.

"Am I satisfied?" said Bunning on the afternoon the season came to its harrowing end. "I should say not. We didn't win the pennant. And that's what we had in mind ten days ago."

In June, when he baffled the Mets with his assortment of sidearm strikes and sliders, both Bunning and the Phils were riding high. Gene Mauch had his team in first place, Bunning already had won seven games ("When he loses, we are shocked," said Dennis Bennett, then a fellow worker of Jim's) and the Mets were performing with the perfect futility everyone expected of them.

As the fans crowded into Shea Stadium that day—32,026 of them were on hand, including Jim's wife, Mary, and his oldest daughter, 12-

year-old Barbara—Manager Mauch had a sneaking suspicion this was going to be more than an ordinary game.

He watched from the dugout as Bunning went through his warmup ritual. Maybe it was hindsight, but Mauch recalled later for the press that Jim seemed "special."

"The way he was throwing, so live and as high as he was. Not high with his pitches. High—himself," said Mauch.

When the game started, Bunning faced the Mets lead-offer Jim Hickman. He threw him two balls that Jim fouled off, both sliders. Then, audaciously, he laughed in Hickman's face, and shouted down at him from his lofty perch on the mound: "You won't get any more like that!"

On the next pitch, Hickman struck out. It was a perfect start to a perfect afternoon.

Once Jesse Gonder, the Mets catcher, hit a hard shot into the hole between first and second base. But agile Tony Taylor was there to gobble it up and throw him out with a good throw. That was the closest the Mets came to a hit all day.

As the game progressed everyone realized Bunning was working to be the perfect Daddy on Daddy's Day. What more could he present to his Missus and his four girls and three boys?

From the fifth inning on, Jim was so aware of his budding masterpiece, that he almost led cheers from the dugout. He exhorted his mates, jabbered incessantly, paced back and forth, tabulated aloud how many outs he had to go for the perfecto, tried to relax by talking about the event. In other words, he did everything to defy protocol and the time-honored superstition that ballplayers don't like to talk about no-hitters while they're happening.

"I knew I had a chance after Tony made that play on Gonder," said Bunning. "If you talk about it you're not as disappointed, if you don't get it."

The way the Mets were walking up there and then sitting down, there didn't seem to be much doubt that Bunning would get what he was chirping about. But even one error in this type of game could spoil Bunning's effort and that meant that the pressure was on everyone in a Philly uniform, not alone Bunning.

"When I heard Jim," said John Briggs, the first-year center fielder, "I kept telling myself that if I had to I'd dive ten feet for the ball." Bunning, however, made such strenuous effort unnecessary.

In the late innings Jim motioned to his infielders and outfielders where to play, much as Mauch himself might. But Mauch didn't resent such usurpation from his crew-cutted hurler. "I think he did it as much to relax himself as he did it to relax his teammates," said the understanding manager.

By the ninth inning, Bunning was so high and hopeful, his catcher, Gus Triandos, could only describe him as "silly."

"I'd like to have Koufax's fast one right now," he laughed, as he trudged to the mound to begin his last mile. He had to get Charlie Smith, George Altman and whoever Stengel would nominate to bat for pitcher Tom Sturdivant.

Smith obliged by popping one up in foul territory to shortstop Bobby Wine. One out. The normally partisan Met crowd roared its approval of the enemy pitcher. Altman swung at a low curve for Bunning's ninth strikeout and you would have thought the Mets had just won the flag.

Now Johnny Stephenson, a lefty, came up to challenge Bunning's big ball game. This young man hasn't broken up many games in his time and maybe in their hearts, to borrow that unfortunate political slogan, the Mets were hoping the kid would get it over with quickly. But in baseball you play it all out, even when you're behind 6–0 and a guy has a fortune riding with one more out, if he gets it.

Stephenson missed a curve, watched a called second strike, then took two balls. On the fifth pitch Jim wrapped a curve around the youngster's bat and the game—the perfect game, from top to bottom—was over.

That night it became official. Jim Bunning appeared as a special guest star on the Ed Sullivan Show, for a cool thousand dollars.

James Paul Bunning, out of Southgate, Kentucky, the same town that gave millionaire jockey Eddie Arcaro to the world, is now 33 years old. Last year was his tenth in the majors, but only his first season in the National League. For nine years, after a minor league apprenticeship in Richmond (Ohio-Indiana League), Davenport in the Three-Eye, Williamsport in the Eastern, Buffalo in the International, Little Rock in the Southern Association, and Charleston in the American Association, Jim had been the mainstay of the Detroit Tigers pitching staff.

In 1957, his third year in the big-time, Jim won 20 games for the Tigers, against 8 losses. If he could have won only one more game in '64, he would have emerged as that rarity—a pitcher with 20-game seasons in both leagues.

In all, Jim won 118 games for the Tigers and on two occasions he led all American League pitchers in the strikeout department. He pitched on five American League All-Star teams, with an impressive mark of four hits yielded in 14 innings.

By all odds his record in the American League had stamped him as one of the genuine pitching stars of his circuit. Yet a succession of Detroit managers were never quite satisfied with his work. For one thing, they felt Jim's temperament could stand a little mellowing. He was alternately rated a hot-head, by his own pilots, and a "head-hunter" by enemy batsmen.

However, nobody ever faulted his intelligence and serious devotion to the game. A stockbroker in the off-season, he represented the American League players in their pension demands.

The year Jim won 20 for the Tigers he gave up 33 home runs. In '63, his final season with Detroit, he won only 12 games, against 13 losses, and threw up 38 home run pitches, to lead all pitchers in the American League.

"I don't care how many homers I give up, if I win," said Jim. But the Detroit management had tired of his gopher problem. Their solution was to ship him out of the league in December, 1963. Lots of eyebrows were raised by the deal. The Phillies gave up Don Demeter, a prodigious RBI man, and minor league hurler Jack Hamilton, for Jim and Gus Triandos.

Those in the Detroit camp who had thought the 6'3" graduate of Xavier University in Cincinnati was washed up, turned out to be sadly mistaken.

By All-Star time of 1964, Bunning was again chosen for the All-Star team. But this time it was the National League club. He pitched two good innings for the Nationals and permitted two singles.

It was obvious the Phils had gotten just what they wanted, a leader for their improved pitching staff. As the Phils moved ahead in the race, Jim became the "stopper" and Mauch, who was playing in the American League when Bunning was a Tiger mainstay, insisted "he's a better pitcher now because he has better control."

"Delivery, that's what Bunning has," said the Philly pilot. "He throws strikes now. Just check his record of walks. It's amazing."

Bunning, himself, thought he was making fewer mistakes than ever before. "I get the ball where I want it more consistently," he said. At season's end he'd given up only 46 walks in 284 innings and his strikeout total was still a bright 219. Jim is now eighth on the list of still-active pitchers in the strikeout department. He has 1,625 Ks on his ledger. The sportswriters voted him the NL's comeback player of the year in a post-season AP poll, but that didn't assuage Jim's feelings about the loss of the pennant.

Obviously Jim Bunning has improved over the years. In July, 1958, he pitched a no-hitter for the Tigers at Fenway park over the Boston Red Sox. He had to throw 132 pitches to do it and two men walked. Six years later, pitching in the other league, he unfolded his perfect game.

If the man keeps on mellowing and learning, as he goes along, there's no telling what's ahead. Maybe a perfect game, with only 27 pitches.

A Week with the Phillies

Arnold Hano

◆ ◆ ◆

In the days before the great collapse of '64, one of baseball's best itinerant free-lance writers, Arnold Hano, author of the vintage A Day in the Bleachers *(1955, 1982, Da Capo Press)—his book-length account of the first game of the 1954 Giants–Indians World Series, with its famous description of Willie Mays's over-the-shoulder catch and even more spectacular throw—spent the first week of September with the red-hot Phillies, who were comfortably in first place and headed toward the pennant.*

The purpose of this piece, written for Sport, was to get an intimate feel as to how a young, aggressive team was handling itself going into the stretch drive. The Phillies exude the confidence and excitement they had shown for the first 150 games of that ill-fated season, unsuspecting of what lay ahead. Hano wrote the story before the collapse, and he published it after the disaster, hence the last line (tacked on at publication). Hano, now in his seventies, worked in the Peace Corps 1991–93 in Costa Rica, where he lives part of the year. A commercial writer for seven decades, he has published 26 books (including best-selling biographies of Sandy Koufax and Willie Mays) and close to 600 magazine pieces, newspaper stories, and columns.

It had been the dryest August the city of Philadelphia had known this century. But not for the Phillies. They'd won 19 ballgames, lost ten, and overwhelmingly increased the first-place lead they'd taken on July 16. As the dry month moved on, the possibility started to become a plausibility, and then the plausibility became a probability.

The Phillies—fourth in 1963, seventh in 1962, eighth in 1961, and eighth in 1960—the Phillies were acting as though they were going to win the 1964 pennant.

From *Sport*, December 1964. Reprinted by permission of Arnold Hano.

And then it was September. The last month. Oh, I know the '64 schedule ran over into October, but September remains the last month, the final lap, the drive to the wire. The stretch.

I flew to New York and rented a car, and drove to Philadelphia, and I watched the Phillies, as they went into the stretch.

But, first, August died with an explosion. On August 28 in this city that is the cradle of western liberty and which calls itself the city of brotherly love, a minor incident on the city's North Side suddenly, furiously, bloodily, tragically erupted into violent rioting. Heads were split open, a man was shot by a policeman—later he would die—looters smashed storefront windows and ransacked shelves. Gangs roamed.

September 1

Connie Mack Stadium stands, or leans, on the north edge of this North Side. You drive through the North Side to get to the ballpark. The aftermath of a riot is, in a sense, almost more tragic than the night of violence itself. The streets had a forlorn look, empty, broken. People stayed indoors. Red police cars quietly patrolled the streets. Boards had replaced broken windows. It looked as if man had been evicted from his dwellings. The city—here—was a silent bomb shelter.

None of this matters, or perhaps it all matters and none of what follows matters. This is a story about baseball, not about riots. But somehow the two may entwine. Practically speaking, one had an effect on the other. People stayed away from Connie Mack Stadium for days afterward, and though the Phillies kept drawing crowds, the crowds were smaller than anticipated, and Bob Carpenter, the man who owns the Phillies, blamed the riots. So did others.

There were other effects. If August was dry, it was nothing compared to the first week of September at Connie Mack Stadium. No beer was sold. This was Philadelphia's solemn and official answer to the rioters. Taverns and liquor stores in the area were shut.

But the truest effect—I think—lay on the field. The Phillies began September with three games against Houston. Jim Bunning went against Hector (Skinny) Brown, and the game should have been tense, should have caught up the 13,306 fans and had them shouting, roaring, swearing, praying. Houston has been a patsy for Philadelphia all season. On this evening, the 39-year-old Brown threw his knuckleball with stubborn skill all night. For four innings, the Phils did not have a hit. Tony Taylor singled in the fifth. Until the seventh, Brown held the Phils scoreless.

So did Bunning hold the Colts.

Yet there was a placid quality about it all. Later, Gene Mauch said, "Shoot, we been in games like this all year long. If we don't beat 'em one way, we beat 'em another. We grind people up. We knew we were going to win it."

So it may have been that, or it may have been the dull aftermath of bloodshed and savagery. Into the seventh they went, swiftly and quietly, and in the seventh, Johnny Callison, who is the best .270 hitter the league knows, hit a knuckleball.

"I felt it was going out as soon as I hit it," he said.

There was a wind blowing that night, toward right field. Callison hit the ball toward the tin-and-wood wall in right, high in the air. But the wind was a bag of tricks, full of currents and dead spots, and the ball began to lag. "I got scared," Callison said.

The ball went over, barely scraping the back of the wall. And the Phils had a run. A batter later, they had another. Wes Covington, right behind Callison, hit one out, and this raised no doubts. One out after that, Frank Thomas hit one out. An inning later, Richie Allen hit one in. That is, he hit a ball to deep center field, where baseballs have been fielded better than this one was, and when it was over, Allen had an inside-the-park home run. Four home runs. Four runs, and Jim Bunning pitching into the ninth. Ho-hum.

Except in the stretch, when it comes up September, nothing is ever ho-hum again. Not until the magic number has disappeared. The Colts put two men on, and Joe Gaines hit a three-run home run, and the Phillies won this silent-ish ballgame, 4–3.

Afterward Gus Triandos talked about pressure, about the tension of the stretch. Triandos knows. He was with Baltimore in 1960 when the Orioles rushed up at the Yankees, and the Yankees smacked them down four times running. "Pressure?" Triandos told a Philadelphia reporter. "Sure there's pressure." But he insisted on modifying it. "There's pressure in every town in baseball There's pressure to win, early or late in the season." And he took a swipe at the notion of men who yield to pressure, and men who rise above it. "I've always hated the word 'clutch' or 'choke.' "

Hate the words all you want to. Until man manages to keep his psyche still, we will have inner urges that propel us, rip us, immobilize us, inspire us. Ballplayers say it differently. Richie Allen is 22 years old. Just a boy. People were saying he was not only the most valuable rookie in the league, maybe he was the most valuable player. Allen demurred. "Johnny Callison deserves the MVP," he said. "He's had more clutch hits than anyone in the league this year."

Allen had some himself. He also had a painful groin injury, and it affected his running. "I'm as quick as my mother," he grunted. But he also said, "I don't want to rest. It's too close to the end. I've got all winter to rest."

So the game was over. The Phils had won one. September had begun. But nothing is soft in September. Bobby Wine, the young shortstop, lay in traction, his back a single throb of pain. Later that week, Clay Dalrymple, the catcher, would hurt his knee. Ruben Amaro, the other shortstop, would land on his right shoulder in a rundown play (he made the out), and by nightfall the shoulder would swell. Cookie Rojas—who looks like a stock clerk—would turn an ankle. "We've bandaged from butt to belly button," manager Mauch would say before the week was out.

This was the stretch.

September 2

The Phillies dugout holds heat like a tin cup. Yet men before a game— players, the manager, coaches, writers, and the hangers-on who always are on a ballfield—congregate in the home-team dugout, and there they talk, or listen.

Wes Covington was asked whether he'd ever been on a team that hit three home runs in a row—the Phils had come within an out the night before—and Covington said, Sure, twice: Mathews, Aaron, and himself, for Milwaukee. Frank Thomas had been in an inning where four men—he was one of the four—had hit consecutive home runs. It lay there like that, the rest of the onlookers eyeing Covington and Thomas. Then Gene Mauch—a man who hit .239 in the majors, and spent 11 of his 16 years in baseball in the minors—said, "The Red Sox in '57 hit four homers in a row." The hitters were Williams, Malzone, Gernert—and Gene Mauch.

But not all the memories on the field were of success. Johnny Callison had been on a pennant winner himself, once before. He was a member of the White Sox of '59 for 49 ballgames. He'd hit a measly .173. "I was disgusted. I was embarrassed to be signing baseballs before games, with the rest of the Sox," he said. He got a half-share cut of the Series money that year, but he remembers—mostly—his embarrassment. The year 1964 will never embarrass Callison. "With my average, I don't think about the MVP," he said. "It'd be nice, but I'm not planning."

Callison is a goodlooking young man, movie-looking, and he is the idol of this city. Because of those clutch hits, much was expected. Yet Callison denied that any tenseness had now held him. "I'm not tense. The team isn't tense. Nobody's panicked yet." He said the last with a grin.

It is a grinning team. The word sportsmen would use is "loose." The men look as though they're enjoying themselves. The year 1950—when the Phils led by seven games as late as Labor Day, and won the pennant only by beating the Dodgers on the very last day of the season—is too many years ago. John Callison was 11 years old.

A grinning team. Laughing. Wes Covington, the team strong man, allowed how once in Cincinnati he'd been hit on the head with a pitched ball. "The ball ended up past the pitching mound."

That's strong.

Gene Mauch said, "This year is the most fun I've ever had in my life. Nobody worries." But as he spoke, in the dugout, he was watching the Houston batters. "We don't worry about the Giant or the Cincy scores. It doesn't matter what they do—if we win." In the hitter's cage—so tattered and torn it looks like something the Flying Wallendas fell through—Houston's huge Walt Bond hit a screaming drive over the right-field wall. "That Bond is strong," Mauch said admiringly. "It's a remarkable thing he's done. Nineteen home runs, in Houston, in that gale."

On the bench, Jack Baldschun—the tireless relief pitcher—smoked a cigaret. Coach Peanuts Lowery smoked a cigar. Manager Mauch chain-smoked. Coach Bob Oldis—who would be re-activated as a catcher before the week was up—chewed tobacco. It is, likely, the most nicotine-stained ballclub in the majors. A Phillie pennant—someone said—would set back the drive on cancer 20 years.

On this warm night, Mauch sent up Chris Short to face the Colts. Short was working with only two days' rest. "The last time I had two days' rest," Short said, "I struck out 14 men."

This time he struck out only ten men. In the sixth, he gave up the second of two walks, and two singles later, the Colts had a run. It wasn't enough.

For three innings, the Phils blew chances. It is the mark of the team. They blow chances, and still win. The other guy blows them, and loses. Call it luck. It is something the Yankees have had for years. Call it what you will. It is also the mark of a winner.

Gonzalez singled to open the Phil first. Dalrymple walked to open the second. Pitcher Short and Gonzalez hit back-to-back singles to open the third. Nobody scored.

Still, they grind away. In the fourth, Wes Covington was fooled by a changeup, and the count was 0-and-2. He singled to right. Clay Dalrymple tried to bunt, missed, tried again and raised a foul pop. Four Colts had a shot at it; all four missed. "A guy gets peeved when he can't bunt," Dalrymple said later. "I got mad." So he singled to right. Frank Thomas bunted ("I'm a good bunter because I work at it. In 1956 I didn't take a lunch hour in spring training. Instead I'd practice bunting. That year I beat out 16 of 20 bunts."), and Tony Taylor looped a single to center for two runs. Thus, the Phils played, for one run—Dalrymple's bunt try—and because they failed, they got two.

But they also held the one-run lead. In the ninth, with one out, Bob Aspromonte hit a bouncing ball toward third. Allen backed up and threw past Thomas for a two-base error, his 34th. "When a man made an error behind me in the past, I'd let down," Short said. "Now I know the guys aren't trying to make errors." Instead of letting down, Short got Joe Gaines and Carroll Hardy, and the ballgame was over.

But the error permitted Philadelphia fans to do something they do better than any other fans in America. Boo.

September 3

Philadelphia fandom is a great beast. Once roused, it is very nearly unmanageable. On September 3 it became truly roused.

It was to be the battle of the playboys, Don Larsen and Dennis Bennett, but before the game, Gene Mauch sat in his office and spoke of many things. On his desk there is a sign that reads: "Isn't This a Beautiful Day? Just watch some bastard louse it up."

He spoke of the personality of his ballclub—"in one word, unselfish"—and he spoke of the development of the team from a floundering second-division dweller to a championship contender. He compared the club with an equally opportunistic team, the Pirates of '60. He did not say his team was going to win the pennant—"I'm not smart enough to know who's going to win a pennant"—and he spoke of the factors that had contributed to this year's success. He ticked them off. The deal for Jim Bunning and Gus Triandos ("for Don Demeter, a platoon left fielder"); the emergence of Cookie Rojas as a uniquely versatile and effective player; the sensational rookie season of Allen; the deal for Thomas. He spoke of his own development from a man who once expected his players to be as dedicated to the game and to winning as he was, and when he found they weren't—in 1953—he fired himself as manager of the Atlanta club. He is 38 years old now, and he feels the change came in him when he could close himself in a room in the dark and say, "This is the way it is. This is the team, these are the players. They are not going to change."

He is an intense man who would still like his players to be cut in his own image, but he does not demand it.

And he has come to understand Philadelphia fandom. "The Philadelphia fan boos," said Gene Mauch. "It is as much a part of Philadelphia as is the Liberty Bell."

The game itself was not much of a game. Dennis Bennett is a young man who has broken curfew and been fined $500 for it, a laughing Irishman who once thought he ought to win 20 games a year for ten years, and instead had won nine games a year for two years, and as of this night, had won nine games in '64. He is good looking and young and a bachelor, with a merry wit and a fine smile, and he is a friend of the evening, especially midnight. But he is just a boy compared to Don Larsen, who has been a friend of many midnights and in many cities throughout the nation.

Larsen until recently had not pitched a complete game for four years. Then, two weeks ago he pitched one for Houston. On this September 3, he not only pitched a complete game, he pitched his first shutout since 1959. Against a shutout there is little you can do except pitch one yourself. Bennett didn't; he gave up seven hits in the first five innings, but once again the hits were wasted. Then the Colts made seven hits in one inning—the sixth—and that was that.

But that is not the story. The story is what happened in the fifth. With two out, Eddie Kasko hit a ground ball to third, the ball striking Allen's glove and bounding away. Charitably, the scorer called it a hit. The crowd booed, first the play, and then vigorously the scorer. Bob Lillis promptly bunted down the third-base line, and young Allen rushed in. The ball had been bunted sharply, and had the third-baseman set himself he could have gloved the ball, and fired out Lillis with relative ease. Instead, Richie charged, tried to scoop one-handed, and let the ball slip away. The scorer called this a hit, and the crowd—which had quickly booed the misplay—now heaped thunderous abuse on the decision.

But it was not all, by a long shot. Every time a ball was hit to Allen, fair or foul, every time he came to bat, the crowd booed. It was not just a few hundred people, but many thousands, perhaps ten or eleven of the twelve thousand people at the game. A bellowing sound in the Philadelphia night, deep-throated, almost frightening.

In the press box, a reporter suggested there was more to it than the usual Philadelphia sporting venom. "Maybe," he said, "we are seeing—hearing—baseball backlash." It sounded foreign in a sport where, as Jackie Robinson had said, baseball has done it. Had broken the color line, smashed it, effaced it. Yet two days later, there would be a column in a New York paper quoting a San Francisco Giant ballplayer—white—who was accusing his Negro and Latin teammates of dogging it, of faking injuries, just to hustle Al Dark out of his job.

And perhaps that was why it sounded so frightening, this abuse of a fine young ballplayer, who happens to be black. Maybe it meant nothing. The time of its occurrences made you suspect, however. Even on a ballfield, a man begins to look about at his neighbor, at his skin. And in the dugout, some time that week, you recall a Phillie coach saying: "That kid on Chicago—what's his name, Campbell—he made out with the winning run on a couple of times in the game with Cincy. What is he, colored?" And that was naked enough for anyone.

Mauch, later, would say, "I don't understand them," even though just a few hours before he had said booing was the key to understanding Phillie fans. "They expect him to be exceptional all the time. It's not fair." Colt players were staggered by the sound, by its volume, its ugliness. Pitcher Hal Woodeshick warned, "The fans could cost the Phillies the pennant." Dick Farrell said, "I never heard anything like it."

In the dressing room, Richie Allen shrugged. "Let them boo," he said. "They can't play third base for me. They paid to get in, so they can boo if they want to. Just so Number 4 isn't booing." Number 4 is Mauch; he wears the number on his back. "I don't hear him booing. There are 25 players on this team. I don't hear them booing."

But—the writer insisted—didn't it bother him in some way? Make him feel mad? Feel hurt? Angry? Sullen?

"It doesn't bother me a bit," Allen said.

Unnoticed, after the booing that greeted Allen's final appearance at the plate, the rookie third-baseman tripled off the boards in right.

September 4

There were 28,149 people at the game Friday night. It was a game of many moments—a golden, classic game, a Philadelphia writer called it the next day, and he was right. You can break this game into its golden shreds, bright as glass. The Giants for one, started a lefthanded boy named Dick Estelle, who had never pitched in the big leagues before. Here he was, starting the season's biggest series, thus far. The Phils were starting Art Mahaffey who two years ago looked like the next great pitcher of the league. Mahaffey had pitched 22 complete games that season, 14 of them in a row. But something had happened since. Before this ballgame, Mahaffey asked his six-year-old son whether he wanted to come to the game.

"Nah," the boy said. "You never get to bat."

That's how fast they'd been getting Mahaffey out of there this year. The boy should have come: his father batted twice (and struck out twice), and for six-plus innings he pitched well. In the second inning, Jim Hart hit a monstrous line-drive home run into the left-field seats. The Giants led 1–0, until the fourth, when with two out, Callison—batting seventh on this day, the lowest he'd been in the order all year—punched a single to the opposite field. Ruben Amaro, a singles hitter, bats eighth.

With Amaro up, Mays played shallow in center field. All things are relative. Mays always plays a shallow outfield. For Amaro it was another 20 feet closer in.

And Amaro lashed at Dick Estelle's fastball and hit it on a curling drive to right-center, toward the big scoreboard some 385 feet from home plate. Mays broke swiftly, which is a redundancy; he always breaks swiftly. This time he seemed to break more quickly, in full flight after the ball. He ran for the scoreboard, at the base of which are advertising signs. One of them reads: PROVIDENT TRADESMENS—yes, without the apostrophe—touting banking services, and as Mays came full tilt toward the sign, he leaped for the ball. Then he crashed into the fence, and fell on his back, and the crowd was silent for a moment. Then Mays danced to his feet and flipped the ball to rightfielder Hart, and the crowd exploded. He had caught the ball a foot from the fence, in the air, and then he had thrust his legs straight out so he wouldn't smash his face against the boards, just his legs, and despite the shocking impact, he held the ball. It was an incredible catch, a catch one felt privileged to witness. For two innings, the stands buzzed with it, but meanwhile, the game had gone on. In the sixth, the Phils got the run back. Allen, who had been booed (and had responded with a walk and a double), now walked again. Frank Thomas sacrificed and Alex Johnson, a powerful young outfielding rookie who platoons against southpaws, doubled to make it 1–1.

In the seventh, Orlando Cepeda—who had said earlier that day: "I don't care if Allen says it does not bother him. It *always* bothers you when they boo"—now hit a single and after Tom Haller failed to bunt and then hit into a double play, Jose Pagan was flattened by a Mahaffey fastball. Pagan stood up and hit the next pitch onto the left-field roof, and the Giants led 3–1.

It seemed enough, 3–1, the Giants still up from Mays' catch, but the Phils scratch away and refuse to quit. Opportunistic, Mauch called the team. Grinds away at you, he said.

Billy O'Dell came in to pitch for the Giants in the seventh. Estelle had broken a callus on his pitching hand. The Phils had played a waiting game, making the boy throw. Estelle threw 32 pitches in the first inning alone.

In the eighth, Allen singled. It marked the fifth consecutive time he had been on base.

And Frank Thomas—who had gone one for his last 14—belted O'Dell's first pitch into the seats for a home run. The crowd roared— roared is too mild a word—and the fans kept it up, and so did the Phils, and before the inning was over, four runs had poured across, the fans chanting Go-Go-Go as they clapped in unison, a short exhausting chant, again almost terrifying. That was the game, though there were other moments, superb fielding plays, gritty relief pitching, and a ninth-inning rally by the Giants that fell short, the tying runs on but Jack Baldschun keeping them on.

The Giants had hit two home runs and two triples, they had seen one of their men make one of the great catches of modern ball, they had seen a first-time pitcher hold the league-leaders to one run in six innings, they had played tightly and well, they had led as late as the eighth. But they had lost.

And when all the golden moments are pieced together they add to another Phillie win. In the clutch. In the stretch. Watching from the stands were Baltimore scouts George Staller and Billy Hitchcock, and White Sox scouts Hollis Thurston and Charlie Metro.

In the clubhouse, Gene Mauch waited until the press arrived, and then—and only then—he marched from his office through the locker room, congratulating the players. It is said that Gene Mauch seldom makes a move that is not calculated.

September 5

Mays did not play. He had landed on his back, and a delayed reaction had set in. He was wearing a brace. He could not swing. So his name wasn't on the lineup card. Nobody's was.

It was Al Dark's turn to play games. He warmed up Bob Hendley and let it appear Hendley was his pitcher, but he did not post a lineup in the Giant dugout, as is the custom. Instead, Whitey Lockman told Phillie public-relations man Larry Shenk what the lineup was, and it was announced by the P.A. man, with Hendley the pitcher.

But when the official lineup was handed in, the pitcher was Bob Bolin. Hendley is a lefthander; Bolin is a righthander. Manager Gene Mauch had loaded up his lineup with righthanders, to face the expected Hendley.

The Giants scored quickly off Bunning, Hart rapping in the run, and Bob Bolin stepped in for the Giants.

You might say Dark had chosen to switch rather than fight; Gene Mauch with the same option—he could, for example, have immediately shoved in Tony Gonzalez in Rojas' spot at the top of the order—had decided he'd rather fight than switch.

More prosaically, Rojas doubled, Callison singled, Allen tripled, and Thomas homered—the cycle—for four runs.

It was exquisite revenge for the Phils. The battles between Mauch and Dark are by now legend, and in the past, Dark had somehow more often than not outmaneuvered Mauch. Not so this day. Gus Triandos slammed a bases-loaded home run in the fifth. The final score was 9–3.

And again more or less unnoticed, Richie Allen had himself a triple, a single and two walks. Now it was nine straight times on base, five straight hits. The booing had not gotten him down; indeed, who is there to say it did not actually challenge him.

September 6

Many of the Giant players ate at Dewey's, a small restaurant near the Warwick hotel, before the game. The waitress at Dewey's who served the Giants, wore a large "Let's Go Phillies" button. On the bus, going to the park, the driver had a small radio which announced merrily that John Callison now had 84 runs-batted-in. And it said further that the magic number—with Cincinnati—was 23. For the Giants, in case anybody cared, it was 19. Nobody seemed to care.

The bus then made a turn and the players stared out at Mt. Peace Cemetery. It seemed appropriate.

It was a Sunday, and the Phils had not been playing well on Sunday. To make it worse, Gene Mauch looked out and there was Pee Wee Reese.

"God-amighty," Mauch said, "it's Game of the Day. When we're on Game of the Day, people don't ask how come we're in first place. They ask how come we're in the league."

Not that Gene Mauch is superstitious. He is not. He had posted a letter in the clubhouse he'd received a few days before.

The letter read in part:

"Dear Gene—I can't wait until you clinch the pennant to offer my congratulations . . . Let the American League bring on the Orioles, the White Sox, or the Yankees—You can take them all." It was from Governor William W. Scranton.

For a team that was 6½ ahead with fewer than 30 games to go, this is perhaps not terribly daring. But teams had blown such leads before, and Mauch—older than Johnny Callison—knew full well how close the Phils had come to blowing the last pennant 14 years before.

Gene Mauch was feeling good. Acting spry. He took batting licks for the first time in ten days or so. He hit a ball into the upper deck—"first time I've ever done that"—and when he fouled a pitch during batting practice, a Phil ballplayer yelled, "Choked again, Gene."

If there was a reason Mauch felt particularly happy, it manifested itself in the dugout before the game. Suddenly Mauch slapped his knee and said, "First time we've been 30 games over!" Thirty games over .500. The Phillies were 82 and 52. They'd won four games out of five in September. This is how they were reacting to the stretch, to the tension that is supposed to arise in September and strangle teams.

Mauch even went so far as to watch Willie Mays take batting practice and say out loud: "He is not swinging right. I don't recall ever seeing him swing so bad."

That Sunday the Phils made five throwing errors—by Amaro, by Allen, by Baldschun, by Thomas, and by Triandos. Willie Mays hit the first pitch thrown him by Chris Short against the light tower over 405 feet from the plate, for a triple. Of the first five Giant hits, three were triples, and two were home runs—by Kuenn and Cepeda. Their next hit was a double.

Five errors to help out, and six extra-base hits, and the Giants had Juan Marichal pitching a tremendous game. Marichal struck out 13 men. In one stretch he fanned seven in a row.

The Giants won the ballgame. Big?

Four to three.

And Gene Mauch locked out the press for ten minutes after the game. He said later it was a custom to keep the press out for ten minutes or so after a game, but if it was a custom, he had violated custom the first five days of September.

Then he let the press in, and when a writer said: "Marichal's pretty tough," Mauch barked: "Sure he's tough. What's his record? He's 17–6 against the National League, and he's 2–2 against the Phillies."

But the Phils were no longer 30 games over .500, and the lead was 5½ games.

September 7

It was Labor Day, and the Dodgers were in. Tommy Davis stood in the lobby of the hotel and he said, "Things are terrible." He shook his head. He had said earlier he never knew what it meant to have "a mental attitude." Now he knew. He wasn't hitting. He wasn't fielding. He was down.

At the ballpark, Mauch was again in a confident mood. He watched Ron Fairly take batting practice, and he said, "When will Fairly get it into his head nobody's going to throw him fast stuff any more?" Fairly, an excellent fastball hitter, was having trouble with curveballs, slow stuff, even in batting practice. Still, it goes against protocol to say such things out loud. "I talk too much," Gene Mauch had admitted a few days earlier.

A woman came to the lip of the dugout and leaned in. "I have a package for you, Gene," she said.

"It's probably a bomb," Mauch muttered—in jest.

It turned out to be a baseball game the woman had invented; she wanted Mauch to have the first one. He thanked her graciously.

The Dodgers were seventh—on Labor Day—and the Phils first, and Gene Mauch, who usually saves Chris Short for the Dodgers, had instead thrown Short at the Giants—who mauled him—and now was reduced to using Dennis Bennett and young Rick Wise. Bennett had not won a ballgame since July 16; he had not pitched a complete game in his last 18 starts. His record—with a leader—was 9–12. Rick Wise would be 19 years old later in September; he was the youngest pitcher in the league.

Everybody was relaxed. The tough Giants had come and gone, and the Phils had won two of three. This was the Dodgers, in seventh. A crowd of 26,390 had arrived; the turnout pushed the total 1964 home attendance to 1,224,172—an all-time Philadelphia record. The crowd was friendlier; the riot was now a week past. Little kids played ball in the streets of the North Side.

And—because "it's as good a time as any"—Gene Mauch did not start Johnny Callison. It was the first time in 244 games Callison had not started. "Damned right I'm tired," the right-fielder said in the clubhouse before the game. So he sat on the bullpen bench for most of the first game—"I smoked two packs of cigarettes"—and he sat out most of the second game as well, and smoked some more.

In the first game Tommy Davis misplayed a fly ball and the Phillies took advantage of it. They won, 5–1. Bennett had won his tenth.

In the clubhouse, Bennett said there'd been a good sign when Jim Bunning hit fungo balls instead of Ed Roebuck. He thought the change might have brought him good luck.

"Are you superstitious?" a writer asked the confident young lefty.

"Nah."

"Well, what do you believe in?"

"Me," Bennett said.

Bennett had been helped by fine Philadelphia fielding. Richie Allen made a superb play on a bunt, racing in, scooping, and firing to second for a force play, in the sixth, and then started a lightning double play when Wills hit the ball down to third a moment later.

The Dodgers had won the second game, 3–1. Gene Mauch was asked why he had used Bobby Wine in both games, instead of replacing him with Ruben Amaro in the second game, at shortstop.

Mauch snapped, "You saw how Ruben could hardly throw to first in yesterday's game."

"But he played yesterday," the writer persisted. "Did his arm get worse overnight?"

"Ask him," Mauch said curtly.

And Mauch again closed the press box—for not quite ten minutes—after that second-game loss.

The week was over. The first week of September. The city had emptied itself over the long weekend, and would start to stream back in again. The next day—Tuesday, September 8—the Phils would start serving beer at the park again. For a week, the part of town where the riot had occurred had been quiet, unusually quiet, the police reported. And they should know. Their red patrol cars were all over the North Side. The taverns and the liquor stores would open.

The Phillies would keep playing baseball, the rest of September, and into October. Gene Mauch wanted to start to play golf—he said—but he figured he could wait. Somebody said he might have to wait about five or six weeks, and everybody smiled. Young Alex Johnson said he hoped it would be the Yankees: he'd always been a Yankee fan. Less young ballplayers and officials were rooting for the Yankees in the other league, because Yankee Stadium was bigger and there'd be more money for the Series teams. Nobody would admit he was thinking of how he'd spend the Series money, but it was on the mind.

Lots of things were on the mind. Managers don't like to see a team make five errors. They don't like to lose to young lefthanders—such as Pete Richert, who beat the Phils in the second game of the Labor Day doubleheader.

And Gene Mauch said to me: "How'd we do while you were here?"

"Five and three."

Mauch nodded and smiled. "Steady."

That was the word. Steady. Nobody was strangling. Nobody had panicked. The word choke was meaningless.

Still, it was just the beginning of September. This is how the Phillies went into the stretch.

You know how they came out of it.

Out with a Whimper

Sandy Grandy

◆ ◆ ◆

"The Year of the Blue Snow," Gus Triandos (by way of Jim Bunning) called it. "The most complete collapse of a first-place club in major league history," wrote Allen Lewis. "The year the National League pennant flew away," Frank Dolson said. Outsiders have written about 1964, but you really had to have been there. I was. "I do not know what caused the fall of Rome / but the Phils fell the night Ruiz stole home," I scribbled in my twelve-year-old's journal. I had some stronger language reserved. I cried the night the team lost its fourth straight game to the Braves. "What's the matter?" my mother asked, a little concerned. "The Phillies lost again," I said. "Oh," she said, "I thought it was something important."

When the Philadelphia Bulletin *was the third newspaper in town, it had the premier sports page (and comics) in the city. The reason: Ray Kelly, who did the play-by-play, and Sandy Grady, who did the color. Grady was bad cop to Kelly's good. His "Man about Sports" column (1960–71) consistently offered some of the best and funniest sportswriting east of the Mississippi. As the collapse unfolded, the always articulate Grady observed it from a variety of angles, and when it was finally over—it was simply over. No crying in the soup. There was a World Series to cover. Here's what Grady was thinking at three crucial moments in the '64 collapse: the night Chico Ruiz stole home; the day the Phillies were dumped out of first place for good (I was there!); and the game that for all intents and purposes ended their season.*

Two ironies unfolded as the Phils were finally eliminated from the pennant race. First, the St. Louis Cardinals, the team that had once threatened to boycott Jackie Robinson, built their world championship squad by deliberate and calculated efforts at integration. Four of the eight regular starters, in addition to star

From the *Philadelphia Evening Bulletin,* September 22, 1964, September 28, 1964, and September 31, 1964. Reprinted by permission of Sandy Grady.

pitcher Bob Gibson, were black. The nearly lily-white Phillies had waited until the 1964 season to have a bona fide black star in their starting lineup. Second, Curt Simmons, the hurler Phillies general manager John Quinn discarded for a buck, shut the Phillies down to put the final nail in their coffin. Damn poetic justice!

A Visit to Managers' Terrace

Now, in that elegant ballyard phrase, The Lump Is Coming Up, the famed Big Apple called fear. Someone is choking, and it seems fair to name the culprits.

Oh, not John Callison, who swears he doesn't give a hoot for magic numbers. Not Wes Covington, whose cold malevolence toward that right-field score-board may yet make it kindling wood. Not Rich Allen, who would laugh if caught in a paddleless canoe in a typhoon. Not Gene Mauch, who thinks pressure is a word for hydraulic engineers, not his brave, noble pros.

The fans are running scared. There were 20,067 anxiety cases in the Connie Mack snakepit last night, and that means 40,134 sweaty palms and shaky knees. A man touring the grandstand had not heard such groaning and cussing and screeching since the last Italian movie. You can't blame the burghers, who remember 1950, a year most of the Phils spent in Algebra I.

They piled out of the parking lots this crisp night, laughing like kids arriving at a wiener roast. There was a fat moon over Lehigh Av., the Phils had a six-and-a-half game lead and all was perfect in the Mauchian world. By 11 P.M., having watched John Tsitouris torment the Phils, 1–0, they hit the sidewalk with the tight mouths, like people who had seen a train hit a car.

Suddenly Pizzas Jammed in Throats
It was all splendid until Cincinnati's Chico Ruiz stole home in the sixth. The ladies waved their Phillies' pennants as pertly as U. of Miami cheerleaders swing pom poms, and you've never seen so many guys in Phillies souvenirs caps whooping it up. A guy in Lower Section 18 blew

a bugle, and it was fun to yell "Charge!" Then suddenly there were a lot of 50¢ hoagies and 25¢ pizza slices jammed in constricted throats.

They began snarling at each batter who lurched hopelessly toward John Tsitouris, who has the pitching motion of your Aunt Maud swatting a mosquito, which made it worse. They booed Art Mahaffey, who left the game biting a fingernail thoughtfully, having heard this music before. They booed each other when customers dropped foul balls. Only in Philadelphia.

But to savor the deep, mortal terror of the last innings, you had to visit the Managers' Terrace. This is the concrete half-moon running behind the box seat–reserved seats, where about 500 guys stand to watch through mesh wire. They manage every inning, and if that idiot Mauch would listen to them he would be 20 games ahead.

These are weather-beaten types, smoking cigars with the name bands left on, wearing colored jackets bearing the names of their bowling teams—"Bombers" or "Champions, 1958." Some of them have malformed left arms from holding the voice of By Saam close to their ears. On Managers' Terrace, though, there are no silly pennants or "Go, Phillies, Go" pins. It has been a hard, weary season for them, and there is no time for jazzy ostentation when you are managing a pennant club.

For the last three innings, they were in trouble on the Managers' Terrace. They wanted a run off Tsitouris profoundly. They tried everything. Three of them, who were observed managing desperately, will be called The Minister, The Advisor and The Judge.

"Get a Hit Off'n This Bum"

The minister prayed to each Phillies deity for deliverance from suffering. He opened the sixth by pleading for mercy from Wes Covington: "C'mon, Wes baby, please get a hit off'n this bum." The Advisor was quick with solid counsel: "Step outta the box and make him nervous, Wes, then knock one off the wall." Covington heard him, and did it. Then John Herrnstein struck out, and The Judge delivered his verdict: "Herrnstein, you no-good bum, I'm gonna send you to Little Rock and bring up Shockley."

The Judge seemed fair about each case. Going to Little Rock was like being sentenced to Eastern Penitentiary, but The Judge was coldly dispassionate about Herrnstein's crime.

The Minister begged Mahaffey not to walk the bases loaded in the seventh. The Advisor yelled to Mauch to get Bobby Locke in there, which Mauch did, thank heavens. The Judge sent Mahaffey to the Three-I League, where he will only be allowed to pitch on Halloween and Lincoln's Birthday.

There was a scary moment in the ninth, because Bobby Shantz pitched well, and The Judge was tempted to fire Mauch for not starting Shantz. There was deep, mute fright down in the stands, though, where people—they often pronounced his name like a sneeze—were saying, "Boy, that Tsitouris is an inhuman machine." They knew his name on Managers' Terrace, okay. They called him Tourist, Curious or Zurich.

They managed hard in the last of the ninth. The Minister beseeched Covington, and got a head-first double. The Advisor told Tony Taylor to walk on a 3–2 count, which he did. Ruben Amaro struck out to end it, and The Judge said with a magisterial rue, "I'm gonna put that bum in the Little League until he learns to swing a bat."

The mob, suddenly pale and aghast, moved slowly out the wickets. "C'mon, Phils, and I can't stand much more of this—you gotta wrap it up," entreated The Minister. "Next time Mauch should know better," said The Advisor. "He's gotta bunt or steal the run like the Reds did."

On the portables, By Saam's voice was saying regretfully that Tsitouris had pitched a wonderful game.

"That Saam would go to a hanging," said The Judge, "and call it wonderful. The bums are gonna blow it if they don't look out."

The moon over Lehigh av. slid ominously behind a cloud as the worried burghers hit the parking lots. The guys from Managers' Terrace chomped their cigars dourly and said they would now play it one game at a time.

Phillies: Tired, Tense and Unlucky

It wasn't really a ball park after this blustery gray Sunday ended. It was an accident ward teeming with victims of an earthquake. Guys padded

around softly, asking in hushed tones: "What happened?" The answer
was usually: "I dunno—but it was awful."

The Braves inspected the wreckage of the Phils' seven-game collapse
and offered a three-part autopsy. The Phils were (a) tired, (b) tense,
(c) unlucky. The victims themselves said nuts to answers (a) and (b),
and said please do not send flowers. The Phils insist they are wounded
but alive for five more games.

"I haven't seen anybody choke up—I feel absolutely no tension,"
said Clay Dalrymple. Then the nude-knobbed catcher compared this
disaster to the 23-game losing botch of 1961: "It's almost as bad. That
was embarrassing but this is disheartening."

It was John Callison who had warned on the plane home from Los
Angeles, when the club was 6½ games ahead: "We'd better keep bearing down." Yep, he remembered it yesterday. "I thought the guys were
spending their World Series money early," John said. "Nah, we're not
tight. If we can go into Cincy those last two days, tied up, we'll win
it."

Callison had struck three homers in that 14–8 final home nightmare—and delivered a blow at clean living. "I chewed tobacco for the
first time in my life, just to loosen things up," Callison said. If that's the
secret, John Quinn may load a ton of Beechnut on the plane for St.
Louis.

Has Milwaukee Brewed Milkshakes?
So their Great Downhill Slalom Run had spilled the Phils from first
place, their first tumble from the peak since July 16. In the Milwaukee
clubhouse, there was glee and sympathy.

"I told Gus Triandos before the game, 'That $7,500 first money may
turn into $750 fourth-place money,'" Ed Bailey cackled. "Funny
game—the Phils expected champagne and may get milkshakes."

"The Phils don't have to feel tight now," Warren Spahn yelled. "It's
all over."

"They're down on themselves because the breaks are going bad for
them," said Joe Torre with a touch of compassion. "They battled us, but
got the bad bounces. Now they'll face tough pitching from the Cards
and Reds—hell, it's fair, if the Phils don't win they don't deserve it."

"I wouldn't want to be in Gene Mauch's shoes—maybe a week from now, but not now," sighed Bobby Bragan. "They've got to be feeling tension. Bad things happen to you when it's that way."

Whatever it was, it wasn't National Brotherhood Week. Bragan and Mauch have been good buddies since they were kid rinkydinks with the 1944 Dodgers. Yet Bragan managed these four games as if it were a World Series, using everything but brass knucks to cool his pal's dream.

"I hated it, but that's the game," said Bragan. "Look, Mauch has done the best job of managing baseball has seen in 20 years. Who else ever came this close without an All-Star on his team? I hate to see it all go down the drain for him."

Also of the compassionate school was Whitlow Wyatt, the Milwaukee pitching authority. "I want to see the Phils win, because I have worked with Mauch and Quinn," said Wyatt. "But their pitching looks sorta tired."

Mauch was in no mood for get-well cards, however. When one analyst wondered what Mauch would do to stop the plunge, Gene growled: "Well, I never could hit and I never tried to pitch." Meaning it was up to his athletes, particularly those in the bullpen, and specifically John Baldschun. "We've got to do in five days what it took Cincinnati 5½ months to do," said Mauch. "But maybe we're better going after something than holding on to it."

Mauch: "Maybe We Need to Get Away"
Mauch knows his baffled people must get untracked against five of the toughest pitchers in the league: Bob (Hoot) Gibson, Ray Sadecki, Curt Simmons, Jim O'Toole and Jim Maloney. "What we've got to do," said Mauch firmly, "is win two in St. Louis and two in Cincinnati. Maybe we just need to get away from home . . ."

"I think a change of environment will help," said Dalrymple. "It couldn't hurt."

"Balls are bouncing crazy for us," said Tony Taylor. "We're not playing bad. Nobody's feeling tight."

"We're starting to anticipate the bad break, and that hurts," said Callison. "We need one good game."

"The whole mess seemed to start with Chico Ruiz' steal of home that beat Art Mahaffey," Bob Oldis said. "I've never seen anything like that run of breaks."

"These guys are gonna explode and hurt somebody," Bob Wine promised, "but it better be quick."

"What it boils down to is that the pitching has to take hold and give guys like Callison and Allen a chance to do their work," Mauch said. "And it will. It will."

Upstairs, there were 34,000 World Series tickets—big as restaurant menus, with the Philadelphia skyline engraved on them—ready for mailing in a few days.

At the moment, they looked like ghastly souvenirs of The Week That Never Was.

Cards Beat Phils as Pirates Defeat Reds in 16

Phils' World Ended with a Whimper

This is the way their world ended, not with a bang, but with a whimper. The darkened bus from the airport that tooled up Rt. 75 at 2 A.M. was mostly silent. The Phils had lost a pennant, though, and in the ghostly lobby guys became noisy with guilt.

"We blew it," said Dennis Bennett, ripping a hotel key out of the brown envelope. "If those kooks in Philadelphia want to boo us, okay, maybe we deserve it. But we all did our damndest and we blew it."

"I don't want anybody feeling sorry for us," said Jim Bunning. "Nobody lost it but us."

"They say this makes us a part of history," said Rich Allen softly. "Maybe nobody lost it as quick as we did. It's a part of the history book I didn't want to be in—but we did it ourselves."

Basically, Gene Mauch had tried a magnificent heist—a steal of a pennant with two solid players (Allen and John Callison) and two pitchers (Bunning and Chris Short). As Stan Musial said at 11 o'clock: "I know it's tough on people in Philadelphia to lose like this—but all year, the pros in the league felt the Phils had the talent of a third or fourth team. Gee, Mauch almost got away with it. . . ."

John Quinn's Great Mistake

There had been this one sliver of a chance, like filling an inside straight against a full house. Failure hits with a stunning bitterness. Maybe next winter when the snow is navel-high the Phils will suddenly cry and/or cuss about this game.

The end began when Curt Simmons walked into the floodlights and said with a wry grin: "I'd like to shut'em out." He nearly did it.

In the first inning, the Phils superscout, Don Hoak said, "He's got our hitters flinching with the off-speed stuff—it looks bad." So, Simmons left with an 8–3 lead, making his record a vengeful 16–2 against the Phils since that night John Quinn told him, "Sorry, Curt, you are released."

Quinn was like the Phillies' hitters. He watched every Simmons' pitch with twitching nerves. Yet, Quinn talked manfully about his great mistake, sitting on the Boeing out of the City of Despair.

"I gave 15 clubs a chance to pick up Curt for One Dollar," said Quinn thoughtfully, "We felt his history of arm trouble was against him. Even tonight I didn't root against Curt personally. He's had an amazing comeback. I would be pretty small to pull against a man like that."

Simmons was more pointed. He feels Quinn—above Bob Carpenter's objections—axed him that May 1960 evening in San Francisco. He shrugs that the old timber was being sawed out, and he was one of the moldy trees. Deals with the Cubs and the Pirates were hanging, but only Solly Hemus of the Cards had faith—"You say your arm is good?" said Hemus. "That good enough for me."

While the Cards bent over transistor radios in the clubhouse, pushing for the Pirates to beat Cincy, Simmons laughed at his dominance of the Phils. He still lives in a North Philadelphia suburb, and makes speeches for a dairy in the winter at high schools.

"They Almost Stole It"—Mayo Smith

"They say, 'who's Simmons—is he still pitching?'" said Curt. "Memories are short in sports. I remember coming home on furlough from the Army to see the 1950 World Series. This time I hope to pitch in one."

So Simmons, his belly a bit potted at 35, his crew cut graying, still hawk beaked, played his cruel shell game with the Phils and knocked them finally away from the prize.

"They didn't have the best ball club, but they almost stole it all," said Mayo Smith, the Yankee scout. "Simmons beats 'em by out-thinking them—but the Phils won't really start thinking about what happened to them until the winter. Talent caught up with them, but it's unbelievable."

Simmons' act was the final curtain of bitterness across the Phils' scene. Yet, the plane out of St. Louis was muted, doleful and blank-eyed. In the front seat, Gene Mauch's wife, Nina Lee, talked softly over the half-eaten supper to her bleak husband.

"Once I thought the season was too short," said Mauch, thinking of the days when every button he pushed poured gold. "Now I wish the son-of-a-gun went 200 games."

The Grand Heist is over. The bank alarm screamed just as the guys with the Grand Design were caught, money-bags open, right at the open bank vault.

The Survivors of '64: Johnny Callison

Stan Hochman

◆ ◆ ◆

If you had to choose three players who were *the '64 Phillies, along with Bunning and Allen you would have to include Johnny Callison. His numbers that year were staggering, and he didn't win the MVP only because back then sportswriters invariably chose players from the two teams that had won pennants (or players who played in New York). Throughout July 1989 Stan Hochman, the voice of the* Philadelphia Daily News *sports page for many years, wrote individual retrospectives on many of the players on the '64 club: where they are now, what they are doing, and what they thought about the '64 season, back then and twenty-five years later. The pieces, read together, provide some of the finest reminiscences of 1964. These players were Philadelphia's Boys of Summer (just as Roger Kahn found Billy Cox tending bar, Hochman discovers Callison doing the same). This essay, written in Hochman's penetrating style, is both poignant and memorable.*

Johnny Callison lit another cigarette.

Somewhere the surgeon who carved away half his stomach winced. Somewhere, the cardiologist who performed the triple bypass groaned.

Callison grinned a crooked, little smile and took another deep drag. If he was going to talk about 1964, he needed to look back through the gauzy haze of cigarette smoke.

He is 50, a bartender at Tomato's in Doylestown. Strangers are always asking him what happened in '64 when the Phillies blew a 6½-game lead with 12 to play.

"I blame Gene [Mauch]," Callison said. "What the hell . . . everybody else does."

From the *Philadelphia Daily News*, July 24, 1989. Reprinted by permission.

He laughs a dry, nervous laugh, to let you know he is kidding.

"It wasn't all Gene's fault. *We* played!"

Callison played. Rightfield. Only the dumb or the darling tried to go from first to third on him.

Little guy with steel-cable forearms and quick wrists.

Kept everything deep down inside him, anxieties rattling around in his stomach like shattered glass, which accounts for the ulcer.

Callison lit another cigarette, trying to dull the pain of 1986.

"My ulcers had been acting up for three or four years," he said. "Finally, one night, I was hemorrhaging, throwing up blood. They rushed me to the hospital.

"They got it stopped finally, but 24 hours later, it started again. They had to take half my stomach out.

"And while I was in intensive care I must have had a heart attack. I didn't even feel it."

"Two days before, I was gonna have a stress test, I'd be carrying the trash cans up from the street and be out of breath.

"Had chest pains. Knew something was wrong. My heart was damaged. They did three bypasses.

"I'm not as strong now. I run out of gas. Hey, at least I've got my weight down."

He is a trim 173, still handsome. Looks a lot like the actor, Allan Ladd.

If you remember Allan Ladd, you remember the year Callison had in '64, 31 homers, 104 runs batted in, 19 too-dumb, too-daring runners gunned down.

"It was a magical year," Callison said.

He won the spring training bowling tournament. An omen.

"Threw three strikes in the last frame," he said proudly.

Hit a three-run homer off mammoth Dick Radatz, using a borrowed bat, to win the All-Star Game.

"Yeah, Billy Williams made me give him the bat back," Callison recalled.

He had the tools to be a star, but not the temperament. Gloomy, introspective, wary of fame, his cup was always half empty, not half full.

And when he looked around the clubhouse on the next to last road trip of the season and saw his teammates fondling new hunting rifles, he grumbled out loud.

"I didn't want to be a black cat," he said, "but I knew anything can happen. Which it did.

"I'd seen too many things happen in baseball to count your chickens. I thought we were gonna win it, I really did.

"But I just wanted to clinch it before we celebrated. I thought we were gonna win, but I didn't go out and buy any fur coats."

Callison went 11-for-40 with 10 RBI in the 10-game losing streak that scuttled the pennant dreams.

Came shivering out of the clubhouse to pinch-hit against the Cardinals in St. Louis.

"I was run-down," Callison said. "Had the flu. Mauch said 'Stay in the clubhouse, just in case.'

"Sure enough, seventh inning, he called me out. I thought, 'This ain't fair.' "

Life ain't fair, but Callison singled. And when he got to first base the bat boy brought him a warm up jacket, and when he couldn't button it, Cardinal's first baseman Bill White reached over and buttoned it for him.

"And then," Callison said, "I had to go out and play the outfield.

"I remember certain plays in some of those games. [Cincinatti's] Chico Ruiz stealing home, a crazy play.

"Doubleplay balls that bounced over our guys' heads. Whatever could go wrong, went wrong.

"Frank Thomas got hurt and we needed that big righthanded bat. We got Vic Power, who never made an error in his life, and he makes two in one game in LA.

"I just think we ended up with the wrong guys in relief, Bobby Locke, was that his name? He became our stopper.

"I didn't understand why he didn't use Ray Culp. Gene would get a thing about a guy and not let up. It was always his way or no way.

"I think Gene was one of the best managers I ever played for, if not the best.

"One thing about him, when you went on that field, you were thinking baseball all the time. There was nothing else on your mind. He didn't let you drift off.

"It was a close team. Closest team I ever played on. Everybody pulled for each other. I don't think there was any jealousy or anything on that club. Just a feeling for each other.

"In the losing streak, Mauch got real nice. We were waiting to get our butts chewed out, and he did the opposite. Maybe he felt he was on us for so long it was time to relax and let us play.

"Ahhh, it cost me a lot of money. I would have been MVP that year if we'd won it.

"And then I still had to deal with [John] Quinn."

Quinn was the general manager, so tight he squeaked. Callison was easy prey, too shy, too uncertain.

Callison lit another cigarette, trying to filter the painful memories through the smoke.

"I was lucky to get a $10,000 raise," he said. "Had to put in attendance clauses and under-the-table stuff. He took all the guts out of me.

"I was doing everything I could, trying, and he didn't want to acknowledge it. Agent? I couldn't afford an agent.

"I didn't know how to argue. I'd talk about my defense and he said it didn't matter.

"He upset me so bad I'd say the hell with it. I'd get depressed. I'd just want to get the arguing over with.

"That year ['64] we had a Phillies cigar deal. And then they cut it out. First commercial and they take it away.

"We played an exhibition against that softball guy [Eddie Feigner]. They were offering $50 if we fouled one back, so I told the catcher to tell him to take it easy.

"The guy thought I was kidding. Blew me away on three pitches and I never touched the ball.

"And then the catcher came into our dugout asking me for my autograph. I told him to take a hike."

Callison finished second to St. Louis third baseman Ken Boyer in the MVP voting. He never would recapture the magic.

"I figured the next year we were gonna be right there," Callison said. "But we got Dick Stuart. And we got Bo Belinsky.

"Bo was great, minded his own business, completely different from what we heard."

The Phillies swapped Callison to the Cubs in 1970. Day baseball, a fresh start.

"I loved it," he recalled, "except for [manager] Leo Durocher.

"He stopped playing me all of a sudden. I was hitting .300. Had a tough night against a lefthander in Atlanta.

"Leo was a funny guy. If somebody said something to him, he was like a parrot, he'd repeat it.

"Someone asked if he was gonna play Callison against lefthanders all year. I thought, 'Oh, bleep, that takes care of me.'

"Next game against a lefthander, sure enough, I wasn't playing. And he wouldn't let me play the outfield the way I wanted to.

"Next year he didn't play me at all. Almost ran me out of baseball.

"I lost about five steps. Couldn't run anymore. Couldn't believe it. My knee was a problem. Taped it every day.

"They sent me to the Yankees [in 1972], and that was great. [Manager] Ralph Houk was a helluva guy.

"I won a lot of games for him. Must have won eight or nine games. He made everybody feel good.

"The next year I didn't play that much. Got released. Don't know if you're ever prepared for it.

"It was like a big block off your back. Finally, it's over with."

He was 34, married, with three daughters, no marketable skills, and a deer-shy personality.

"I thought I was in pretty good shape with investments," Callison said sadly, snapping his fingers. "Inflation took that away like that.

"I'd been promised some jobs I didn't get. There were five years there where I didn't think we were gonna make it.

"Two years after I got out, I tried to get back into baseball. I didn't want to go to the minor leagues. I'd liked to have been a big-league coach. Nothing came of it."

Dianne, his wife, still pretty, still petite, joins us on the back patio of their Glenside home. She had endured enough lonely, ominous nights when Callison was on the road.

"I was scared," she remembered with a shudder. "We got a burglar alarm. We got two dogs, then three."

The Callisons have three daughters, six granddaughters. One of the girls calls to him from behind the screen door. He waves, another cigarette stuck between his fingers.

"I sold cars," he said. "I sold electronics. Just what I needed to sell, huh?

"Now, I tend bar. I've always been lousy with people. Things get bad, I don't feel like talking, I walk down to the other end, wash glasses."

He had superstar skills from the eyebrows down. It hurts to watch today's players squander their skills, waltz through whole games, entire seasons.

"I watch a little baseball on TV," he said. "Second-guessing. What's the fun in that?

"I don't go down there. I couldn't sit through a game."

"He took me to one game," Dianne said. "Said he was going down to the clubhouse.

"Came back in the fifth inning and said, 'Let's go.' I didn't want to leave.

"He said it was the last game he'd take me to. I told him, 'This is the first game you've ever taken me to.'"

"The players were so different," Callison sighed. "There were only a couple of old guys left I played against.

"I just didn't like the atmosphere. When I played, the kids always looked up to the older players.

"Now, they don't look up to nothing. I never went back."

Johnny Callison lit another cigarette, searching in the smoke for that magic that was 1964.

Uecker's (Next-to) Last Hurrah

Bob Uecker and Mickey Herskowitz

◆ ◆ ◆

By 1966 the Phillies were a team searching for identity. In the days before free agency the only way to build a team, if your farm system was, like the Phillies', in disrepair, was to trade for players. Gene Mauch and John Quinn never stopped wheeling and dealing. A six-player deal in October 1965 brought the later-to-be-famous broadcaster/actor/Rodney Dangerfieldesque Bob Uecker to serve as back-up catcher. This piece, from Uecker's The Catcher in the Wry *(1982, Putnam), is more than a series of anecdotes and one-liners. The tone seems to remind us that all of baseball, not just the Phillies, was in a period of transition, and that certain deep-seated resentments and momentous changes were waiting to explode. There is a lull-before-the-storm quality to Uecker's retrospective here. Nineteen-sixty-six was the year of the Koufax–Drysdale holdout— the precursor to Curt Flood's challenge to the reserve clause, predicated on his trade to the Phillies before the 1970 season, and the McNally–Messersmith arbitration ruling that would change baseball forever less than ten years down the line. The nation was experiencing turmoil as the Vietnam War intensified. Jim Bouton's career was on the decline, and his baseball-debunking* Ball Four *(1970, World) would come along just as the decade was coming to a close. Uecker remembers the Phillies in the last years of Connie Mack Stadium and Gene Mauch. Thirty years later, his words still ring true—and hilarious.*

The Phillies, like the Cardinals, were a team trying to regroup. No manager had survived more adversity than Gene Mauch. His first team had established a major-league record by losing twenty-three straight games in 1961. Near the end of the streak, they came off a road trip to find a large crowd waiting for them at the airport in Philadelphia. They figured, obviously, it was a lynch mob. A pitcher named Frank Sullivan called out, "leave the plane in single file. That way they can't get us with one burst."

But the fans came to welcome them home alive, to cheer, to give them support. There is no way to know what makes a Phillies fan tick. They rallied behind Gene Mauch, and in time he gave them a contender, only to see the Phillies blow a ten-game lead in the nightmare season of 1964. The next year they were never a factor, and now Mauch had decided to retool the club.

I felt at home with the Phillies, when I reported to camp at Clearwater in March. The roster included such cashews as Richie Allen, who liked everything about a ball park except getting there; Bo Belinsky, the flamboyant left-hander who thought he had been Rudolph Valentino in a prior life, and John Boozer, a pitcher whose idea of fun was to eat bugs and worms and watch people gag. He did a better job in the clubhouse than D-Con. He would be talking to a writer and one of the players would hand him a live worm or a beetle. Some of the reactions were terrific.

Belinsky reported to camp two days late, explaining that he had been trapped by a snowstorm in Texas on the drive from California. Those Texas snowstorms can be murder.

In addition to the ex-Cardinal trio, Mauch had traded for Phil Linz, an infielder the Yankees had fired for playing the harmonica on the team bus after a loss, and Jackie Brandt, who once watched part of an All-Star Game while sitting in the dugout in the nude.

The Phillies had a terrific roster. I don't mean in talent, but in names, the kind that headline writers loved, like Wine and Boozer, and the kind that just had a certain ring, like Ferguson Jenkins, Cookie Rojas and Clay Dalrymple.

I had been brought in to back up Dalrymple, a seven-year vet and an underrated fellow, whose .213 average in 1965 was well below his form. Clay hit from the left side, which meant that once again I would have a chance to start against the left-handers. It was hard to tell if I had made any progress. I had been traded to my third team in three years. The

Phillies issued me uniform Number 10. I had worn 9 in St. Louis and 8 in Milwaukee. Was this progress?

When the players talked about the best and the brightest managers, the name of Gene Mauch often came up. He was quick-tempered, but he did not give up on people easily. His career as a player had been similar to mine. He was a shortstop who always seemed to line up behind someone better, such as Phil Rizzuto, with the Yankees, or Pee Wee Reese, with the Dodgers.

Frustrated, still a kid, Mauch once confronted his manager, Casey Stengel, in the dining room of a hotel where the Yankees stayed. "Dammit, Casey," he blurted, "I've got to play."

Stengel looked up from his soup and nodded. "Go talk to Mr. Rizzuto," the old man said. "If it's okay with him, it's okay with me."

Mauch was the most intense manager I ever knew. He would sit on the bench with his arms folded and his eyes never stopped moving. He didn't miss a thing. They used to tell a story about when Mauch was playing for the Red Sox, and on the way to the airport the team bus got stuck under an overpass. The driver and the team got out to study the problem. Finally, Mauch said, "Let the air out of the tires and fill them up on the other side." And so they did.

I was in the lineup on opening day, 1966, caught Chris Short and drove in a run with a single as we beat the Reds and Joe Nuxhall, 3–1. Then a really uncharacteristic thing happened. I hit home runs on consecutive days at the end of April. In my first six games, I had produced four hits, half of them homers, and driven in six runs. A curious start, it was worth three stars and a full, hand-lettered page in the scrapbook:

TWO HOMERS
IN TWO
DAYS!

BIG UKE
IS STARTING TO
FIND THE RANGE

ONLY 505 CAREER
HOMERS BEHIND
MAYS & OTT!

Ah, yes, the future stretched ahead as smooth and inviting as the Pennsylvania Turnpike. When I connected for my third homer on Memorial Day, against the Mets, Mark wrote a story for the school paper at Drury, and mailed a copy to Bob Howsam. The Cardinals were in the process of sending Mahaffey and Johnson to the minors. The trade was looking rather one-sided for the Phillies.

The story went like this: "Bob Howsam has finally, publicly, admitted in May that he was completely wrong in October. The story we got then was that we were trading White, Groat, and Uecker for Johnson, Corrales, and Mahaffey because we (the Cardinals) were fully committed to our youth movement.

"Well, it doesn't look too good for smiling Bob. How can you say you're in a youth movement and trade a thirty-one-year-old slugger like White and then keep a broken-down, thirty-seven-year-old pitcher named Curt Simmons, who only pitches against the Phillies and can't beat them?

"With his homer, double, and three runs batted in on Memorial Day, and his two singles two days later, Uecker raised his average to a lusty .266. With three homers . . . he seems likely to get a new career high in every hitting department, and last year had been his best. He's hitting better than either Bill White or Dick Groat, the men he was traded with, and that ought to make him the big man in the deal. The key man in the deal!

"Howsam, you're an idiot."

With aplomb, Howsam wrote back:

Dear Mr. Stillwell,

Thank you for sending along the article which appeared at Drury.

It's nice to know, too, that you have remained Cardinal fans.

We hope you and your Fan Club will have the opportunity to visit the new Busch Memorial Stadium and see the Cardinals play. I think you'll enjoy it.

Kindest regards,
Bob Howsam
General Manager

The first time the teams met in 1966, the Phillies edged the Cards, 5–3. Bill White singled home our first two runs. I singled to open the winning rally and scored the tie-breaking run on a bases-loaded walk to Groat, who had two hits. It's true, hitting well is the best revenge.

On June 3, I slugged my fourth homer of the year, equaling the total for my entire big-league career. The blow was off an ex-teammate, Ray Sadecki, then pitching for the Giants. By the All-Star break I had raised my total to six, the same number as John Callison, a guy who was usually good for twenty-five to thirty a season.

I would have felt great, except that everybody around the Phillies kept wondering what was wrong with Callison. Four teams figured to stay in the pennant race most of the way, the Dodgers, Giants, Pirates, and the Phillies. We needed a big year from Callison. In fact, we needed a big year from everybody.

The point should be made right here that it can be harmful for a fellow who doesn't hit homers to suddenly start banging a few. It is like a guy who discovers girls late in life and thinks he can catch up all at once. And the next thing you know, you are in a jar at the Harvard Medical School.

But sooner or later you have to try. You see a Richie Allen twitch a muscle and the ball flies off the bat and lands five hundred feet away. And you think, is there any reason I can't do that? The next thing you know, your hands are down at the end of the bat and all your weight is on your heels.

In a way, those homers, hitting in the .270's, and getting four (4) votes for the All-Star Game may have been my undoing. Up to then my theories had stood the test of time, like milk of magnesia: 1) The more I played, the closer I was to getting shipped out, and 2) the better I performed, the more they expected.

If I had been content to just hit .200 every year, all singles, and throw out a runner now and then, I might have played as long as Gaylord Perry. Your body doesn't wear out very fast when you catch a game every four or five days.

On July 17, I tagged my seventh homer in what turned out to be a fifteen-inning win over the first-place Giants. On the Phillies, only Allen and Bill White had more, even though a total of twelve players had started more games.

I had no personal goals in mind, which was just as well because I did not hit another homer during the rest of the season.

We stayed in the race until September, then became the first of the four contenders to fade. Chris Short won twenty games and Jim Bunning finished with nineteen. A late-season slump by Bill White was costly, but he drove in 103 runs and popped twenty-two homers.

Seasons that end badly tend to blur, a series of pitches half-forgotten at the moment they are half-missed, in games that are half-played. But it was a thrill, that year, to watch Richie Allen, young and untamed, blossom into a superstar. He hit forty home runs and fought Hank Aaron for the title down to the final days. He drove in 110 runs and batted .317. And he was going to get stronger and better. He would in time overpower this game and, unfortunately, himself.

Allen was one of baseball's raw talents, a prodigious long-ball hitter. He preferred horses and cars to the company of people, but he was seldom loud or rude. He asked only to be treated like a man. In view of what Richie accomplished, the request did not seem unreasonable.

Part of his problem was that no matter how much he accomplished, it was never enough to satisfy all of his critics. Some just didn't like him, his color, his style, his habits. Others simply felt that he didn't get the most out of his huge gifts. Many a time, on his way to the plate, Richie would tell us he was going to take two strikes and see if he could hit one pitch. He would do this against some of the best pitchers in the league. He drove Gene Mauch wild, but more often than not he came through. He was just that good.

Richie did not take direction well, he was careless about the time, and he liked to sip the cooking sherry. We would get in the back of the plane, glowing slightly, and sing harmony, all the old barbershop songs. We were a happy pair.

I was a witness to the events that led to Richie's famous car pushing accident, which left him with a mangled hand. Someone had given him an old stock car. He had it at the ball park one day, and he invited Dick Groat, Bob Skinner and myself to ride back to the Presidential Apartments with him. On the way, he tried to show us how to speed shift a stock car, and going from first to second he jammed the gears into reverse. The gears locked. We pushed the jalopy over to the side of the road and that was where it stayed, until Richie had it towed to his apartment.

I don't know how long the car stayed there, but at last he decided to move it. He tried to push the car from the front and his hand slipped and went through the headlight. From then on his hand was like a claw, after the surgeons did what they could to repair the tendons. After that I called him "Crash" Allen. A lesser man would have been finished. Richie regained the use of his hand and played ten more stormy seasons.

My own season was a deceptive one, as my seasons sometimes were. In the final weeks my average shrank to .208. But I had almost as many runs batted in (thirty) as I did base hits (forty-three). I saw the most action of my career, catching seventy-six games and playing one inning at third base, although I no longer remember why. It probably had to do with whatever strategy Gene Mauch was using that night.

I figured I had done well enough to go another year, and that was as far as I ever planned. Big-league baseball players, as a group, fool no one but themselves. We are like Oskar in *The Tin Drum*, the little boy who would not grow up.

My fan club was growing older. It had somehow acquired 476 members, and the hard core were now seniors preparing to graduate. We were bonded, in a curious kind of way. They were like having your own private gag, my Pookah, my Harvey the Rabbit made real. They redeemed my view of life; that the world belongs to those who know when to laugh at it. I am not sure what they got in return, other than a hero without the trimmings, a hero who could never let them down.

Well, almost.

The problem with being a fringe player is that just about the time you get comfortable with a team, you're gone again. Wherever I had played, the scrubs banded together and developed our own esprit de corps. I don't think any of the teams ever suffered for it, although I am not sure all of my managers would agree. On the Phillies, we called ourselves The Avengers, and the group included Bobby Wine, Phil Linz and Jackie Brandt. Richie Allen was an honorary member. He was a great player, but he had the heart of a truant.

The career of another fellow, who was to become a special friend of mine, ended that year. Harvey Kuenn batted .296 for the Phillies and decided to call it a career. He was thirty-six, had played fifteen seasons and finished with a lifetime average of .303.

He had been a principal in one of the most publicized trades ever made. Harvey won the batting title at Detroit in 1959, and then was swapped for the man who had won the home run title, Rocky Colavito of Cleveland.

I admired Harvey as a fine agitator and one of the smartest hitters I had ever been around or caught behind. He stood in the deepest part of the batter's box and defied the pitcher to throw the ball on the outside corner of the plate. That was a pitch he could kill. He was an all-fields, line drive hitter, but if his team needed a run in the late innings to tie or win, he could take you downtown.

After our playing days, both of us came home to Milwaukee. Harvey joined the Brewers as a coach. I'm on the radio crew. And our friendship continues.

In February, three years ago, his right leg was amputated because of a circulatory problem. By the end of spring training, he was walking on an artificial limb. By winter, he was playing golf every day. Sometimes a fellow as big and active as Harvey Kuenn finds it hard to accept such a blow. But those who knew him as a great athlete found out he was much more. He wouldn't let life slip one over the outside corner, either.

We were not far into the 1967 season when I knew my days with the Phillies were numbered. I went to the plate one night as a pinch hitter, and when I looked to the third-base coach for a sign he turned his back on me.

The trade that sent me back to the Braves, my original club, for another catcher, Gene Oliver, was announced on June seventh. In truth, I felt a little guilty about leaving Philadelphia. Richie Allen was brooding and threatening not to play. I felt like a hostage who had been released early.

The next morning, Rich said he wasn't going to the ball park anymore. I called Donald Davidson, the Braves' road secretary and an old friend, and told him I couldn't report right away. He pleaded with me: "Uke, dammit, you got to get your ass down here. Joe Torre is hurt and you're the only catcher we have."

When I left, Allen was still boycotting the ball park. Soon I heard from Charlie Meister, in the Phillies' front office: "You have to talk to Richie. He hasn't suited up since we made the trade." I called, reminded him that the Braves would be flying into Philadelphia for a three-game series that weekend, and convinced him to go back to work.

Of course, it didn't take much to keep Richie away from the ball park. He didn't like to practice. Always felt it wasn't in his contract. He had signed up just for the games.

I was fortunate to room with great, normal players like Eddie Mathews, and an occasional pure flake like Roger Craig.

Craig, my roomie in St. Louis, had one of the most uneven careers any pitcher ever had. He helped pitch the Dodgers to a pennant in 1959, and in two seasons with the Mets lost a total of forty-six games.

Influenced, perhaps, by his term with the Mets, Roger loved horror movies and sometimes imagined that he was in one. He had a problem with his neck for a while and wore a brace. I would open the closet door to put away my coat, and find him hanging on the inside of the door, his brace looped over the hook.

Those are the pictures you take out of baseball, more than the runs, hits, and errors. You remember the players and the people and the rhythm of the towns.

I honestly liked Philadelphia. The fans there were smart and mean and you could count on them. One of my biggest thrills in baseball was watching a guy fall out of the upper deck in Connie Mack Stadium. The crowd booed when he tried to get up.

The Lucchesi Interlude

Thoroughly Modern Phillies

Roy Blount, Jr.

◆ ◆ ◆

The Phillies left the confines of Connie Mack Stadium (née Shibe Park) at Twenty-first and Lehigh on October 2, 1970. The management handed out slabs of brightly colored wood (dated, along with the words "I was there") to fans as a memento of that last, historic night. The problem was that fans not only proceeded to rip up the stadium to get real souvenirs, but also began swinging the slabs around like war clubs, causing a near riot. The following year, the Phillies entered Veterans Stadium and thus began the legacy of skipper Frank Lucchesi, arguably the most popular Phillies manager of the last fifty years. Roy Blount, Jr., now a nationally known essayist and humorist, but a writer for Sports Illustrated *in the 1970s, was present at the dawn of the age of concrete horseshoe stadia, Astroturf, and brightly colored uniforms. It was the time of "mod." It was awful, but it was fun. Here is the story for all of you who never knew, or would like to forget, Philadelphia Phil and Phillis.*

George (Stud) Myatt, the Phillies' venerable third-base coach, stood in brand-new Philadelphia Veterans Stadium last Saturday, resplendent in his innovative red shoes with white stripes and his bright red-and-white uniform with a mod small "p" on the shirt. He shifted his venerable chaw and spat liberally on the latest-model wall-to-wall AstroTurf. Was there anything, he was asked, to the rumor that Phillies who chew had been urged to avoid getting tobacco juice on the artificial surface?

"If they don't want me to spit on it," Myatt replied, "they're going to have to give me a spittoon. My wife gives me one so I don't spit on the carpet when I'm home."

More generally, how did Myatt feel about plying his trade against the backdrop of the new $50-some-odd million facility—with its usherettes in mini-culottes and hot pants, its $15,000 "super boxes," its gaudy scoreboard and its other extravagant features? For instance, the "dancing waters" behind the centerfield wall, which were just then coming up green. "How would you like to have green spots on you?" he was asked.

"I've had those," he said.

Whatever obscure condition the old coach may have been recollecting, the drift of his remarks was reasonably clear, Baseball has broken out in a rash of new looks this spring—from the red socks currently being affected by the White Sox to the new uniforms and home of the "Thoroughly Modern Phillies" (as they have been called). But that doesn't mean that there is anything profoundly new under the tentative early-season sun.

The point was made more specifically a few minutes later by Gene Mauch, who used to manage the Phillies and now manages the Expos. (Montreal, incidentally, started the current fad of using all lower-case letters in its logo; the Phillies and the California Angels have taken up such trendy typography this year.) Mauch had brought his Expos into town for the new stadium's inaugural game, and his attention was directed to Philadelphia Phil and Philadelphia Phillis, the mammoth kewpie dolls in Colonial garb whose function has been described by Phillies special-effects executive Bill Giles as follows:

"They are part of my home run spectacular. When a Phillie hits a homer, Philadelphia Phil will appear between the boards in center field and hit a baseball. It will travel toward the message board in right center and strike a Liberty Bell. The bell with glow and its crack will light up. The ball will continue and hit little Philadelphia Phillis in the fanny and she will fall down. As she falls, she will pull a lanyard on a cannon and the cannon will explode. After smoke and sound effects, a Colonial American flag will drop down. Then my dancing waters will come into play to the tune of *Stars and Stripes Forever.*"

As it happened, when Third Baseman Don Money produced a Phillie homer against Mauch's Expos, "the ball" (a light running unobtrusively along a track between Phil and Phillis) was barely visible, the bell failed to glow, Phillis struck a thoroughly warranted blow for Women's Liberation by declining to fall down and the cannon smoke and the cannon noise went off independently of one another. The assumption before the game, however, was that the home run spectacular would captivate the sellout crowd. How did Mauch feel about baseball's greater and greater reliance upon such gimmickery?

"It's here," said Mauch resignedly. He sounded like Ethyl Barrymore at a performance of *Oh! Calcutta!*

"It's here," he said, "and just like in the Astrodome, the fans will come to see it at first, but after a while they will come to see a ball game."

Fortunately, not to say surprisingly, a ball game is what the Expos and the Phillies gave the spectators on Holy Saturday. It was a competent 4–1 victory by the Phils—featuring a triple over the drawn-in outfield and three fine fielding plays by wispy young Shortstop Larry Bowa (who isn't called Bowa Constrictor because he doesn't choke); an over-the-shoulder catch in left field by John Briggs; a 220th lifetime win by 39-year-old Jim Bunning (the oldest starting pitcher in baseball, performing in the youngest park); and an inning and two-thirds of hitless relief by whippy Joe Hoerner.

And glory be. The 55,352 fans in paying attendance (all 56,371 seats were sold in advance, but nippy weather caused a few no-shows) did not boo. Well, they did boo Phillies General Manager John Quinn, Phillies President Bob Carpenter, Baseball Commissioner Bowie Kuhn and even, to some extent, national anthem singer Mike Douglas in the pregame ceremonies, but they did not boo the ball game. They did not even boo Philadelphia Phil and Phillis or the Liberty Bell. They acted as though they could take Philadelphia Phil and Phillis and the Liberty Bell or leave them alone. They cheered the ball game.

This from a constituency that traditionally boos everything for miles around. "When there was an Easter egg hunt before a game in Connie Mack Stadium," claims former Phillie Catcher Bob Uecker, now a member of the Braves' speakers bureau, "there would be a few kids who wouldn't get any eggs. The crowd would boo them. I've seen people in Philadelphia standing on street corners booing each other."

The Quality of Mercy Is Not Strained

Tom Cushman

◆ ◆ ◆

Covering the Phillies in 1971 (the year Frank Rizzo first ran for mayor) was painful enough, but sitting through a game that seemed as though it would never end was beyond human endurance. But then most of us are not sportswriters, and if something historic (the longest game, a no-hitter, or whatever) is in the making, we just might want to stay there for the whole thing. That's why there are still those of us who never leave until the last out. This particular game, covered by the Daily News's Tom Cushman, did not make the record book, but it was the occasion for a celebrated piece of writing. It might call to mind that home game the Phillies called off against Sandy Koufax in August of '64 because, so went the official announcement, storm clouds were threatening over South Jersey; or, conversely, the fourth game of the 1977 National League Championship series, when for the sake of the almighty Television Dollar, a flood almost as bad as the one Noah and Utnapishtim endured could not get the game called off.

Shortly before the Phillies and Cardinals waded out to resume the 12th inning yesterday, a message wiggled across the Veterans Stadium scoreboard, which was one of the few things in South Philadelphia still above water.

The message read:

"Shag, this is God speaking. The sun will be out in 10 minutes.

It is comforting to learn that there are some connections that even a million dollar scoreboard can't manage, and a hot line to heaven obviously is one of them. The sun never really made it again yesterday and neither did the ball game although umpire Shag Crawford and his crew certainly gave it every opportunity. It took two rain delays, six

From the *Philadelphia Daily News*, August 2, 1971. Reprinted by permission.

hours, 11 and one-sixth innings, and an attack of indigestion by The Great Zamboni for the Phillies to salvage a 3–3 tie in a game that eventually will be replayed from the first pitch.

Or, if you're so disposed, you could say that the Cardinals won a 6–3 tie. It was that wild.

In summary, the Phillies and Woodie Fryman were just about to snuggle up to a 3–2 victory when the Cards scored a run in the ninth inning to force the deadlock. In the top of the 12th, it was still 3–3 with Lou Brock on third, Julian Javier on first, no outs, and the late afternoon monsoon in progress when Crawford called the first halt.

Under National League rules, there must be a wait of at least 50 minutes before the contest can be called. Play eventually resumed one-hour-and-49-minutes later, courtesy of the Zamboni Vacuum, which had sucked up the deepest puddles and gotten its pipes jammed with ice cream lids in the process.

"I wanted to give them every chance to get this game in, " Crawford was to explain between delays. "That's why they put the Astroturf down. That's why they've got this Zamboni, or whatever it is. I wouldn't care if we had to stay here until midnight."

As he spoke, the last traces of crimson were still ebbing from Crawford's face. After the resumption of play the Cardinals had promptly scored three runs, the final two with a new shower drifting down into the stadium. The climax came when the Phils' Billy Wilson walked Cardinal reliever Darry Patterson on four pitches and then wild-pitched Joe Torre home with the sixth run.

Wilson arrived at the plate shortly after the ball did to inform umpire Stan Landes that the mound was—in his opinion—an unplayable lie. "I told him if he didn't think so to go out there and try to pitch himself," Wilson said later.

Crawford was already on his way down the line from third base with his arms raised, apparently to call another halt. When he arrived, Frank Lucchesi was there to meet him and the thunder that followed was not rolling down from the heavens.

"Who the hell knows what he was saying, he was yelling so loud," Crawford said "Before he came out I had my arms up. We were stopping the game."

Lucchesi had a chance to cool his motor before he reviewed the incident. "I inspected the mound before we resumed play, and I had complaints then," he pointed out. "After it began raining again, my contention was that my pitcher couldn't stand on the mound.

"I misunderstood Shag," Frank said, with a sly smile, "and he misunderstood me, and pretty soon we had a little beef going."

Landes, who assumed the role of arbitrator, explained it like this. "They were talking about Rizzo and Longstreth," he said.

After that came delay number two, this one lasting 31 minutes. The game eventually was called after the umpires inspected the field, and learned that the Great Zamboni still had a bellyful of ice cream lids and was inoperable. The Cardinals, who had devoted the first recess to watching Jack Nicklaus and Arnold Palmer win the PGA team championship on television, sizzled like they had been struck by lightning after the game was called. They protested, claiming that Zamboni's jockey had split the scene.

It is sad that Zamboni should be hung with a rap like this, because without him the Cardinals would never have had the chance to float those three runs across after the first delay.

As it happened, the game nearly took an ironic twist following the long wait. With Brock and Javier repositioned at third and first, pinch-hitter Bob Burda ripped a Wilson pitch just inside the first base bag. Deron Johnson made a diving knockdown and while sprawled, picked up the ball and tagged the base.

His throw to second then caught Javier in a rundown, but with the swift Brock edging down the line at third, second baseman Denny Doyle elected to chase Javier back toward first. Brock broke for home and scored easily while Javier, with a dive, got into first ahead of Doyle's tag.

Joe Torre, who had singled the three previous trips, then bounced a low liner just to the right of Larry Bowa, who would have needed a periscope if there had been any more moisture on his side of the infield.

"Maybe you couldn't see them from upstairs," Bowa said later, "but there were puddles out there. There's no way you could play. Torre's ball was a routine out, but you start to move and you sink. That stuff's dangerous when it's wet."

Torre's ball skipped through and Matty Alou plunked one up the middle for another hit, then Billy Wilson started throwing everything high. That's when the rain started coming down harder and the Phillies began taking their time.

What if play had been resumed a second time, would it have been too far-fetched for some of the Phillies to start slipping and tumbling in the turf.

"We would have done the best we could under whatever the circumstances were," Lucchesi said. "If it is in the cards for us to get beat that way, then we get beat. I won't make a farce of the game."

Since baseball is a game of statistics, perhaps you would be interested in filing this one. From the time that play was first halted, it took 2:36 to not finish the 12th inning. It would seem that heaven and the Cardinals had been given a reasonable chance.

The Axman Cometh

Frank Dolson

◆ ◆ ◆

I met Frank Lucchesi once in an elevator at the Holiday Inn in Baltimore. He was coaching with the Rangers then and on his way to the hotel bar. "Frank Lucchesi!" I said. "Yeah?" he said, surprised anyone would even recognize him, let alone without a uniform on. How could anyone forget him, this warm, garrulous man who bled Phillies red? Had he been given any sort of a team, things might have been different. ("You can't serve water with a pitchfork," he once said about what it was like to manage one dreadful team after another.) Frank Dolson, the dean of Philadelphia sportswriters, who retired from his long years of service with the Philadelphia Inquirer *in 1995, captures all of Lucchesi's virtues—his good-heartedness, his patience with players—in this brief profile, and, in turn, delivers an acerbic commentary on the callous way in which Lucchesi was discharged by the people he thought were his friends and supporters. Baseball was Dolson's favorite sport, and his book about life in the minor leagues,* Beating the Bushes *(1982, Icarus Press), has become something of a classic. This excerpt is from his first book,* The Philadelphia Story: A City of Losers Winners *(1981, Icarus Press).*

He was a charismatic guy, this bouncy, little Italian with the heart of gold, who had spent a lifetime in the minor leagues helping kids, making friends, dreaming of the day when the big leagues would beckon. The Phillies may have had managers who won more games than Lucchesi, but never in the city's history had there been a manager who won over the fans as quickly as he did. The people seemed instantly to identify with this long-time minor leaguer who had fought his

From *The Philadelphia Story: A City of Losers Winners* by Frank Dolson (South Bend, Ind.: Icarus Press, 1981). Reprinted by permission of Frank Dolson.

way to the top. Some would have considered managing the Phillies in the early '70s a thankless, virtually hopeless job; Frank Lucchesi considered it the greatest job in the world, a fantasy come to life. His enthusiasm and his joy were catching. Lucchesi had a way of communicating with people. He liked the press, and the press liked him; and as a result even before he arrived in town from his first spring training, the Philadelphia public felt they knew the man, and they liked what they knew. As long as he lives, Lucchesi will remember the opening of the 1970 baseball season at Connie Mack Stadium. They introduced him to the big crowd, and he popped out of the dugout in that jaunty way of his, a stranger in a big, supposedly tough city, and the people showered him with affection.

Lucchesi doffed his cap, and the applause grew louder; many of the people stood to welcome the new manager. Frank, a highly emotional man, was nonplussed. Here he was, in a place where the natives supposedly devoured Phillie managers for lunch, and they were cheering him before he'd managed a single game. His eyes filled with tears. It was a welcome he would never forget . . . a welcome that would make it extra difficult for him to accept his forced departure in July of 1972.

Before he left, Lucchesi must have signed a million autographs, made a zillion friends. If somebody wanted him to make a speech or visit a hospital or make a phone call to a sick kid, he did it . . . and seemed to love doing it. From a public-relations standpoint, the Phillies never had a manager who was more effective than Frank Lucchesi. At a time when the Phillies were in the early stages of a long, hard rebuilding program, he was a perfect man for the job. He was patient with the kids—most of whom he had managed in the minors—and he was great with the press and the fans.

At least one player who went on to become a National League All-Star owes his big-league career to Lucchesi and isn't reluctant to say so. Larry Bowa played for Lucchesi in the Double A Eastern League and again in the Triple A Pacific Coast League. Frank loved the fiery, little shortstop. He understood him. And he was determined to stick with him.

There's every reason to believe that another manager, one who didn't know Bowa the way Lucchesi did, would have given up on the kid when his batting average seemed stuck somewhere below .200 in the early stages of his rookie year. Lucchesi kept playing him, kept building him up. And it paid off.

"I've worked for everything I have in baseball," Bowa said one day during 1981 spring training, "and I'll work when I get out of baseball, and I'll work when I'm getting ready to die. That's the way I am. I don't want anybody to do any favors for me. As far as my salary is concerned, every penny I've earned. Just one guy gave me a break, that's how I look at it. Frank Lucchesi gave me the biggest break of my life, and if I owe anything to anybody, I owe everything to Frank Lucchesi. If not for him, I wouldn't have had the opportunity to play in the big leagues. He gave me that opportunity. We were in last place, and he died with me, and I owe it to him. I've written him letters [to tell him]. And I sent him my World Series glove at the end of the [1980] season for his son. I'm breaking in a glove now because I gave him my 'gamer' that I used for three years. That's what the man means to me."

As much as Lucchesi meant to Bowa, the Phillies' job meant even more to Lucchesi. Under any circumstances, his firing would have been sad. The way the Phillies did it, it was brutal. Funny, you'd have thought with all the practice they'd had at getting rid of managers by 1972 they would know how to conduct a decent firing.

Naturally, Lucchesi had heard the rumors that began circulating as the long, losing summer of '72 commenced. One of those rumors seemed based on hard, cold fact. A most reliable source—it was, of all people, Dallas Green—told Allen Lewis of *The Inquirer* that a managerial change appeared to be in the offing. Lewis, who was no longer covering baseball, gave the information to his office, and his office notified the man who was covering the Phillies at the time.

That man was Bruce Keidan, and he wasted no time seeking out the truth. In the course of the investigation, a phone call was placed to the home of Dave Bristol, believed to be one of the leading candidates for the Phillies' job. Dave wasn't there, but a member of the family passed along the information that the Phillies had, indeed, been trying to get in touch with Bristol. The evidence seemed overwhelming: Lucchesi was out, and Bristol was in.

The Phillies were playing a Saturday-night home game, and Keidan informed Lucchesi that his paper had learned from an "unimpeachable source" that Frank was about to be fired and that Bristol was about to be hired. Lucchesi was jolted. Despite the rumors, he had forced himself to think that his old friend and new Phillies' general manager, Paul Owens, would never do such a thing to him. That night I spoke to Lucchesi long-distance from Eugene, Oregon, where I was covering the Olympic Trials. Frank was terribly upset; he didn't know what to do next.

"I told him [Keidan], 'I don't believe it,' " Lucchesi told me over the phone. "I don't think they'd do a thing like this. The last week or ten days they indicated I'd be all right, at least through the end of this season. I've been with the organization eighteen, nineteen years. I don't have to go in and ask them, 'Am I all right? Are you getting ready to fire me?' I don't have red blood in me. I have Phillie blood in me."

But Keidan's words haunted him. Lucchesi went through a sleepless Saturday night, and something that happened early Sunday morning didn't soothe his nerves.

The Phillies had been planning a Sunday-night cookout in Delaware. All members of the official family and their families were invited. For days Frank Powell, assistant to the Phillies' president, had made it a point to remind Frank of the gala event every time he saw him. "Don't forget Sunday night, Frank," Powell kept saying.

Then, as luck would have it, Lucchesi ran into Powell at the ball park on Sunday morning, following that sleepless Saturday night. This time, instead of reminding him for the umpteenth time about the cookout, Powell told Lucchesi that the affair had been called off. "Bob [Carpenter] can't make it," Powell explained. "And Paul's tied up."

Maybe it was Lucchesi's imagination, but Powell seemed a little nervous when he relayed that information. Now the manager was really worried. Perhaps it was all a coincidence that the Phillies had phoned Dave Bristol's home and that the cookout was canceled. On the other hand, there seemed to be a distinct possibility that the Phillies had decided to move their cookout to Monday with Frank Lucchesi as the main course.

The manager sought advice; I told him there was only one thing to do, only one way to put his mind at ease. Confront Owens with the latest batch of rumors and speculations and ask him, point-blank, if the decision had been made to fire the manager the following day. The worst that could happen was confirmation from Owens. At least then Frank would know; he wouldn't have to go through another night of twisting and turning and wondering. Lucchesi agreed. That was the thing to do.

Paul Owens and Dallas Green, then farm director of the Phillies, were in Paul's office that Sunday morning when Lucchesi walked in to find out if he was about to be replaced by Dave Bristol.

"I said, 'Look, I've known you fifteen, sixteen years, and you've never conned me,'" Frank told me a few minutes later, relating the conversation. "'I'd like to know the story.'"

So Owens told him the "story." He told him Bristol had been contacted for information on an American League player the Phillies were trying to get in a waiver deal.

"Paul told me there's nothing going on," Lucchesi said over the phone shortly before the Sunday game began. "If something does happen now, it would be unbelievable. If it isn't true, you'll have a heartbroken man here."

For the first time in quite a while some of the spark had returned to Lucchesi's voice, some of the bounce was back in his walk. He was convinced that the rumors were all false, that there was, in fact, "nothing going on."

And so the next day, when the ax fell, Frank Lucchesi broke down and cried as he faced the press. His friend had fibbed to him, misled him. It was a rotten thing to do.

The Phillies, of course, said they had done nothing of the kind and played a little semantics game to prove it. "If I thought for a minute I'd lied to Frank Lucchesi, I'd feel worse than you do," Paul Owens told me. "I have to live with Paul Owens. I have to look at myself in the mirror in the morning."

Then why wasn't Frank told the truth Sunday morning when he sought it?

"He asked specifically about the Bristol thing," Dallas Green explained. "I said, 'Frank, we tried to contact Dave Bristol to find out about an American League player. That's the only reason. He's the only guy I know who would give us the information with no ax to grind. . . .' Frank said, 'Fine, that's all I want to know.'

"If Frank had come right out and asked, 'Am I going to be fired tomorrow or next week?' we'd probably have broken down."

"I could not have looked him in the eye [and lied]," Owens said.

"These two guys," Ruly Carpenter added, "there's no way they would have lied to Frank Lucchesi if he had asked them, 'Am I a goner?'"

Beautiful, right? All Frank Lucchesi had to do was ask the right question in the right way, and he would have been spared the agony of being built up Sunday for a brutal letdown on Monday. The Phillies' official version of the deception was ludicrous. Why did they think he was asking them about Bristol? Did they really think that Frank gave a damn whether the name of his successor was Bristol or Stengel or Durocher—or, as it turned out, Owens? Lucchesi was there to find out one thing: Did he still have his job? In the most literal sense, they may have given him an honest answer when he asked, "Am I going to be replaced by Dave Bristol tomorrow?" and they assured him there was nothing to it. But the truth was they intentionally deceived him into thinking the job was still his. Frank Lucchesi deserved something better than that.

The
Ozark
Era

Schmidt Hits Four Home Runs

Allen Lewis

◆ ◆ ◆

It's hard to believe how many exciting "shootouts" (three of them against the Cubs) have been a part of Phillies history. There was the 26–23 game in 1922 and the wildest one ever, the 23–22 victory in 1979, not to mention the 15–14 defeat in Game Four of the 1993 World Series (see pp. 284–302). The April 17, 1976, brouhaha at Wrigley Field, in which the Phillies were down by eleven runs at two points, featured four consecutive home runs by the great Mike Schmidt, the third Hall of Fame Phillie to connect for four homers in a single game.

Allen Lewis was the heir to Stan Baumgartner on the Phillies beat for the Philadelphia Inquirer, *and one of the best pure sportswriters this city has ever had. A suburban Philadelphia boy, Lewis graduated from Haverford College in 1940, with letters in baseball and football. After stints on a Connecticut weekly and the* Philadelphia Evening Ledger, *and then four and a half years in the army during World War II, he joined the* Inquirer *sports staff in 1946 and never looked back. He retired in 1979 and now resides in Clearwater, Florida. He is still the reigning expert on Phillies trivia and writes a "This Week in Phillies History" column for the* Phillies Report.

Third baseman Mike Schmidt was demoted in the batting order yesterday—and promoted in the record book.

Dropped from third place to sixth in the lineup for the first time this season, the Phillies' all-or-nothing slugger became the 10th player in major league history to hit four home runs in one game and the first National Leaguer in modern times to hit four in a row.

His fourth homer of the day produced the decisive run in the 10th

From the *Philadelphia Inquirer,* April 18, 1976. Reprinted with permission from the *Philadelphia Inquirer.*

inning of an 18–16 victory over the Chicago Cubs before 28,287 at Wrigley Field.

The Phillies rallied—whoo boy, did they rally—after falling behind 12–1 and 13–2. Schmidt was the big producer, of course, batting in eight runs.

The major league home run leader for the past two seasons, Schmidt hit a two-run homer in the fifth inning and a solo homer in the seventh, both off righthanded starter Rick Reuschel; a three-run homer off right-handed reliever Mike Garman in the eighth and, finally, a two-run homer off righthanded Paul Reuschel in the 10th.

The wind was blowing out and the "friendly confines of Wrigley Field" shrank to the proportions of a telephone booth. In all, the Phillies hit six homers, the Cubs three.

Garry Maddox homered in the second, and Bob Boone tied the score when he led off the ninth with a homer against ex-Phil lefty Darold Knowles. Steve Swisher tied the score at 1-all with a blast in the Cubs' seven-run second inning in which Rick Monday also connected for a three-run homer.

The Phillies' clubhouse, heretofore subdued with only one victory in the first four games, bubbled with enthusiasm after this one. Almost everyone had a hand in the affair, it seemed. Steve Carlton started, only to be knocked out in the second inning, and seven more Philadelphia pitchers followed.

The victory went to lefthander Tug McGraw, who pitched the eighth, the two-run ninth, and then departed for a pinch-hitter following Schmidt's fourth homer. The Phils then had to call upon Tommy Underwood and, finally, Jim Lonborg to end the tug-of-war after the Cubs scored once and had Bill Madlock on second base in the last half of the 10th.

Lonborg threw one pitch. Jerry Morales bounced it to Mike Schmidt and the third baseman threw low to first. But Dick Allen dug the ball out of the dirt for the final out in the three-hour 42-minute game.

"Smitty never would have done it without me," McGraw said in laughing reference to the two runs he yielded in the ninth, sending the game into overtime and thus providing Schmidt with another time at bat.

"I wasn't thinking anything special when I went up there," Schmidt said. "I was feeling good and was nice and relaxed. I don't think moving down to sixth (in the order) meant anything.

"I did use a Tony Taylor bat today, and I wore a Terry Harmon T-shirt that he said had a lot of hits in it."

Schmidt, who flied out to deep center in the second inning and singled in the fourth, was reminded that in the last game he played here he hit two homers.

That stood as his career high until he became the first Phil to hit four homers in one game since Chuck Klein did it in 1936 at Pittsburgh, also in 10 innings. Delahanty hit four for the Phils in 1896. the last major leaguer to hit four in a game was San Francisco's Willie Mays at Milwaukee in 1961.

Schmidt, who has now five homers and 10 RBIs for the season, said his third homer—a tremendous shot that landed high up in the center field bleachers—was the ball he hit best and the line-drive to the left center in the 10th was the runnerup. His other homers cleared the left-field barrier.

"I hit a curve ball for the first one," Schmidt said, "a fast ball down and out over the place for the second and the third, and a fast ball up and in for the fourth."

"The last one was the best swing for me because I didn't try to be too fine."

Asked if he thought the Phillies still had a chance when they were 11 runs behind, Schmidt said, "Really, deep down you don't think so. But maybe the lack of pressure helped. You just go up there and work on your swing. I needed a game like this to take off some of the pressure."

Schmidt had struck out nine times and hit a mere .167 in the four previous games.

The Phillies banged out a total of 24 hits, but didn't appear to have a chance when the Cubs jumped out so far in the front.

In the seven-run second the Cubs put together five hits in addition to the homers by Swisher and Monday. Ron Schueler replaced Carlton but had to be relieved in their five-run third after three of the first four Cubs reached base.

Gene Garber relieved, loaded the bases with an intentional walk, hit a batter and gave up a two-run single to Manny Trillo and a two-run single to Dave Rosello that made it 12–1.

Dave Cash knocked in a Phil run with a fourth-inning single, but Monday's opposite-field homer to left off Ron Reed got that right back.

Then Schmidt went into his act. Jay Johnstone, who had hits his first four times up, Dick Allen, Larry Bowa and Boone all helped out.

Allen's two-run single preceded Schmidt's three-run homer in the eighth, and Boone tied it with his first homer of the year to left center at the start of the ninth.

Bobby Tolan, whose pinch single touched off the Phils' five-run rally in the eighth, looped a single off sub shortstop Nick Kelleher's glove with the game tied and came home one out later when Bowa tripled to right center. Johnstone's squeeze bunt scored Bowa and the Phillies were ahead 15–13.

Not for long. With one out, Morales singled and Andy Thornton doubled, putting the tying runs on base. After Trillo flied out, Bowa came to the mound.

"He asked me how I wanted him to play Swisher," McGraw reported. "I said, 'How many years you got in the big leagues?' He said, 'Seven.' I said, 'Well, I got 10 and that's 17 and we ought to be able to figure out something."

"So he went back and I threw the same pitch I did to lose the opener, and with the same result."

Swisher singled in both runs to tie the game and put it up to Schmidt once again. He didn't miss.

A Flag for Betsy Ross's Town?

Red Smith

◆ ◆ ◆

When the Phillies were making their first run for the National League pennant in almost a dozen years and seemed nearly invincible, Red Smith, then writing the "Sports of the Times" column for the New York Times, *reminisced about his days covering the Futile Phils and put in one good cheer for the old hometown boys. The contrast was too striking to pass without comment from Red. Despite the way things turned out for the Phils in the postseason, 1976 was a banner year. Smith compressed all of the highlights of the season into one hopeful column and presaged even better times ahead.*

Baker Bowl in Philadelphia was a stately pleasure dome when Al Reach built it for his Phillies in 1887 but by the 1930's and '40's it bore a striking resemblance to a run-down men's room. This made it a perfect setting for a run-down team that called the park home. The press box was a fenced-off section of the upper deck directly behind the plate, rather narrow and perhaps a dozen tiers deep. Stan Baumgartner had been a left-handed pitcher with the Phillies, and it tells something about the team that when he became a sports writer on the Philadelphia Inquirer he considered it a step up in the world. Stan had a seat in the front row of the press box, which enabled the working press behind him to while away the intervals between Chuck Klein's home runs by throwing peanuts at his large, bushy head. One day when the Cubs were in town, somebody started throwing paper cups of water, somebody else retaliated, and soon little rivulets were finding their way through the floor to the seats below. This brought a visit from Gerry Nugent, the Club President, a tall, courteous gentleman who never raised his voice.

"Gentlemen," Gerry said, "please! After all, we have patrons down-stairs."

"My God!" said Warren Brown of Chicago, reaching for his type-writer. "What a story!"

In those days, the patrons went to see the Phillies for laughs. This year nobody finds them amusing, least of all the managers of the other teams in the National League. The team, whose two pennants in 100 years constitute a record that will never be broken on purpose, has more victories and fewer defeats than any other club in the majors. Winning 50 of their first 70 games, the Phils made the fastest start since the Brooklyn Dodgers of 1955, whose won-lost figures at the end of June were 52–19. Those Dodgers won the pennant on Sept. 8, the earliest it had ever been done.

Home Runs and Strikeouts

Recently the Mets won six straight and gained half a game on the Phil-lies. Nobody makes up much ground on them because of their ability to win by whatever means is necessary. Larry Shenk, the resident drum-mer boy, likes to say they can do it with lumber, leather or legs. For clients who do not share Mr. Shenk's sweet tooth for alliteration, that translates as "power, defense or speed."

Last Tuesday night's game in Montreal offered an example. Phila-delphia made nine hits including three doubles but the score was only 1–1 when Dick Allen led off in the ninth inning. He singled and took third on a single by Jay Johnstone. Then the muscular Bob Boone, who had hit two of the doubles, squeezed Allen home with a bunt.

Boone is one reason for the Phillies' new look. This is the big catcher's fourth season with the team. His batting average over three summers was .251. Now he is hitting around .315. He and Garry Mad-dox, the center fielder obtained from San Francisco last year in ex-change for Willie Montanez, have the highest averages but in the league tabulation published last Sunday five Phillies—Allen, Dave Cash, Mike Schmidt, Greg Luzinski and Johnstone—were listed one after another with averages from .299 to .295.

Ask anybody in the organization why the Phillies of 1976 are so un-like the Phillies of 1975, who finished second in the National League East, or the Phillies of 1974 or 1973 or 1972, who finished third, sixth, and sixth, and he will mention Boone, Luzinski and Schmidt and Jim Kaat and Ron Reed. The first three are just realizing their potential; the other two, acquired in trades with the White Sox and Cardinals, have given depth and class to a pitching staff that was better than an empty clubhouse in the first place.

Luzinski led the league last summer with 120 runs batted in, the first Philadelphia player to head this category in 25 years. Schmidt was the home run champion for the second straight time but he also led the league in strikeouts with 138 in 1974 and 180 last season. One more year as the strikeout king and he'll match Hack Wilson's mark, two more and he'll tie Babe Ruth.

Visible Means of Support

The Phillies are second in team batting, second in team pitching and second in fewest errors. They have sent nine or more men to bat in an inning 19 separate times, have had 16 four-run innings, eight five-run innings and six six-run innings.

With support like that, the pitchers have prospered. Kaat, who has eight victories and two defeats, is on a six-game winning streak. Jim Lonborg, who had eight victories for all of last season, won his first eight games this year. Steve Carlton won five in a row and so did 22-year-old Larry Christenson.

Tug McGraw has won four, lost four and saved five games but in the bull pen the boss bull has been Reed. One day he walked in against the Reds with the bases filled and nobody out. He struck out Tony Perez, struck out Johnny Bench and retired Ken Griffey on a fly.

As all history students know, the Phillies last won a pennant in 1950, and lost the World Series to the Yankees in four straight. They had won for the first time in 35 years earlier, and had lost to the Red Sox in five games. However, things are looking up in Father Penn's "greene coun-trie towne." Philadelphia gets the All-Star game this month. The Phillies' Robin Roberts will be inducted into the Hall of Fame in August. And when we speak of the Bicentennial we're talking about Philadelphia, because that's where this nation started.

Bicentennials come once in 200 years. Pennants come oftener to Betsy Ross's town, but not much.

The Ten-Minute Collapse

Bill Conlin

◆ ◆ ◆

This might or might not be Bill Conlin's most famous piece. The stalwart Daily News *columnist has written so many good columns over the years, but this memorable account belongs in any anthology of good sportswriting and, indeed, has appeared in two others. Conlin records with a minimalist's eye for detail the second of Danny Ozark's three strikes in the 1977 playoff games. With victory one out away, the Futile Phils seemed to rise from the grave—in record time— and blast all hopes of taking a two-game lead on the Dodgers.*

Dusty Baker hit a tough chopper to third, and Mike Schmidt pounced on the wicked short hop like a jaguar running down a rabbit.

That was one out in the top of the ninth, seven straight ground balls thrown by Gene Garber. And 63,719 fans were on their feet, a shrieking chorus that all afternoon had roared with the blood lust of a Roman Coliseum mob rooting for the lion.

Rick Monday bounced out to Teddy Sizemore. The Vet throng was chanting "DEEEFENSE." Eight straight ground balls by Geno. Game three was history. One more out, Geno, baby, and this was a 5–3 Phillies' victory. The Dodgers had coughed up two eighth-inning runs to go with three the crowd and plate umpire Harry Wendelstedt had bled from starter Burt Hooton in the second.

The Dodgers were down to their suspect bench. Ancient Vic Davalillo hauled his well-traveled bones to the plate, more wrinkles on his leather face than there are base hits left in his bat.

From the *Philadelphia Daily News*, October 8, 1977. Reprinted by permission.

On deck was Manny Mota, thirty-nine years old, one final straw for Tommy Lasorda to clutch at should Davalillo reach first base.

Thus began the shortest, most devastating nightmare in the history of a town steeped in an athletic tradition of flood, fire, and famine, a town where some seasons even down seemed like a long way up.

A funeral dirge would be appropriate at this point, Beethoven's *Eroica,* perhaps, or a few choruses from *Lohengrin.*

You thought the *Titanic* went down fast!

The 1964 Collapse took ten games. This one took ten minutes. It was like watching the shambles of 1964 compressed into an elapsed-time film sequence.

With two outs, the Phillies met the enemy, and it was them.

Davalillo legged out a superb bunt to Sizemore, as if that is the normal play for a thirty-nine-year-old man with just forty-eight at bats after the Dodgers picked him up for late-season insurance.

"If he had hollered, 'Hey, I'm gonna lay one down,' we still couldn't have stopped it," First Baseman Richie Hebner said after the incredible 6–5 loss. "It was just a perfect bunt, a great play on Vic's part."

Mota came up swinging for a home run. He hit one in the final regular-season game last Sunday, hadn't hit one before that since the 1972 season.

He fouled a pitch back, then fell behind 0 to 2 with a swing so lusty it almost dislodged his batting helmet.

"Two strikes I am trying to just protect the plate," Mota said over the joyous babble of the winner's clubhouse. "I'm not a power hitter; I try to hit line drives. He threw me an inside slider."

Mota jumped on the pitch like a Santo Domingo street urchin putting the touch on a well-heeled gringo tourist. "Thank you, *señor,* may God bless you for this gift."

The fly ball carried, driving Greg Luzinski back toward the bull-pen fence in left. There was enough controversy in this schizophrenic game to keep a Warren Commission busy for weeks, and this was one chapter.

Luzinksi leaped at the fence. The ball lodged briefly in the webbing of his glove, then jarred loose, hit the fence, and nestled back into Bull's grasp. Wouldn't it have been a much easier play for fleet-footed Jerry Martin, often Luzinski's defensive caddy?

"He was the third batter up in the ninth," Danny Ozark said, wearing the dazed look of a train-wreck survivor. "I wanted him in the lineup in case the game was tied."

Davalillo was being held at third when Luzinski threw to second. The ball skidded through Sizemore's legs. Davalillo scored, and Mota huffed to third on the second baseman's error.

The inning reached a ten on the Richter Scale of natural disasters when Davey Lopes roped a one-hop shot off the heel of Schmidt's glove, off his knee, deflecting to Larry Bowa at shortstop. Bowa made a brilliant pickup and gunned a strike to Hebner. First-base umpire Bruce Froemming double-clutched, then spread his hands palm down. Hebner shrieked and stamped. Ozark erupted from the dugout. The veins in Bowa's neck bulged like telephone cables.

"If he had called the play right, both me and Hebner would have been thrown out," Ozark seethed in his office after a calm performance in the mass interview room. "He didn't know what the bleep to call it, so he called it safe. He was stunned by Bowa's throw, as far as I'm concerned. He just anticipated Bowa couldn't make the throw. He's got his hands stuffed in his pockets half the bleeping time."

For the second time in the tense war, the unwavering eye of the TV replay cameras would show Lopes out by a narrow margin, just as they proved from two angles that Steve Garvey never touched the plate on Bob Boone's superb block in the second.

Garber unfurled a pickoff move that skidded past Hebner, and Lopes jetted to second. "It was a sinker that exploded," Hebner said. "I should have got more body in front of it."

The Phillies fiery Götterdämmerung was complete when Bill Russell bounced a single up the middle.

Mike Garman, sixth Los Angeles pitcher on an afternoon of baffling selection by Lasorda, retired Bowa and Schmidt, then drilled Luzinski with a high, tight fastball.

Hebner bounced Garman's first pitch to Steve Garvey, and the crowd stood in a collective silence reserved for the demise of a great matador in a jammed Plaza de Toros.

Death had come to the executioners. The Phillies had met the enemy, and it was them.

Life and Death through the Years with the Phillies

James A. Michener

◆ ◆ ◆

*One of our nation's most distinguished authors, James Michener put the Phils'
third straight postseason playoff loss in 1978 into historical and personal perspective for this* New York Times *op-ed piece. An octogenarian, Bucks County,
Pennsylvania, resident, and long-suffering Phillies fan, Michener not only got
that "one great year" but also got to throw out the first ball in the second game of
the 1980 World Series. For that occasion he wrote a bit of poesy called "Line
Composed in Exaltation over the North Atlantic," the title referring to the fact
that he was flying to Bangkok when the pilot announced that the Phillies had
won the World Series.*

Like any prudent man, I try from time to time to take stock of
myself, and this year, at the close of the baseball season, I decided that I was not charismatic, not especially brave and not many
other things. But, by damn, I had character.

Since 1915, I have been cheering for the Philadelphia Phillies, and if
that doesn't take character, what does? In such circumstances, it is tra-
ditional to say, "I supported them in good years and bad." There were
no good years. I cheered in bad and worse.

Of the 16 teams in the original big leagues, none ever had a chain of
such disastrous years as the Phillies. Year after year they wallowed in last
place, and I remember my friend Marvin saying one October with real
hope, "Next year's gotta look up," and a listener said, "There ain't no up."

In those years, we loyal fans had to hold our tempers as sportswriters coined such nifty phrases as "The Phainting Phils" and "The Pheckless Phils." Did you ever see Baker Field in those days? It was the smallest, crummiest, most ridiculous field in baseball with a right field so close that left-handed hitters pulverized it. Philly outfielders used to play leaning against it, and if they took six running steps they were in the infield.

The Mets Were Different

But still we went to the games. In later years, the New York Mets had a team almost as inept, and their fans too remained loyal, but what a difference. The New York fans played it for comedy, orchestrated by that master jokester, Casey Stengel. We Philly fans played it for real, bleeding when our team went down, not joking.

And we had much to bleed about. Remember the 1964 finish? I was working in Egypt that September, with the Phillies so far ahead in the National League that I felt no apprehension when I had to go into the desert for a long trip. I told Marvin, "Only way we can lose this year is drop 10 games in a row while somebody else wins 10." When I returned to Cairo and looked at The International Herald Tribune to see how the Phils were doing in the World Series, I saw to my astonishment that St. Louis was playing the Yanks.

"What happened? I yelled, and Marvin said, "We blew 10 in a row."

People forget that back in the miracle year of 1950, when the Phils did get into the World Series, they ended their regular season losing eight out of 10 games until the final day. Only on the last Sunday did they eke out an extra-inning victory over Brooklyn to squeeze home.

It's Been Embarrassing

The Phillies did not do well in that World Series: Yanks four games, Phils none. In fact, none of the original 16 teams has done worse than the Phils. In 1915, they played Boston in the World Series, won the first game, then lost four. Their standing in World Series play is 1–8.

In league playoffs, they have done the same. In 1976: Phillies none, Cincinatti three. In 1977 and 1978: Phillies one, Los Angeles three. In all post-season games, the Phillies have won three and lost 17.

We Philly fans have watched in embarrassment as newcomer towns like Milwaukee, Los Angeles, Baltimore and Oakland have carried off the championship while our fine old town accomplishes nothing. Even the St. Louis Browns, when they played in the World Series in 1944 with a one-armed outfielder, did better than the Phils have done. They won two games in that Series before bowing to the Cards.

But my team waited until this year to play its quintessential end-of-year doubleheader. It had led the National League by comfortable margins—no Philly fan should ever use that term—when Pittsburgh, 11½ games back, caught fire. As it usually does, the race came down to the wire, and on the final Friday, the Phillies faced the Pirates in a do-or-die situation. Two games. They had to win one to clinch the pennant.

Another One Down Drain

First game, bottom of the ninth, score tied at 4–4. Ed Ott lofts an easy fly to right-center for the final out and extra-innings. But the Philly center-fielder, Garry Maddox, and the right-fielder, Bake McBride, allow the ball to fall between them. Still, Ott should have been held to a triple, but Maddox heaves the ball past third base and that game goes down the drain.

Second game, bottom of the ninth again, score tied at 1–1. Pittsburgh batting. Dave Parker slams a double to center, then an error by Maddox turns into a triple. But all is not lost. Two Pirate batters are intentionally walked and a relief pitcher, Warren Brusstar, marches to the mound . . . and balks. Yep, in a crucial game, he balks in the winning run.

Third game, bottom of the ninth once more, Phillies leading by 10–4. This time, the Pirates start to swing from the dugout, and with only one out the score is 10–8 with the tying run at the plate in Willie Stargell. I was watching this game with Marvin and other faithfuls, and not one of us expected our team to get the Pirates out. We expected disaster, and when our boys finally eked out the victory that clinched the pennant, Marvin said: "Don't worry. They'll blow it in the playoffs." Which they did.

A Sense of Tragedy

A young literary critic asked me the other day:

"Mr. Michener, you seem to be optimistic about the human race. Don't you have a sense of tragedy?"

I thought a minute and told him:

"Young man, when you root for the Phillies, you acquire a sense of tragedy."

Marvin must have been thinking of this when he handed me a slip of paper to be used in case he died before me. On his tombstone he wants:

"Here lies a Phillies Phan, still hoping for that one great year."

Schmidt Just Made It Look Easy

Jayson Stark

◆ ◆ ◆

"If you saw Mike Schmidt play baseball," wrote Dave Anderson, the Pulitzer Prize–winning sports columnist for the New York Times, *"you can always say that you saw baseball's best third-baseman. Even the old-timers might not argue." Added Thomas Boswell, Mike Schmidt "did what so many great athletes have failed to do; he left us wanting more."*

Though he played across two decades for the Phillies, Schmidt will always be linked to Danny Ozark, whom Schmidt did not think much of as a manager. "When Schmidt came to the Phillies, in 1973," Tony Kornheiser wrote, "Ozark saw something special in him—some perfect flash of marble. And, with Ozark's sculpting, there would someday emerge a full-blown David, ensuring the manager's place in baseball history as his Michelangelo." Schmidt didn't reach his potential fast enough for Danny Ozark—and for some fans. (There is a distinctively dishonest brand of Phillies fans: those who claim to have been at some game they never were and those who now claim never to have booed Mike Schmidt.) It is fittingly ironic that Schmidt entered his prime just as Ozark's years in Philadelphia were coming to an end.

When the fire finally went out of Schmidt after seventeen years and he retired on May 29, 1989, the Inquirer*'s Jayson Stark glowingly recalled the man and what he meant to baseball and the city of Philadelphia.*

There will come a day, sometime in the next century, when you will tell your grandchildren you saw him play.

You will get to reminiscing about the great Mike Schmidt. And once you get started, you will find it hard to stop.

From the *Philadelphia Inquirer,* May 30, 1989. Reprinted with permission from the *Philadelphia Inquirer.*

You will tell them of the four home runs that were gone with the wind on that magical Saturday afternoon at Wrigley in 1976.

You will tell them of the home run in Montreal on a long day's journey into an October night, the home run that pierced a hole in the 38-degree glop and sealed up the NL East for a 1980 Phillies team that was bound for greatness.

You will tell them of No. 500, a moment not just of history but of poetry. A game-winning, three-run home run with two outs in the ninth inning. A home run hit in the most pressure-packed of settings, at a moment when his team needed him most.

But it won't be just those highlight-film clips you remember when you get to thinking about Mike Schmidt. You will remember the image of the greatest third baseman of his time. Perhaps you will remember that above all.

It will be the image of a man who made his sport look almost too easy. He may have fired those home runs off into the night, but he never shook the earth trying to launch them.

He never went tumbling to one knee like Reggie. He never glowered like Frank Robinson or towered like Willie McCovey.

They just came flowing out of him—so smooth, so easy, so natural. Dick Allen hit lightning bolts. Greg Luzinski hit moon shots. Mike Schmidt just hit baseballs that wouldn't come down.

And how will you describe the way a 10-time Gold Glove-winner played third base? With many of those same words: *smooth, easy, natural.*

He wasn't much for flopping around in the dirt, making a lot of plays that looked more spectacular than they were. That wasn't Mike Schmidt's style.

His style was to make the spectacular plays look *easier* than they were, not the other way around. And that was a trick only the great ones could turn.

He had the quick step to either side and the arm to gun you down from the parking lot. He made the barehanded charge play as brilliantly as any third baseman of his generation.

He could outthink you, too. How many runners took that turn around second as Schmidt charged those little swinging bunts and cocked to throw to first, only to find themselves out when the throw to first turned into a fake, followed by a seed to the second baseman?

More than a few. It was a play that came to bear Mike Schmidt's unique signature, the signature of the thinking-man's third baseman.

The thinking. In time, maybe you'll forget about the thinking. But for the 17 years that he wore a uniform, the thinking was an issue that would never go away.

Did Mike Schmidt really think too much? Even a lot of people who admired him told him he did. They saw a Hall of Fame home-run hitter try bunting for hits or inside-outing the ball to the right side, and something inside them rebelled.

Hall of Fame home-run hitters didn't have to do those things, they said. He would be better off if he just let it happen, they said.

But it wasn't Mike Schmidt's way merely to let it happen. He was a man who hit 548 home runs, and yet he spent his entire career trying *not* to hit them.

He had his ideas about the way this game was meant to be played. And he was determined to live out those ideas. But it wasn't until the end of his career that the people who watched him most closely came to accept that—and, in turn, accept him.

"Heck, for years I've told them that [that approach] must be doing a *little* something for me," Schmidt said in 1986, at the close of a season that won him his third and final MVP award. "But all I heard about was what a great player I would be if I just got out there and let it happen.

"I'll tell you what," he said. "If I just went out there and let it happen, I'd be a mediocre player. I'd be a major-leaguer, but a mediocre one."

Well, whatever it was that made him the player he became, mediocre is not the word you will use when you tell your grandchildren about the man you saw.

He reached 500 home runs faster than all but four players who ever lived. He hit 35 home runs in 11 different seasons, a number bettered only by a legend named Babe Ruth. He hit 30 home runs in 13 seasons, a feat surpassed only by Henry Aaron.

He hit more home runs than any third baseman in history. He led his league in homers more times than any player except Ruth. He won more Gold Gloves than any third baseman except Brooks Robinson.

He started eight all-star games. He was the most valuable player of a World Series. He was once voted the greatest player in the history of his franchise.

And he ticked off those glittery seasons with the consistency of an assembly line. Toss out the harsh initiation of his 1973 rookie year (.196, 18 homers) and the injury-riddled farewell seasons of 1988 and '89. What you find in between is a brilliance that never quit.

In between, Schmidt hit at least 31 homers in every year but one (1978). And scored at least 88 runs in every year but one (the 1981 strike year). And drove in at least 87 runs in every year but one ('78).

So how will you explain some day why they booed him as much as they cheered him in the town he called home for every game of his career?

Oh, maybe by the next century, no one will care anymore that he once described the fans of Philadelphia as "uncontrollable," and "a mob scene," and "beyond help."

Maybe by then, no one will be offended by his suggestions that he would have had a much better career in a city "where they were just grateful to have me around," or by his theories that people were "jealous" of his money and success.

Maybe by then, they will only laugh at the memory of Schmidt wearing a shoulder-length red wig at first base, trying to win back the hearts of those same people.

But at the time, it wasn't always cheers, and it wasn't always chuckles. He was so good, people expected more than he could give. And in turn, he expected more from them than he got.

And there got to be a few days where he couldn't take it anymore. Then all his feelings came spilling out in the papers, or on the radio, or at the podium. And the next day, there he was, trying to grin and explain that when he said these Philadelphians had eaten too many cheesesteaks, he hadn't meant it like it sounded.

He wasn't your typical superstar, and Philadelphia never treated him like one. They loved him. They hated him. Often they did both on the same day.

But in the end, when he began to talk of calling it quits or of signing with the Mets or Reds or Dodgers, Philadelphia couldn't bear the thought of life without him.

When he signed his final contract with the Phillies just last winter, he actually gave credit to the people of Philadelphia for bringing him back. He got the impression, he said, that those people "would be hurt if I left." He heard that message on the streets and in the shopping malls. And the Phillies heard it in the offices where the big decisions were made.

By the end, he was more than just a superstar whose numbers dwelled alongside those of men named Gehrig, Ruth and Mays. He was a symbol of the most glorious era in Phillies history, an era of which he was the centerpiece.

The most famous photograph in the life of the Phillies still hangs on many a wall. It was taken moments after the last out of the 1980 World Series.

A throng of Phillies had just converged around the pitcher's mound to celebrate the championship they had played their whole careers to win. On top of the heap, riding aboard the shoulders of Tug McGraw, was Michael Jack Schmidt, the greatest third baseman of his time.

There will be a day, sometime in the next century, when you tell your grandchildren about the moment captured in that photograph. And you will tell them, too, about the man who rode atop the heap.

Thin Mountain Air

Pat Jordan

◆ ◆ ◆

As Jayson Stark observed in the Sporting News *of August 1, 1994, "If there is a certain aura that surrounds men who make the Hall of Fame, it is hard to name a modern pitcher who exuded that aura anymore than . . . the invincible, inimitable Steven Norman Carlton." Carlton and Mike Schmidt were the two dominant Phillies players during the Ozark era. Before the notorious "Big Silence," there were more or less predictable puff pieces written about Carlton, the man reporters once labeled "The Franchise" and everyone called "Lefty." While there is no question about either Carlton's greatness or his famous reticence, Pat Jordan, one of the country's most talented freelance magazine writers (and a former Milwaukee Braves' bonus baby, who never made it to the show and chronicled his three years of frustration in the baseball masterpiece* A False Spring *[1975, Dodd, Mead]), in this controversial April 1994 piece for* Philadelphia Magazine, *depicts a less taciturn but no less inscrutable Steve Carlton living in a bizarre kind of retirement in Durango, Colorado.*

Carlton repudiated the piece and accused Jordan of misquoting him. But as Carlton's friend and battery mate Tim McCarver wrote about him in Oh, Baby, I Love It! *(1987, Villard): "Steve may not be a complete recluse, but he comes close. If he hadn't wound up in the majors, he probably would have been a hunting guide in a desolate cabin back in the mountains fifty miles or so from any paved roads."*

Whatever one feels about this profile, it is a stellar piece of writing, reminiscent of Jordan's other fine essays on pitchers collected in The Suitors of Spring *(1974, Dodd, Mead). And we might say of Carlton what Stephen Jay Gould wrote of one of the game's genuine misanthropes, Ty Cobb: "Baseball is a beautiful game, and an important part of our history as a nation, and a joy and*

From *Philadelphia Magazine*, April 1994. Reprinted with permission of Pat Jordan.

comfort in the lives of millions. . . . And excellence in any honorable form—that rarest and most precious of human accomplishments—must be praised, despite the toll often exacted on the achievers and the victims of their obsessions."

Durango, Colorado, is a cold mountain community 6,506 feet above sea level. It is known for its thin air, which can make residents light-headed, disoriented. It is surrounded by the La Platta mountain range. Built into the foothills of those mountains is a domed concrete house covered with snow and dirt. No one but its owner can explain what he was seeking with that house.

"I came to Durango in 1989 to get away from society," he says. He is a big man, 6-5, 225 pounds, dressed in a Western shirt, jeans and cowboy boots. He is standing beside his truck in the thick snow that covers the land around his bunker and rests gently on the branches of the low-lying piñon trees that dot his 400 acres. It is a few days before Christmas. "I don't like it where there are too many people," he says. "I like it here because the people are spiritually tuned in." He glances sideways, out of the corner of his eyes. "They know where the lies fall."

He makes a sweeping gesture with a long arm, encompassing his bunker, his barn with its turkeys, pheasants and horses, and more than 160 fruit trees he has planted. "This is sacred land," he says. "We're self-sufficient here. There's no one around us. We grow our own food." He points to sliding glass doors that lead inside his bunker to the greenhouse off his bedroom. "We have our own well," he says. "And 16 solar batteries for heat and electricity."

Even his telephone works on cellular microwave transmitters. That way no one can tap his wires.

"The house is built with over 300 yards of concrete," he says. "Three-feet-thick walls covered by another three feet of earth." Why? He looks startled, like a huge bird. His small eyes blink once, twice, and then he says, "So the gamma rays won't penetrate the walls."

Built under the house is a 7,000-foot storage cellar. He's stocked it with canned foods, bottled water, weapons. "Do you know if you store guns in PVC pipe, they can last forever underground without rusting?"

he says. He glances sideways again. "The Revolution is definitely coming."

He believes in the Revolution, only he isn't precisely sure which of a myriad of conspiratorial groups will begin it. Possibly, he says, it will be started by the Skull and Bones Society of Yale University. Or maybe the International Monetary Fund. Or the World Health Organization. There are so many conspiracies, and so little time. Sometimes all those conspiracies confuse him and he contradicts himself. One minute he'll say "The Russian and U.S. governments fill the air with low-frequency sound waves meant to control us," and the next he'll say "The Elders of Zion rule the world," and then "The British MI-5 and -6 intelligence agencies have ruled the world since 1812," and "Twelve Jewish bankers meeting in Switzerland rule the world," and "The world is controlled by a committee of 300 which meets at a roundtable in Rome." The subterfuge starts early. Like the plot by the National Education Association to subvert American children with false teachings. "Don't tell me that two plus two equals four," he once said. "How do you know that two *is* two? That's the real question."

He believes that last eight U.S. presidents have been guilty of treason, that President Clinton "has a black son" he won't acknowledge and that his wife, Hillary, "is a dyke," and that the AIDS virus was created at a secret Maryland biological warfare laboratory "to get rid of gays and blacks, and now they have a strain of the virus that can live ten days in the air or on a plate of food, because you know who most of the waiters are," and finally, that most of the mass murderers in this country who open fire indiscriminately in fast-food restaurants "are hypnotized to kill those people and then themselves immediately afterwards," as in the movie *The Manchurian Candidate.* He blinks once, twice, and says "Who hypnotizes them? *They* do!"

Maybe he isn't really contradicting himself. Maybe he is just one of those people who read into the simplest things a cosmic significance they may or may not have. Conspiracies everywhere to explain things he cannot fathom. The refuge of a limited mind. "The mind is its own place," John Milton wrote in *Paradise Lost.* "And in itself can make a Heaven of Hell, a Hell of Heaven."

Steven Norman Carlton, "Lefty," discovered his first conspiracy in 1988, when he was forced to leave baseball prematurely and against his will, he says—after a 24-year major-league pitching career of such excellence that he was an almost-unanimous selection for baseball's Hall of Fame on his first try, this past January. He received 96 percent of all baseball writers' votes, the second-highest percentage ever received by a pitcher (after Tom Seaver's 98 percent) and the fifth-highest of all time.

Carlton, who pitched for the Phillies from 1972 to 1986 after seven years with the St. Louis Cardinals, has—after the Braves' Warren Spahn—the most wins of any left-handed pitcher. Carlton won 329 games and lost 244 during his career. Six times he won 20 games or more in a season, and he was voted his league's Cy Young Award a record four times. His most phenomenal season, one of the greatest seasons a pitcher has ever had, came in his first year with the Phillies: Carlton won 27 games, lost only ten and fashioned a 1.98 ERA for a last-place team that won only 59 games all season. In other words, he earned almost half of his team's victories, the highest such percentage ever. For almost 20 years, he was the pitcher against which all others were judged.

The secrets to his success were many. Talent. An uncanny ability to reduce pitching to its simplest terms. An unorthodox, yet rigorous, training regimen. A fierce stubbornness, and an even fiercer arrogance. All contributed to his success on the mound and, later, to his inability to adjust to the complexities of life off the mound.

As a pitcher, Carlton knew his limitations. A mind easily baffled by intricacies. There were so many batters. Their strengths and weaknesses confused him, so he refused to go over batters' tendencies in pregame meetings. He blocked them out of his consciousness and reduced pitching to a mere game of toss between pitcher and catcher—his personal catcher, Tim McCarver. He used only two pitches: an explosive fastball and an equally explosive, biting slider. He just threw one of the two pitches to his catcher's glove. Fastball up and in; slider low and away. He worked very hard to let nothing intrude upon his concentration. Once the third baseman fired a ball that hit him in the head. He blinked, waved off the players rushing to his aid, picked up the ball, toed the rubber and faced his next batter. His parents, Joe and Anne Carlton, claim they've never seen their son cry.

It was not always easy for him to be so singularly focused while pitching. "Concentration on the mound is a battle," he says. "Things creep into your mind. Your mind is always chattering."

To prevent any "chattering" before a start, he had the Phillies build him a $15,000 "mood behavior" room next to the clubhouse. It was soundproof, with dark blue carpet on the floor, walls and ceiling. He'd sit there for hours in an easy chair, staring at a painting of ocean waves rushing against the shore. A disembodied voice intoned "I am courageous, calm, confident and relaxed . . . I can control my destiny." Carlton, said teammate Dal Maxvill, lived in "a little dark room of his mind."

His training routine was just as unorthodox. He hated to run wind sprints, so instead he stuck his arm in a garbage pail filled with brown rice and rotated it 49 times, for the 49 years that Kwan Gung, a Chinese martial-arts hero, lived. By then, Lefty himself was a martial-arts expert. He performed the slow, ritualized movements in his clubhouse before each game. He also extensively read Eastern theology and philosophy. Those texts discussed the mysteries of life, the unknowable and how a man should confront them. Silence, stoicism and simplicity.

Those tenets struck a chord in him because, increasingly, his life off the mound was becoming more complex than a game of catch. People constantly clamored for his autograph. Waitresses messed up his order in restaurants, so he tore up their menus. Reporters began to ask him questions he didn't like, or didn't understand, or maybe he just thought were trivial. They even had the effrontery to question him about his failures.

"People are always throwing variables at you," he said in disgust, and refused to talk anymore. The press called it "the Big Silence." From 1974 to 1988, Carlton wouldn't speak to the media. (It wasn't just *Daily News* sportswriter Bill Conlin's stories, as many assumed, but a series of articles, Carlton says now, that drove him to withdraw.) One sportswriter said there would come a time when Lefty would "wish he'd been a good guy when he'd had the chance." But he didn't have to be a good guy. He wasn't interested in the fame being a good guy would bring him. He wanted only to perfect his craft, which he did, and to become rich.

Over the last ten years of his career, Carlton earned close to $10 million, almost all of it in salary because he didn't want the annoyance of doing endorsements. It was demeaning, he thought, for him to hawk peoples' wares. Then again, thanks to the Big Silence, there weren't a lot of sponsors beating down his door. He already had a reputation for sullen arrogance. When he went to New York City once to discuss a contract for a book about his life, he told the editors he really didn't care about the book, that he was just doing it for the money and because his wife, Beverly, thought it was a good idea. The editors beat a hasty retreat.

Carlton didn't need a publisher's money, or a sponsor's, because he had a personal agent who promised to make him so rich that when he retired he could do nothing but fish and hunt. He had his salary checks sent directly to the agent, David Landfield, who invested them in oil and gas leases, car dealerships and Florida swampland. Since Carlton couldn't be bothered with the checks and often had no idea exactly how big they were, Landfield simply sent him a monthly allowance, as if he were a child. Those monthly allotments would be all Carlton would ever see out of his $10 million. Not one of Landfield's investments for him ever made a cent. By 1983, all the money was gone.

During the nine years that Landfield worked for him, Carlton's friends tried to warn him off the agent. Bill Giles, the Phillies' owner, and Mike Schmidt, Lefty's teammate, pleaded with him to drop Landfield. But he wouldn't listen. One time, he even got into a fistfight with Schmidt in the clubhouse because of Landfield, and the two, formerly close friends, stopped speaking. Carlton said it was because he was loyal to Landfield, whom he trusted. Others said he was just being stubborn and arrogant because his success on the mound had led him to believe he was invincible off it. McCarver once said that Lefty "always had an irascible contempt for being human. He thinks he's superhuman."

When the truth of what Landfield had done with his money finally intruded into Carlton's psyche, it was too late. He went through the motions of suing Landfield in 1983, but by then Landfield had declared bankruptcy. Worse, Carlton never had a chance to recoup his money, because only a few years later his career was on the downswing and those big paychecks were a thing of the past. He began to lose the bite on his slider in '85, and people told him he should try to pick up another pitch. But he refused. He continued to throw the only way he knew how. Fastball up and in, slider low and away.

Between 1986 and 1988, Carlton was traded or released five times, until finally, after being cut by the Minnesota Twins, no club would sign him—even for the $100,000 league minimum. Carlton was furious. At 43 he insisted he could still pitch. That's when he uncovered his first conspiracy.

"The Twins set me up to release me by not pitching me," he says today. "And the other owners were told to keep their hands off. Other teams wouldn't even talk to me. I don't understand it." To understand it, all Carlton has to do is look at his pitching record from 1985 to 1988: 16 wins, 37 losses and an ERA of more than five runs per game. It was a reality he didn't want to face. So, sullen and hurt, Carlton decided to punish those who had hurt him. He retreated to Durango and soon afterward began building his mountain bunker, turning his back on the game and the real world that had betrayed him.

Steve Carlton, 49, dressed in a T-shirt and gym shorts, is standing on his head in the mirrored exercise room, performing his daily three hours of yoga.

"I don't even feel any weight above my neck," he says, upside down. Just then a screaming flock of children runs into the room with their female yoga instructor, who is dressed in black tights. Immediately Carlton takes out two earplugs and sticks them in his ears. "It takes the bite off the high-end notes," he says, smiling. He is still a handsome man, his face relatively unlined. His is a typically American handsomeness, perfect features without idiosyncrasies. Except for his eyes. They are small and hazel and show very little.

"I spend my summers riding motorcycles and dirt bikes," he says. "I work around the house. It's taken us three years and we're still not finished. (It is rumored that he doesn't have the money to do so.) In the winter I ski and read books, Eastern metaphysical stuff. All about the power within. Oneness with the universe. I want to tap into my own mind to know what God knows." He rights himself, sits cross-legged on a mat and begins contorting into another yoga position, the ankle of his left leg somewhere behind his ear.

"You ought to try it," he says. "Yoga for three hours a day. And skiing, too." He says this with absolute conviction, as if it has never crossed his mind that there are those who do not have three hours in the morning to spare for yoga, and three more hours in the afternoon to ski.

In fact, Durango seems to be the kind of town where people have unlimited leisure time. At 10:30 on a weekday morning, the health club is packed. Durango is one of those faux-Western towns whose women dress in dirndl skirts and cowboy boots and whose men, their faces adorned with elaborately waxed 1890s handlebar mustaches, wear plaid work shirts rolled up to the elbows. It has a lot of "saloons"—not bars—with clever names, like Father Murphy's, that have walls adorned with old guns, specialize in a variety of cappuccinos and frown upon cigar smoking. Clean air is an important subject in Durango. When the town's only tobacco shop wanted to hold a cigar smoker, its two owners were afraid it would be disrupted by protesters chaining themselves to their shop door. It's a town for people who cannot countenance the idiosyncrasies of their fellow man. So they come to this clean, thin mountain air where they can breathe without being contaminated by the foulness of the rest of the world.

Carlton believes he is in better physical shape now than when he left baseball six years ago. "In a month I could be throwing in the 80s [miles per hour] and win," he says. "There's nothing wrong with me. I was labeled 'too old.' But you can still pitch in your 50s. It's not for money but for pride, proving you can perform. That's the beauty of it. Then to be cut off . . . It's disheartening. If only they let you tell them when you know you're done. It hurts. But I haven't looked back. No thought of what I should have done. Maybe I should have learned a circle change-up in my later years. But I didn't think I needed a change."

Most great pitchers intuit the loss of their power pitches before it actually happens. Warren Spahn, for example. He could see, in his early 30s, a time when his high, leg-kicking fastball would no longer be adequate. So he began to perfect an off-speed screwball and a slow curve. By the time Spahn lost his fastball, he had perfected his off-speed pitches, and his string of 20-victory seasons continued unbroken into his late 30s and early 40s. But Carlton was both luckier than Spahn and less fortunate. Because he did not lose his power pitches until late into his 30s, he was deluded into thinking he would never lose them, and so didn't develop any off-speed pitches.

Carlton, lying on his back now, pulls one leg underneath himself and stretches it. "Baseball was fun," he says. "But I have no regrets. Competition is the ultimate level of insecurity, having to beat someone. I don't miss baseball. I never look back. You turn the page. Eternity lies in the here and now. If you live in the past, you accelerate the death process. Your being is your substance."

As a player, Carlton was known for his conviviality with his teammates. He spent a lot of his off-hours drinking with them, and there were hints in the press, most notably by Bill Conlin, that his drinking contributed to some of his disastrous years, such as the 13–20 '73 season. After he left baseball, Carlton, who used to be a wine connoisseur, with a million-dollar cellar, gave up drinking.

"I had nobody to go drinking with anymore," he says. "Now when I see old baseball players, I have nothing to talk to them about. All that old-time bullshit. It bores me. I live in the here and now. I'd be intellectually starved in the game today." Still, Carlton would like to get back into it. He sees himself as a pitching coach in spring training.

"I'd like to teach young pitchers the mental aspect of the game," he says. "Teach them wisdom, which is different than knowledge. Champions think a certain way. To a higher level. They create their future. The body is just a vehicle for the mind and spirit. Champions will themselves to win. They know they're gonna win. Others hope they'll win. The mind gives you what it asks for. That's its God."

Then he relates a story about a friend in Durango, who, years ago, didn't want to play on his high school basketball team because he knew it was going to have a losing season. Before the season began, the friend was hit by a car, destroying his knee.

"See," says Carlton, as if he's just proved a point. "If you have an accident, you create it in your mind. That's a fact. The mind is the conscious architect of your success. What you hold consciously in your mind becomes your reality."

If this is so, then Carlton must have willed his own failure in the twilight of his career. When such a possibility is broached to him, he looks up, terrified. He blinks once, in shock, and a second time to banish the thought from his psyche. "Why do you ask such questions?" he says shrilly. He has so carefully crafted his philosophies that he can become completely disoriented when they are challenged. That's why Carlton has withdrawn from the world into the security of his bunker. There he is left alone with only his thoughts, his dictums, his conspiracies, with no one to question them. Such questions strike fear in Carlton. And above all else, Steve Carlton is a fearful man.

"Fear dictates our lives," he has said. "Fear is a tremendous energy that must be banished. Fear makes our own prisons. It's instilled in us by our government and the Church. They control fear. It's the Great Lie. But don't get me started on that."

For a man who, for 15 years, was known for his silences, Carlton now talks a lot. In fact, he can't stop himself. When he was voted into the Hall of Fame this past January, he held a press conference. At the end of its scheduled 45 minutes, the sportswriters got up to leave. Carlton called them back to talk some more. "I don't mind," he said. "It's been a long time." When he is inducted, with Phil Rizzuto, into the Hall in late July before the assembled national press, it will be interesting to see if he will still be so loquacious.

A lot of people are suspicious of his motives for talking so much now. Carlton claims, "It's all Bev's idea." He says his wife wants him to get back into the world. For years, Beverly Carlton ran interference for her husband during "the Big Silence." After Carlton won his 300th game, in 1983, he surrounded himself with a police escort and fled the clubhouse to avoid reporters. He left it to Bev to talk to the press.

"Steve would like to play another ten years," she told them. "He just might. Baseball's been great to us." Then, to humanize her distant husband, she revealed a little intimacy. "Well," she said, "he likes Ukrainian food."

In Carlton's final season, when he began to rethink his silence, he said it was because "my wife convinced me that if I want to find a job after I'm through playing, having my name in the paper doesn't hurt." Even today, Bev Carlton schedules her husband's interviews. (He no longer has an agent.) When reporters show up in Durango, Carlton will feign surprise at their presence. "I didn't know you were coming," he says. When told that his wife said she confirmed the interview with him, he blinks, once, twice, and says, "I didn't pay any attention." In this way, he can lay off the distasteful prospect of being interviewed on his wife. He can maintain, in his mind's eye, the lofty arrogance of "the Big Silence" while no longer adhering to it. ("Bev likes to read about me," he says.)

It is likely that Carlton is talking now because he needs money, looking to reassert his presence in the public's consciousness so he can do endorsements. "We'll probably do some of that stuff in the coming years," he says. It's a distasteful position his old agent put him in, and one he doesn't like to be reminded of. "It's one of life's little lessons," Carlton says of David Landfield. "I don't want to talk about it. I no longer live in the past." Then, after a moment of silence, he adds, "It all came down to trust. You're most vulnerable there. When your trust is breached, it affects you."

Most of Carlton's money for the past few years has come from his two businesses. He claims he is a sports agent, but won't mention the names of his clients. (It is hard to imagine anyone, even a ballplayer, entrusting his money to a man who lost millions of his own.) The bulk of his money, a reported $100,000 or so per year, comes from autograph shows and the Home Shopping Network, where he peddles his own wares. Caps, cards, T-shirts, little plaster figurines of himself as a pitcher—all emblazoned with the number 329, his career victory total. He sells these objects by mail, too, out of a tiny, cluttered office in a nondescript, wooden building a few miles from town. A sign out front lists the building's occupants, lawyers and such. But there is no mention of Carlton's enterprise, Game Winner Sports Management, and he likes it that way. "We didn't want a sign up so people would know where we are," he says, smiling. In fact, even the occupants of the building aren't sure where "the baseball player's" office is.

"We have a toll-free number [1-800-72LEFTY]," he says. "We accept VISA and checks. Just send me a check and don't bother me."

Now as Carlton finishes with his yoga, the instructor in the black tights ushers one of the children over to him. The teacher is smiling, giggly, blushing, a vaguely attractive woman who seems to have a crush on Carlton. She leans close to him and says, "I have someone who wants to meet you." Carlton shrinks back from her even as she urges the uncomprehending child toward him. "Go ahead," she says. The child looks up at the towering man and says, "Happy birthday." Carlton blinks, confused. "I don't celebrate birthdays," he says.

At the foot of a steep, winding dirt road rutted with snow, Steve Carlton stops his truck and gets out to engage its four-wheel drive. When he gets back in and begins driving carefully up the path, he says, "I've been lucky. I've had teachers in my life. One guy began writing me letters, four or five a week, in 1970. That's the year I won 20 games with the Cardinals. He told me where the power and energy comes from. He was a night watchman. We talked on the phone a few times and met a couple times. He was a very spiritual guy. All I knew about him was that his name was Mr. Briggs. Then he was gone as quickly as he came into my life. It was a gift."

When he reaches his bunker, at twilight, he stops and gets out. He looks out over his land and says, "There's nothing like being by yourself. I'm reclusive. I want to get in touch with myself." He glances sideways, and adds, "But society is coming." That's why he is preparing by being self-sufficient. He is not so self-sufficient, however, that he's ever mustered the courage to butcher his animals for food. But, that's a moot point now. All his chickens were killed by raccoons last winter.

It's late. Carlton has a dinner appointment. But he's not sure what time it is now, because he doesn't wear a watch. "I never know what time it is," he says. "Or what day it is. Time is stress. Pressure melts away if you don't deal with time. I don't believe in birthdays, either. Or anniversaries. I don't watch television. We don't read newspapers. We don't even have a Christmas tree. Those things hold vibrations of the past, and I exist only in the now. Bev is even more into it than I am."

He trudges through the snow to the side door of his odd, domed bunker. Inside, he puts the flat of one palm against the concrete and says, "I'm waiting for the coldness to come out of the walls." Bev is waiting for him in the living room. She is a small, sweet, nervous woman, sitting in a chair by a space heater. She used to bleach her hair blonde, but now her short cut is its natural brown. She smiles as her husband sits down across from her. She jugs herself from the cold, and then drags on a cigarette.

Their home is starkly furnished, not out of design but necessity. A few wooden tables, a bookcase filled with Carlton's Eastern metaphysical books, a patterned sofa and easy chair, hand-me-downs from their son Scott, 25, a bartender in St. Louis. Their other son, Steven, 27, lives in Washington state, where he writes children's songs.

Carlton doesn't like to talk about his kids. "Why do you have to know about them?" he says plaintively. He doesn't talk much about his parents, either, whom he rarely sees or speaks to. They, it seems, are another part of Carlton's past that he has cut out of his life.

"The correspondence lacks," admits Joe Carlton, 87 and blind. "We don't hear from him much. It's okay, though."

"We keep up with him in the newspapers," says Anne Carlton, who says of *her* age, "It's nobody's damned business."

The elder Carltons are sitting in the shadowed, musty living room of their small concrete house in North Miami, where they raised their son and two daughters, Christina and Joanne. From the outside, it looks uninhabited. The drab house paint is peeling, and the yards out front and back, dotted with Joe's many fruit trees, are overgown, rotted fruit littering the tall grass.

Inside, the furniture is old and worn, and thick dust coats the television screen. Even the many photographs and newspaper articles on the walls are faded and dusty, like old tintypes. The photos are mostly of their son in various baseball uniforms. As a teenager—gawky, with a faint, distant smile, posing with his teammates, the Lions. With the Cardinals, his hair fashionably long, back in the '60s. Then with the Phillies, posing with Mike Schmidt, captioned MVP AND CY YOUNG.

"No, I haven't heard from him," says Joe, a former maintenance man with Pan Am. He is sitting on an ottoman, staring straight ahead through thick glasses. "I can't see you, except as a shadow," he says, staring out the window. He is a thin man, almost gaunt, with long silvery swept-back hair. He is wearing a faded Hawaiian shirt.

"It's no special reason," says Anne, sitting in her easy chair. "He just doesn't call anymore."

"He called when Anne's mother died, at 101," says Joe. Then he begins to talk about his son as a child. How Joe used to go hunting with him in the Everglades. "We used to shoot light bulbs," he says.

"Steve was a natural-born hunter," says Anne. "Tell what kind of animals you hunted in the Everglades."

"Lions and tigers."

"Oh, you didn't. There are no lions and tigers in the Everglades. Tell what kind of animals."

Joe, confused, says, "There were lots of animals." Anne shakes her head. "Steve was always quiet," adds Joe, trying to remember. "He wasn't very talkative around the house when he was a boy." He fetches an old scrapbook and opens a page to a newspaper photograph of his son in a Phillies cap. There is a zipper where his mouth should be.

"Can I bum a cigarette off you?" Anne says to their guest. "Oh, you don't have any. Too bad."

"The last time we saw Steve was five years ago," says Joe.

"It wasn't that long ago."

"Yes, it was. Time flies."

"It was only four years."

"He never told us about his house."

"We don't even know where Durango is. I never heard of it. Have you seen his house? Really, it's built into a mountain?"

"Steve got an interest in his philosophies when he got hold of one of my books when he was in high school," says Joe.

"He doesn't believe in Christmas trees anymore?" asks Anne. "We *always* had a Christmas tree. Bev *liked* Christmas trees.

"No, we never asked him for any money," Anne continues. "He would have given it to us if we asked, though."

"He never helped us financially. I didn't need it." Joe, who is also hard of hearing, cups a hand around an ear. "What? His sons? You mean Steve's sons? No, we never hear from them, either."

"Our daughters call, though," says Anne.

"They came down for my 85th birthday," says Joe. "They gave me a surprise party. Steve didn't come."

Joe gets up and goes into a small guest room where, on a desk, dresser and two twin beds, he has laid out mementos of his son's career. A photograph of a plaster impression of Steve's hand when he was a boy. A high school graduation photo of Steve with a flattop haircut.

"Steve doesn't collect this stuff," says Joe. "He's too busy. Here's another picture of Steve. I got pictures all over. I got another picture here, somewhere, when we took Steve to St. Augustine, where Anne is from. It's a picture of Steve in the oldest fort in America. He's behind bars." Joe rummages around for the photo, disturbing dust, but he can't find it. He leafs through one last scrapbook; on its final page is a photograph of a burial mound of skulls and bones, thousands of them, piled in a heap. Joe looks at it and says, "We took it in Cuba. See here what I wrote at the bottom: *The end.*"

There are no photographs of Joe and Anne in their son's living room. No photos of his and Bev's children. No photos of themselves when younger. No wedding photos of smiling bride and bridegroom. No photos of Carlton in a Phillies uniform or on a hunting trip. There are no keepsakes of their past. No prints on the wall. No Christmas tree, no presents, nestled in cotton snow. There is nothing in that huge, high, concave, whitewashed concrete room except the few pieces of nondescript furniture and the space heater. Bev and her husband seem dwarfed by the cavelike room. They huddle around the space heater like a 20th-century version of the clan in the movie *Quest for Fire.* Mere survival seems their only joy, their only beauty, except for the view through the sliding-glass living room doors of the La Platta mountain range, all white and purple and rose in the setting sun, which Beverly has turned her back on.

Bev tries to make small talk as she drags on her cigarette. Curiously, her husband no longer hates cigarette smoke as he once did as a ballplayer, when he claimed he could taste it on his wineglass if someone in the room was smoking. Of course, in those days he didn't eat red meat either because of the blood. His thinking has changed now, he has said, because he realizes "that the juice of anything is its blood, that the juice of a carrot is the carrot's blood."

Bev is talking about the time she and other Phillies' wives met Ted Turner. "Oh, yes," she says, "he kept putting his hand on the behinds of the wives."

"He was crude and vulgar," says Carlton. "What's wrong with America?" He shakes his head in disgust and begins a long monologue on the unfairness of the American government, primarily because it won't allow its citizens to walk around armed. Bev listens patiently smiling her thin smile, her head nodding like a small bird sipping water. Her husband is right. She is a lot like him. Frightened. When it is time to meet their guests for dinner, Carlton stands up. Bev remains seated hugging herself against the cold.

"Oh, I'm not going to dinner," she says with explanation. "Just Steve."

It's confusing to their guest, until he remembers Carlton's words: "Bev wants me to get out into the world," Carlton had said. Which is what she is doing now: sending him out into that fearful world in order to make a living for them. It's something she knows he has to do on his own if they are going to survive, like a mother bundling her tiny child off to school for the first time. Meanwhile she sits at home in their stark bunker huddled close to the space heater for warmth, worrying about him out there, alone and scared, in the real world he shunned for so many years.

The Wizard of Oze, Through the Years

Ted Silary

◆ ◆ ◆

Ah, Danny Ozark! What is there to say about the much-harried Phillies manager of the 1970s? All writers had to do was follow him around with a tape recorder. But even that took some doing. Never well liked by his players, the fans, or the press, Ozark nonetheless brought three near-championship teams to Philadelphia after inheriting a quintessential last-place club from interim manager Paul Owens. Whatever his true accomplishments, Ozark will be remembered as the media's whipping boy and the local master of the malaprop—a manager who would not be "co-horsed," who had a wonderful "repertoire" with his players, and whose "limits were limitless." When morale was low on the ballclub, he insisted that "morality is not a factor."

Though much of the following piece was indebted to Bill Conlin, Ted Silary, Conlin's colleague at the Daily News, *compiled what he described as "a romp through the years with the Wizard of Oze." The press always expected Ozark to be fired and was surprised that he lasted as long as he did. This article was written the day after the ax fell.*

When Danny Ozark left the Phils' employ last night he not only led the National League managers in length of service but also in brushes with turmoil and most times second guessed. What follows is a romp through the years with the Wizard of Oze.

1972

Nov. 1—Ozark is named Phil's manager though writers covering the team had all but conceded the job to Dave Bristol. Bill Conlin writes, "Danny Ozark talks baseball like he invented it. The only trouble here

From the *Philadelphia Daily News*, September 1, 1979. Reprinted by permission.

is that he's going to have to uninvent baseball the way the Phillies have been playing it."

1973

March 25—In spring training, Ozark says, "You could throw a blanket over the Pirates, St. Louis, Chicago and us."

April 6—Ozark's debut is ruined as Steve Carlton loses to the Mets and Tom Seaver in New York, 3–0.

May 10—Ozark has already begun to confuse the media. Bill Conlin writes, "Ozark says a lot of things. He says so many things that figuring out what he is trying to say is like trying to crack the White House code. David Eisenhower (then working for the *Bulletin*) may be the only guy in town with enough experience in doubletalk to understand him."

June 1—In the early morning hours in Los Angeles, a group of Phillies' players meets with GM Paul Owens and asks him to return to the field, reciting a long bill of indictment against Ozark. Owens: "I know there are problems. That's why I'm making these road trips. But I've got to find out for myself. Go out there and hang in there tough and show me you're professionals."

June 12—After 56 games, Phils are 10½ games out and in last place. Daily News adopts "Danny's Blanket" as symbol of team and uses cartoons to spice up stories the rest of the season.

Sept. 26—After relations had become strained between the two, Cesar Tovar tells Ozark he will not start a game at third base. Tovar tells Owens, "Danny Ozark will never win here. He has treat me very bad all season. He don't know how to get along with players. He manage very dumb."

Oct. 3—After Phils finish 71–91, third worst record in the majors, Conlin writes an assessment of Ozark: "What surfaced was a man who had none of (Gene) Mauch's current tactical brilliance and all of Gene's early inability to communicate with young players. His conduct of a ballgame showed the inconsistency of the born hunch player, mixing whim with baseball logic, prestidigitation with percentages." Owens roars, "The only problem is you bleeping sadists who get some kind of weird thrill out of ripping us when we screw up."

1974

Jan. 23—After Phils' annual mid-winter media luncheon, Ozark says, "I feel optimistic again. I still think it's going to be a blanket this year." Conlin writes, "It is a piece of work, Danny's Blanket, a magic carpet with a bum engine. Ozark should have read the fine print on the warranty, which guarantees it only for five months or 90 losses, whichever comes first."

July 31—During a 9–8 loss to the Cardinals, the Phils—tied for first—distribute a five paragraph announcement: Ozark has been re-hired for two more years. Ozark, grinning after the game: "You have to suffer with me for two more years." "That's a two-way street," somebody suggested.

1975

June 18—Injuries leave the Phils with infield nightmares, especially at third. Ozark: "What it boils down to is that I don't want to get into a Galphonse and Astone situation at third base."

Aug. 22—After Inquirer's Frank Dolson "fires" Ozark while Conlin is at the shore on vacation, Conlin gives him a vote of confidence. Jaws drop. Conlin: "Maybe I'm mellowing. But I've learned to enjoy Danny Ozark."

Sept. 5—Daily News introduces poll entitled, "Help Save Super-team." Almost two weeks later, Richie Ashburn is declared a landslide winner: "I have no ambition to manage at all. If I become a manager, I couldn't pursue a lot of the things I like to do."

Sept. 22—Pirates beat Phils to clinch division title and AP writer asks Ozark, "What now?" Ozark: "Try to win tomorrow. We're not out of it yet." Reporter: "Danny, you're out of it." Ozark: "That's news to me. If we win the rest of ours and they lose the rest of theirs we tie." Reporter:

"Danny, you're seven down with six to play." Ozark: "Well, that's very disheartening."

1976

April 25—Ozark uses Jerry Martin to pinch-hit for Tommy Hutton in the ninth inning of a 3–2 loss to the Braves. Dick Allen was available and had even been listed as a starter on the original line-up card. After being second-guessed, Ozark orders all of the writers from the locker room, but AP's Ralph Bernstein stands firm. Obscenities fly and they almost come to blows.

April 27—NL President Chub Feeney orders Ozark to resume granting interviews.

July 29—After several strange days, Dick Allen does not show up for a game with Cubs and is docked two days' pay and fined. Ozark: "It's a low blow to the players who've admired the guy, a low blow right in the gut."

Sept. 29—Ollie Brown, who started in right field all year against left-handers, is held out as Phils beat Expos to clinch division title. Several members of team are quoted along racial lines. Ozark: "Ollie knows why he wasn't in the lineup." Ozark gives Allen permission to go home after Montreal series. Again, the players bicker.

Oct. 13—Ozark named Manager of the Year by Sporting News.

Oct. 14—Ozark signs contract to manage Phils for two more years. Owens says, "I think everybody has known Danny was coming back. There was never any doubt in my mind."

1977

May 9—After Phils were rained out in LA on a Sunday, they were forced to stay over for Monday makeup. However, the game was called at 10 A.M. though field appeared playable. Ozark fumes at Dodger President Peter O'Malley: "I'm damned upset because you said the field is unsafe and you can walk out there and not even get your shoes wet." Later, he says, "I just lost my Dodger Blue."

May 24—Again, Ozark banishes the media from the clubhouse. Conlin writes, "If we knew as little about baseball as the anointed ignoramuses who wear baseball uniforms know about the function of a newspaper there would be a total blackout of baseball news."

June 12—After Phils lose to Atlanta, Owens rips Ozark's manuevers.

June 27—In an interview with Stan Hochman, Ozark says, "I could have been gone after my first year. Or my second year. Or even my third year. But they had enough faith in me, that I was doing the right thing, using the players the right way, not overusing the younger players on the club."

1978

Aug. 8—Phils are in midst of slump and Conlin calls them a "kennel club of a team." He asks Ozark, "What can a man with less than two months left on a contract tell a bunch of guys who have years and years and years and years left on theirs?" Ozark, after hesitation: "Well, I put in an order for a new Lincoln and I may have that SOB paid for before the year is up and that's not too bleeping long."

Oct. 1—Following much strife and hard charge from Pittsburgh, Phils clinch division title in Pittsburgh. Conlin writes, "Ozark did a helluva job this season, more impressive in the clubhouse than on the bench, more memorable in his handling of people and situations than for brilliant field strategy." Ozark: "You guys know I don't blow my own horn much, but I'm gonna blow it just a little now. I did a helluva job."

Oct. 3—Ozark says, "I think we'll win the first two (playoff) games here (with Los Angeles) and go out there and win Friday and sweep this thing."

Oct. 8—Ozark says, "If I'm not back next season, I'll probably come back on my own and watch a game at the Vet. I'll enjoy the game. I'll enjoy second-guessing the guy who takes my place."

Oct. 13—After Ozark is rehired Mike Schmidt says, "I don't have any negative feeling about that at all. . . . Whatever happened, it wasn't his fault we didn't win in the playoffs."

1979

April 18—A fan follows Ozark and Owens onto the team bus in Pittsburgh and winds up shoving Ozark and throwing an unsuccessful punch at him. Ozark responds with a right to the guy's midsection. "I can't rate it as much of a scuffle," Owens says. "I usually lose my hat if it's a good one and I still have my hat."

June 11—The question is, "Is Danny Ozark in trouble?" Owner Ruly Carpenter: "Is that what they're saying? They've been saying it ever since he got here. . . . There isn't a player on this team who can look in a mirror and say that it's the manager's fault."

June 30—When being taken out by Ozark in St. Louis, Steve Carlton spikes the ball at the manager's feet. Ozark levies a heavy fine. "The guy tried to show me up out there and I'm damned upset about it."

Aug. 7—Ozark pinch hits Greg Cross for Greg Luzinski with the bases loaded in a game the Phils will win over Montreal, 4–2. Ozark keeps his door closed for 66 minutes, waves good-by to media men as he departs and says, "Sometimes, you have to walk away from good friends." Speculation points to him quitting.

Aug. 31—The end.

Championship Seasons

1980: It Wasn't Pretty
But It Sure Was Fun

Thomas Boswell

◆ ◆ ◆

The nearly hundred-year drought was finally over on October 21, 1980. The Phillies were World Champions for the first time, having defeated the Kansas City Royals in the World Series four games to two. "Tens of thousands of long-suffering Philadelphians took to the streets," wrote Don Kimmelman on the front page of the Inquirer, *"for a raucous, tumultuous, horn-blowing, firecracker-exploding celebration." It wouldn't have been Philadelphia, though, without at least one person getting killed (it happened at about 2:35 that morning).*

Considered by many to be the best sportswriter in America today, Thomas Boswell, a syndicated columnist for the Washington Post, *has written four books on baseball, including* How Life Imitates the World Series *(1982, Doubleday), from which this splendid essay was taken.*

Boswell's account understands the Phillies' victory in the context of baseball in 1980: the down-to-the-wire division title, which the Phils clinched on the penulti-mate night of the season, and the incredible National League Championship Series, which Ron Fimrite of Sports Illustrated *described as "five of the most amazing baseball games ever strung together."*

What if the attack dogs had been brought into play just one out sooner? Then what would Pete Rose have done?

After all, before the final inning of the 1980 World Series, umpires gave the most bizarre ground rule in baseball history: "Animals are in play."

What if that menacing menagerie of dogs and horses had made its massed entrance with two outs left to go, instead of only one? When Frank White's foul popped out of the hands of Bob Boone, his gold glove turned alchemically to lead by the black magic of Phillies' history, would Rose's lizard tongue of a mitt have flicked out so quickly to gobble the fly?

Or would that baseball have been appropriated by the fangs of a devil-dog sent to insure that the Phillies remained destiny's doormats?

That, you see, is how our winter mind recalls a baseball season, not with chalk-dry statistics or records, but with a few vivid, richly associative moments of truth. Of all those moments, perhaps the most lustrous is Rose's reflex catch. It may not have been the best or most important play of 1980—or even of that sixth and last game of the Series—but it was the most symbolic. That tenth-of-a-second grab earned Rose all of his $2.98 million contract, for with it he absolved the Phillies of being themselves. Washed them clean of a century of baseball sins, he did, all in a tingling instant. "Not this time," his innermost synapses said.

This was the ultimate game when the Phillies' life passed before their eyes—all ninety-seven years of it. This was a team that not only had to defeat the best-hitting club in thirty years—the Kansas City Royals—but had to renounce its own anti-tradition as well. Born to failure in 1883 and entrenched as the sport's ninety-seven-year weaklings ever since, the Phillies survived an October in which they had a dozen chances to drown.

Their last two chances to gasp for breath, swallow deep, and die came in the sixth game of the World Series as the Royals loaded the bases in the eighth and ninth with the Phils ahead by a 4–1 margin that felt like half a run. What Phillie fan could help but think back on fifty-one seasons in the Baker Bowl, thirty-two years in Shibe Park (later Connie Mack Stadium), and finally another decade in the antiseptic Vet, and still nothing in the way of diamond-centered rings? That is how you measure real failure—not in seasons, but in buildings crumbled under the weight of defeat, parks that lasted longer than the lives of men and now are gone.

In the eighth, that ancient premonition machine began to chug. If

Macbeth's first witch had commandeered the PA system and said, "Here I have a pilot's thumb, wrack'd as homeward he did come," no one would have doubted Dallas Green was the pilot and the thumb in question was the one he had used to send Steve Carlton to the showers. Why, in the name of Gavvy Cravath, Wild Bill Donovan, Kaiser Wilhelm, and Danny Ozark, had Green yanked Lefty, the Sphinx of the Schuyl-kill, the man Rose proclaimed, "the best pitcher in the world, unless the Russians have got one I haven't seen"?

On came the only relief pitcher with a tugboat named after him: Tug McGraw. He was beyond the help of Tylenol. This was a frazzled man on a solitary mound with only his savvy and guts to preserve him. "I'm mentally exhausted," McGraw had said. "It's a good thing I don't pitch with my brain, or I'd have to soak my head in a bucket of ice."

McGraw had a right to his sore brain. In Montreal, he pounded the dirt with his open palms when he won the division clincher in the next-to-last game of the season. In Houston, he embraced his mates after he saved the fourth and series-tying game. And he would, in a few min-utes, lead the Phillie cotillion as it danced off the diamond amid hooves, helmets, and truncheons after he had saved the World Series.

But first all the threads of the Phillies' championship skein had to tangle themselves into one ball, and that ball had to plot itself squarely into Rose's hand. In that split second when White's foul ball squirted from Boone's glove to Rose's, everything went from fast-forward to stop-action. "Cut . . . that's a take . . . print it," said the director. "Bring on the animals. Unsheathe the billy clubs. Anybody wants to kiss these guys, they got to get maced and beaten. Oh, Tug, one last thing. Yeah, I know you're tired. Just strike out Willie Wilson, will you? Sure, just like the other eleven times."

Thus, so tired that "if I hadn't gotten Wilson, I'd have called Dallas out to get me," McGraw finally saved the Phillies. Just as Rose had saved McGraw, and they both had saved Green. That was the proper triumvirate: Green, plus his left- and right-hand men. When baseball comes to its last turn of the screw, it is still aggressive leadership that is of primary importance. That's when ballplayers revert to atavistic tribal habits, particularly leaning on a few old chieftains. For the Phils, that meant Green setting a policy of close-order drill and blunt home truths, with Rose and McGraw testifying loudly that such a system could work. Rose demonstrated what it meant to hustle and play hurt. "Jeez," he said, "we got guys who think they're toughin' it out if they play with a headache." While Rose talked attitude, McGraw talked tactics, calling Green the best handler of a pitching staff since Gil Hodges. And Green himself . . . well . . . he just talked: "Players don't like to look in the mirror. Well, I'm their mirror. I told this team in spring training that I was going to give them one more chance to live up to their talent. A lot of guys are on their last hurrah here, but somebody had to remind them."

And how long did it take this doctrine to sink in among the Phillies? "We had a meeting in August after we lost four in a row to Pittsburgh and looked like dead meat," said Green. "I aired 'em out as good as I know how to chew. Maybe that helped a little. But I can't honestly say we sniffed it, really got after it, until the last week of the season."

Huhhhh?

That heretical statement gives a clue to not only the Phils but the whole 1980 season. If this baseball year opened as a Broadway play, it would get an ambivalent review: aesthetically and technically erratic, sometimes even abominable, yet dramatically wonderful, almost unsurpassed. For such a theme, the Phils were perfect protagonists.

This was a season when our baseball characters seemed particularly vivid, because they seemed especially isolated and vulnerable. That's why, when the curtain dropped, we felt an unexpected sadness that the long, weird season—with its odd juxtaposition of tense individual virtuosity against a backdrop of slapstick—was finally done.

This was the year when all twenty-six major league teams showed up without a destiny. How dull are those seasons when we realize that one team has swaddled itself in a cocoon of protective myth-making, calling itself a "team of destiny," or the like. A club can shield itself with its own fabulous tale-telling, a sort of group hypnosis. In 1980, nobody could hide within the camouflage of a Family, least of all the Astros, Royals, and Phils, whose histories were laminated in failure. After six months of assuming they were dukes and princes of their sport—but probably not kings—these clubs, which ranked third, fourth, and sixth in victories, suddenly found themselves in water over their heads. And they sensed it.

Under such conditions, baseball is a brutally difficult and solitary game. Under pressure, each man stood alone, pinned in a limelight radiance. At times, these sound, but self-doubting teams played as though they were standing in a mine field.

Appropriately, the most memorable Series play was a ball clanking from one glove to another. This was a Series of snafus as much as game-winning RBIs, a championship that, truly, was Left on Base. Never have two October foes hit so well when it didn't matter, or so atrociously when it did. These teams with the highest combined batting average for a six-game Series (.292) put 168 runners on base but only scored 50 of them. With no one on base, they batted .300. With runners in scoring position, .236. That trend worsened as pressure grew. In the last four games, the Phils batted .356 with none on; .175 with men in scoring position. Let's not hear too much about The Team that Wouldn't Die. For the last five Series games, this Kansas City club with the highest team average since '50 (.286) batted .340 with the sacks empty; .191 with runners in scoring position. Said one Kansas City official, "We're so tight we squeak."

The regular-season trademark of both these swift teams was their explosiveness. Yet, in the Series, they become implosive, collapsing into themselves like dying stars turning into black holes. As the Series progressed, both emitted less and less light.

The progression of the Series conspired to tie K.C. into knots. In the opener, 20-game winner Dennis Leonard blew a 4–0 lead and lost 7–6 to Whirlybird Walk, a rookie who, in his short career, had gone to bat without a bat and taken the mound without a glove. Perhaps Walk's true calling was to be one of the young Red Sox pitchers of 1980 who got Don Zimmer fired. Like Wilhelmus ("Last Call for . . .") Remmerswaal, who, after establishing precedent at Pawtucket by missing three of the team's first four flights, was called up and immediately missed the Bosox bus to Yankee Stadium. Asked why he was late, Remmerswaal said, "I took a taxi." Unfortunately, the taxi took Last Call to Shea Stadium. Remmerswaal's first victory of 1980 came in a game when Zimmer called the bull pen, barked "Get Win up," and was told, "He's out in the bleachers buying peanuts."

The Royals then put 19 men on base in Game Two, 18 of them against Carlton, but scored only 4 runs and lost 6–4 when the Phils filibustered for 4 runs in the eighth against quippy reliever Dan Quisenberry.

After these two days in Philly, the Royals were ready for every sort of self-flagellation. Catcher Darrell Porter tiptoeing into home plate to avoid a collision with Boone was just the outward symbol of a suddenly meek and disoriented team. "We seem intimidated by the crowds, intimidated by being in the Series," said K.C. rookie manager Jim Frey. His solution was to call a pep-talk team meeting, then invite a Howard Cosell imitator into the clubhouse to insult and ridicule every Royal in sight.

You could say it helped. That is, if you didn't happen to see the next game. The Royals won (4–3) in 10 innings only because the Phils lost in 9. In a kind of reverse classic, the Phils put 20 men on base in their 200-minute agony of clutch failure. Thirty Phils stepped up with runners on. Only 2 could drive home a run. A single in any of 12 different spots would have meant a win. The perfect Phillie emblem was Mike Schmidt, the eventual Series MVP. Schmidt hit .381 for this 77th "Classic" with 7 RBIs, but he also stranded 11 runners in the Series, including 9 in this game. By contrast, Brett came to bat with only 14 men on in the whole Series, compared to Schmidt's 23. Sometimes, luck is fate.

That humble victory loosened up the Royals—for exactly 1⅔ innings. Of the first 14 Royals to bat in Game Four, 1 walked, 2 singled, 3 doubled, 1 tripled, and Willie Mays Aikens—who had already hit 2 homers in the opener and won Game Three the night before with a sudden-death single off McGraw—crushed two 450-foot home runs. In that nightmare, the Phils saw the Royals take five extra bases on them. Philadelphia starter Larry Christenson left with an ERA of 108.00. The Royals hit the ball between outfielders, into three-cushion pin-ball corners, into water fountains, and over the car parked in the Kansas City bull pen.

Then, suddenly, the Royals abated like a Kansas twister blowing itself out. The Phils helped. They waited until Brett's next at-bat, then had

Dickie Noles throw a 90-miles-per-hour fastball that missed Brett's temple by inches as he cartwheeled, foot-to-the-sky. It was the perfect tactical message to a team that charges the plate and defies opponents to retaliate.

"I believe in Hammurabi's Code," said Brett. "An eye for an eye and a tooth for a tooth." However, Frey doesn't. It's annoyed his traditionally pugnacious team all year. Frey is from the Earl Weaver School and never orders a knockdown pitch because he doesn't want it on his conscience. So when Brett pinwheeled, Frey put his best face on matters, charging onto the field to point at Noles and scream with Rose. Nevertheless, the Royals came out looking like genial slow-pitch softball noncombatants. From the moment Brett went down, then fanned, the Royals hit .083 with men in scoring position for the rest of the Series, and Brett, after starting 6 for 12, went 1 for his next 10.

All the tension, insecurity, and worry pent up within this Series came to a head in the pivotal ninth inning of the fifth game. A season without destiny resolved itself into an inning constructed of coincidence and dumb luck. Of all the minimal art rallies in this Series, the Phils' 2-run ninth for a 4–3 win was the pip. Philadelphia hit 6 consecutive grounders or line drives, all of which could or should have been caught—and this turned the Series for the Phillies.

In one lone Series game, everything is luck. Or nothing is luck. You can watch for decades and never quite decide. That's how it was with Schmidt's lead-off grounder that smacked Brett's glove as he dove left, then bounced away. And with Del Unser's one-hop bullet that Aikens should have blocked at first had he not committed the cardinal sin of bad fielders: He tried to make a good play instead of a safe one and got nothing but air. And, finally, Manny Trillo, the dependable Phillie MVP of the play-offs, cracked a liner that Quisenberry got both hands on at his navel, but couldn't grasp as it trickled away.

The fans of Kansas City, who join with the PA tape deck in an unselfconscious seventh-inning rendition of "Take Me Out to the Ball Game," may say, "Shucks, just a little bad luck." But don't try that bunk on Philadelphia folk. They know baseball. The box score has to add up. You must lose for a reason. If there isn't one, you gotta start inventing. Those with sharp eyes and hard hearts will convict the Royals of terminal jitters and use that final inning of the fifth game as Exhibit A. Ill fortune attendeth the team that thinks it's going bad. And just how bad were the Royals going?

You know you're going bad when your wife takes you aside and tries to change your batting stance. And you take her advice. Ask superstar Wilson (230 hits, 79 steals), who hit .111 before his wife told him, "Stand up straighter, dear," and .176 thereafter.

You know you're going bad when an usherette calls you to the box-seat railing, hands you a bat, and says, "You gave this to me on June 2 when you were hitting .333. Now, you need it more than I do." And you see the bat in the game. Ask Porter, 1 for 20 in postseason before getting two hits with the new-old bat.

Plenty of Royals were going bad and couldn't forget it. So, when Game Five reached its apex—Phils ahead by a run, bases loaded with Royals, 2 outs in the ninth—K.C. needed the perfect star-crossed character.

That's right. Jose Cardenal.

This Series spotlighted two quintessential journeymen—Cardenal (37, vet of 10 teams, glad-hand bon vivant in cowboy regalia) and the Phillies' Unser (35, vet of 5 teams, shy gent in corduroy and patches). Both, in repose, have the hound-faced look of too-frequent defeat. Both came to their current roles as last resorts before retirement. And each finally had the feast of fame set before him. Four times Unser delivered in the postseason pinch, once with the season-saving, game-tying single and three times with doubles that were the nub of game-winning rallies. After thirteen years, you're entitled. But, after eighteen years, wasn't Cardenal entitled, too? Unser got the candy. Cardenal just got the fuzzy end of the lollipop.

Many managers have pet reclamation projects. Cardenal is Frey's. So Jose materialized in right field in Game Two, went 0 for 4, and let Schmidt's eminently catchable game-winning liner land on the warning track while he pulled up short so as not to be too near the scene of the crime. And, in the final crisis of Game Five, Frey stuck with Cardenal, instead of .305 hitter Duke Wathan.

One reason that men like Unser and Cardenal have lengthy, unspectacular careers is The Book. The Book on Cardenal is all in capital letters: JAM THE LITTLE FELLOW. So McGraw did. Every pitch. Cardenal's rebuttal was a weak foul as his bat flew to the mound. McGraw and Cardenal met at the foot of the hill. Until that instant, Cardenal had been thinking, "One hit and you will be everywhere, even on the 'Good Morning' talk shows." As Cardenal reached McGraw, the southpaw said, "Here's your bat," then, holding the bat handle forward, jabbed Cardenal in the stomach. Had that bat been a lance, the rally could not have been slain more effectively. After the game, after his final strikeout, Cardenal still came back, again and again, to McGraw. "Everybody knows McGraw is crazy," he said. "Jab me in the stomach with my own bat."

If this Series seemed blessed in scenes from a Theater of the Absurd, and if the Phillies seemed more at home in such surroundings, there was a reason. During October and the Five Games War against Houston, the Phillies had stepped through the Looking Glass and into a baseball world inhabited by mad hatters, dormice, and Cheshire cats. Game after game, the line score should have read: winning pitcher— Alice; loser—sanity. These Phils make a science of finding diamonds in the garbage.

The night when the Phillies began to arise from a century's sleep was a miserable, dank evening in Canada. The Phillies slunk into town dead-tied with Montreal with 3 games left. They were still burdened by the ignominy of losing 2 of 3 to the Expos in the Vet the previous weekend. That series had ended with the Philadelphia fans in their customary autumn pall, growling in disgust as they bent, folded, and mutilated their programs into paper airplanes which they used to pepper the beloved Phils from the upper deck. Between innings, it took six hustling grounds crewmen just to clean up the debris. With that as prologue, plus a week of warfare between Green and veteran players, the Phils were expected to perform a patented Philadelphia dive. "We just have a different form of exercise," said McGraw. "We flush our minds in public."

All that Friday night in Montreal, the Phils played like men of stone. All except Schmidt, the Phil heretofore most petrified by late-season adrenaline overdoses. This was a game that the Phils could have lost 1– 0, and quietly died. But Schmidt, who has spent his life ardently pursuing relaxation—through meditation, feigned coolness, religion—had discovered the ultimate relaxant. Germs. "Probably just what I need. I'm so miserable I'm limp as a rag doll," he said after a sacrifice fly and a sixth-inning homer had created a 2–1 win. "You know me," he said, clenching his fist and biceps into a knot. "Can't get loose (cough, cough). Whenever I feel blah, I always make out like a bandit [hack, wheeze]. I figure my temperature is about 111½."

Schmidt, who set a major league record for homers by a third baseman (48), had gotten the Phils to the hump, but the Expos helped them over. On the final regular-season Saturday, in a seven-hour, rain-delayed game that tasted like swill, the Phillies ended up drinking champagne. The Phils made 5 errors, had 4 men trapped between bases in rundowns, and had another thrown out at the plate. The coup came when Greg Luzinski got a 2-run, bases-loaded single that ended up as an inning-ending double play (DP 8–6–5–4–5–3–2).

The Expos were worse. Don't ask particulars. After all, the Montrealers, playing without injured Ron LeFlore (broken wrist) and Ellis Valentine (sprained ego), were shorthanded. Suffice it to say that one normal-speed ground ball somehow rolled directly between the legs of both the Expo third baseman and left fielder on the same play. Finally, Schmidt's 2-run homer in the eleventh clinched the pennant and began a celebration that was equal parts wine and spleen. The Phils smashed champagne bottles into garbage cans so violently that players were ducking flying glass. The team split in three parts. Some, filled with vindication and fury, screamed and led obscene chants. Some were numb and perplexed, looking at a side of their mates that they had known about, but perhaps wished had stayed hidden. And a few sequestered themselves in a small room. "If we don't get to the Series," said a subdued Schmidt, "then all of this doesn't mean shit. We'll still be the same old fucked-up Phillies."

Eight days later, the Phillies would have their cathartic evening for the washing away of bad dreams and bad blood in a bath of sweeter champagne. Some said the Phils would never in this world reach the Series. They were right. By the time the Phils had escaped the Astros, they had discovered that the land of their dreams was on the other side of normal baseball reality. When the final Astro flyball came down out of the dungeon grayness of the Dome roof, Bowa had the right idea. He jumped up and down in one spot as though touched by some Pentecostal gift of tongues.

The final two NL play-off games—both breathless extra-inning Phillie wins—were something out of a hookah dream. For those two days, it seemed that baseball was playing the men, not the men playing the game. The sport itself seemed to be showing off for the 100 million watching eyes, as though saying, "Now that I've got these silly humans totally in my control, watch what I can do." Would you believe three double plays in one game, all started on balls hit to the outfield? What about Maddox's soft liner back to the feet of Houston pitcher Vern Ruhle with men on first and second. For fifteen minutes, as umpires, managers, and the NL president had a sequence of terrified meetings, no one in America was certain if he had just seen a triple play, double play, or just one solitary out.

But Game Four was just the stage-setter. Game Five was the goosebump champ. The Phils had many escapes, but none nearly so improbable as their 5-run eighth inning against Nolan Ryan in the last game. Few things in baseball are more certain than The Ryan Express with a 3-run late-inning lead, especially when he is gusting up to 99 m.p.h. Since the 1972 season, Ryan has protected 97 percent of the leads that his teams have given him from the eighth inning forward. It is a statistic no one can fathom, a sort of natural phenomenon. Like Ryan's fastball.

The Phillies' great uprising was classic because it happened primarily in the mind. The Phils may be fatalistic, but Ryan is a walking snake pit. Bowa bit him first with a single. Next, Boone rapped a one-hopper back to Ryan that should have been a double play. But Ryan has as many Achilles' heels as a spider, fielding being one. His tragic flaw is that he refuses to master any aspect of the game not directly related to throwing unhittable pitches. The ball clanked off his glove for a scratch hit. Sensing Ryan's ruffled state of mind, Greg Gross laid down a bunt. Ryan never budged. Stage set: bases loaded, Rose at bat.

The Phils could have asked for no better man. "It was Rose who led us in the play-offs," said Schmidt. "I was just a spectator." That October may have been the last vast chunk of baseball fun that Rose could

gobble like a greedy child. For the first time, he talked about his forti-
eth birthday and the need to start taking days off in 1981. "The older
you get," said Rose, "well, the days are coming to an end, so you want
to enjoy them all. You can't bear to give one away."

Rose savored his showcase, redeeming his .282 season by hitting .388
from the final Expo series to the end. Here we thought that no living
man could enjoy a game, or embody it, more than Rose-in-bloom did
baseball. And now we discover that a fading Rose loves it even more.

In his previous at-bat, Rose had smoked a liner to Ryan's glove, then
got into a needling match with one pitcher few hitters would dare annoy. "Aw, we were havin' fun," explained Rose. "I just told him if he was
so fuckin' proud of the fuckin' curveball, why don't he throw it to me
the next time up and we'll see if he catches that one."

Perhaps only Rose could figure out how to get a man with a 100
m.p.h. fastball to throw him 90 m.p.h. curves with the pennant at stake.
Insult him, challenge him, and smile the whole time like it's just a
picnic and you're too dumb to have an alterior motive. And believe it
or not, with the bases loaded, Ryan threw curveballs. Rose gratefully
took them, putting Ryan in a hole. Finally, after a full-count foul tip,
Rose walked to first and a run walked home. Ryan walked to the
shower. Against mere mortals from the Astro bull pen, the Phils finished the great comeback. Nolan Ryan, so proud—so proud of his no-
hitters, and strikeouts, and his lead-protecting stats. Take your base,
Pete. Take your pennant. Take everything.

But not easily. Not against the Astros. Twice, Houston was 6 outs
away from the Series—leading by 2 runs in Game Four and 3 in Game
Five. Twice the Phillies rallied against the team with the best ERA in
baseball (3.10) to go ahead, with 3 in the eighth on Saturday and 5 in
the eighth on Sunday. And twice the Astros came back to force extra
innings, with a run in the bottom of the ninth Saturday and with 2 runs
in the eighth Sunday, the latter time against McGraw, whose ERA had
been 0.59 for six weeks.

For ninety-seven consecutive years, it was always the Phillies who slept
the winter on the cold floor of hard reality. Never were they permitted
illusions or heroes or the occasional benediction of harmless exaggera-
tion. For a century, Philly had to face the facts. For one short winter,

the thought of baseball can be pure pleasure. Now that the season has ended, all fans can glance back with a slow appraising eye over a vast blurred exhibition.

The City of Brotherly Love will remember only masterpieces.

Those Malevolent Phillies

Pete Axthelm

◆ ◆ ◆

The Phillies' world championship was met with disdain throughout the rest of the baseball world, especially as concerned inside the Phillies' clubhouse, which Roger Angell said "resembled a private sanatorium for privileged depressives—a place of moneyed calm and secret self-doubt." Despite the joy and jubilation, the 1980 season had also been one of acrimony and discontent between Phillies players and their "bleeping" (to quote Larry Bowa) fans. In his account of the series, Newsweek's Pete Axthelm demonstrated his contempt for the "churlish and thin-skinned" Phils and his partiality for the Royals: "Except for the eloquent power in the swings of [George] Brett and [Willie] Aikens, the ragged, dead-even series could hardly be ranked as an artistic triumph." In this analysis of the series, which appeared the following week, Axthelm bestowed a new name on those previously "depressing" and "futile" Phillies. This is the sort of sour grapes piece—by a first-rate writer—that Phillies fans take great pleasure in reading. As for Dickie Noles, the notorious brush-back pitcher told Rich Westcott fifteen years later that he wasn't throwing at George Brett in the celebrated incident of Game Four. "I was just really trying to move him off the plate. The only effect I think the pitch had was to embarrass Brett. I think . . . his whole team was embarrassed by it." Right. And the Iranians only wanted to throw a surprise party for the Americans at the U.S. embassy that summer.

At the end, even Tug McGraw got the Philly spirit. All season long the ebullient relief pitcher had been one of the few Philadelphia players to stand apart from his embattled mates, bantering with friends and actually intimating that playing baseball could be fun. But when the World Series was won, and the Phillies were paraded before thousands of their fans—the same fans with whom many of them had shared a mutual hatred all year—McGraw seemed to finally absorb the squad's malevolent message. In his triumphal moment at the microphone, Tug thought back to his past with the New York Mets, those glorious times when he gave a city and a whole nation of underdog lovers their slogan: "You gotta believe!" McGraw had this to say to the folks who had cheered him through those wonderful, innocent days: "New York can take this world championship and stick it!"

Perfect. One of the last holdouts was in the fold. The Philadelphia story was complete. The Phillies celebrated as they had played against Kansas City, in bullying and abrasive style. Shortstop Larry Bowa sneered that the boos of the fans had inspired him. Outfielder Lonnie Smith led a few teammates in obscene chants directed at the press. Ace pitcher Steve Carlton withdrew in sullen splendor to the off-limits trainer's room, while sycophants hurled beer at the reporters who maintained their demeaning vigil outside the door of the sanctuary. When McGraw belatedly joined in the mood, there seemed to be only one flaw in the script. The police attack dogs who snarled at the fans during the final inning were aimed in the wrong direction.

Disco: Can the world champions of the national pastime really be as joyless, juvenile and obnoxious as they seem? In fairness, it should be noted that the World Series in the media age places teams under a distorting glass. The winning Oakland A's and the New York Yankees of the past decade were probably not as disunited and explosive as they appeared in the series glare. Nor were the 1979 Pittsburgh Pirates and their wives precisely the "fam-a-lee" that brought only love and disco music to television last fall. So surely there must be some things to admire about the Phillies.

Pete Rose's enthusiasm. McGraw's post-game humor. Most Valuable Player Mike Schmidt's refusal to quit when he seemed consumed by a playoff slump. There it is. A list almost as long as the tale of Willie Wilson's series heroics. And poor Willie, the Kansas City leadoff man, set a record with his dozen strike-outs.

History has much to do with the Philly phenomenon. This franchise existed for 97 years without winning a world title. At times its pursuit has been poignant and appealing, as it was when the Whiz Kids of 1950 raced to a pennant and bowed in four straight series games to the New York Yankees—or when the anguished 1964 team bumbled away a pennant with a closing ten-game losing streak. But sometime around Year 93, the quest unraveled from the quixotic into the cutthroat. The modern Phillies have boasted talent almost as imposing as their payroll. When they have failed, they have astutely blamed the fans, the press or one another.

It is fitting that the most memorable image of this World Series is a nasty one—that of reliever Dickie Noles firing a fast ball toward the jaw of Royals superstar George Brett. At the time, the Phillies were busy losing the fourth game, and Brett was hitting just under .500. The Phils did not lose again, and after that pitch, the mighty Brett hit a very mortal .273.

To old-timers who recall managers' cries of "Stick it in his ear," the knockdown pitch stood as a turning point. Brett angrily denies that suggestion, and I am not about to argue about batting with a .390 hitter. But the incident pointed out an unfortunate situation. Under the rules, the umpires warned both teams that if there were any more knockdowns, the guilty pitcher and manager would be ejected. That prevented retaliation and a potential riot. But the fact remained that Noles had gotten away with a cowardly, dangerous move. Brett may be correct when he says that the Royals were not intimidated by it. But it is hard to imagine that the unavenged assault did not help the Phillies to feel all the more like the bullies on the block.

Whatever the reasons, the Kansas City decision makers grew increasingly tentative as the Phillies took charge. Third-base coach Gordy MacKenzie waved runners toward disaster with a frequency that made George Steinbrenner's least favorite Yankee coach, Mike Ferraro, resemble the second coming of John J. McGraw by comparison. Manager Jim Frey seemed too quick to call for his hittable reliever Dan Quisenberry and far too slow to insert a defensive replacement for immobile first baseman Willie Aikens. Frey also displayed an uncanny instinct for ordering Brett to play deep at third when the Phils bunted—and moving George in close when slugger Schmidt was swinging away.

Victory: In contrast, burly Dallas Green managed the Phillies in the style they deserve. He awakened them with a tirade of curses in August, and he drove them relentlessly through the stretch with the promise that they could all be shipped out at his command. When he was informed last week that one of his many complainers, Greg Luzinski, was unhappy about being benched, his reply was vintage. "I love Greg," Green snapped sarcastically. "I'd love to play him. But I'm not the one who hit .228 this year."

With victory in sight, Green made the simplest decision of all. He handed the ball to Carlton. There may be something puzzling about a 35-year-old pitcher so reclusive that he may refuse Hall of Fame induction unless he is promised a soundproof cubicle for his statue. But Lefty is overpoweringly straightforward on the mound—and he never let the Royals into the ball game. By the time he let McGraw finish up, the excitement was limited largely to watching the awesome police array of dogs and horses on the carpeted field. I don't know much about the esthetics of attack dogs, but I can testify that the horses were sleek and spirited. There, I've done it. I've found one more thing to like about baseball in Philadelphia.

What Money Hath
(and Hathn't) Wrought

Wilfrid Sheed

◆ ◆ ◆

Philadelphia was the first stopover for the masterful essayist Wilfrid Sheed, whose family, he later recalled in My Life as a Fan *(1993, Simon and Schuster) "had left England just before the German bombs came looking for us." Baseball was his American baptism and Shibe Park "the scene of [his] Baseball Mitzvah." He would further remember, "I must, just for openers, have been the only kid on hand in short pants and an English accent . . . who didn't yet understand or much like anything about America except for this gorgeous beautiful game."*

The following article on the 1980 World Series, borrowed from Sheed's collection Baseball and Lesser Sports *(1991, HarperCollins), "may be," he wrote, "the only baseball piece ever to appear in the* Nation. *Hence the emphasis on class struggle, dialectical materialism, economic determinism—and their ultimate subordination to the Percentages which rule baseball with the iron whim of a pagan God."*

When he mistakenly wrote that "neither cast had been in [a World Series] before," Sheed told me that he was thinking of those days of baseball when teams seemed to be teams for life and players stayed on the same club for nearly their entire careers. Anyway, Sheed remarked, there wasn't an editor at the Nation *who had ever played baseball, let alone been to a ballgame, so it's no surprise this little glitch snuck by.*

The 1980 World Series was supposed to feature the spoiled millionaires of Philadelphia versus the enlightened millionaires of New York. I don't know what sort of millionaires they have in Kansas City—this was written before we received the definitive answer in 1989: "overpaid" ones. But money and the modern ballplayer has been the talk all season, even when the lads fall to fighting over beanballs. (Nobody that rich wants to be hit in the head, goes the reasoning.)

Thus the Yankees put up with the bully-boy ravings of George Steinbrenner because they can't afford not to. New York is such a lucrative playground, in TV commercials alone, that Steinbrenner can chew out the help with impunity. Philadelphia apparently does not cast quite the same spell, so there the players chew out the manager instead. The question the World Series was *supposed* to answer was, which is better for you, to chew or be chewed?

The Series we got did suggest that perhaps these are not baseball questions at all, but messy fallout from the gossip culture. The Phillies were supposed to hate their manager so much that they might well lose four straight, or whatever it took, just to spite him. The Kansas City Royals, who, it seems, only mildly dislike their manager, should have cashed in on this quirk of brotherly love handsomely—everybody else has who's had the good luck to encounter the Phils in October, by which time they must be a ball of seething hate.

Yet when the blather had cleared, one team had made sixty hits and the other fifty-nine; one team (a different one) had outscored the other 4.5 to 3.9 per game—which I believe comes close to the average score of all ball games played anywhere since the beginning of time. In short, the verities triumphed over the froth of the press. Baseball is so finely calibrated that the super teams win three out of five, and the dogs two out of five. It is not the least surprising to find two teams with exactly the same records after *160 games.* So a series between *any* two big-league teams could be close. Yet in a World Series, these percentages fly out the window and everything is supposed to come down to character, as if ballplayers were prisoners of their nerves, like the rest of us. Arnold Palmer once remarked that laymen who talk about "choking" under pressure have no idea how many things can go wrong with your golf game besides fear. However jumpy he may feel, a professional athlete can call on a reserve of sheer skill, as a musician can: e.g., you don't praise an Isaac Stern performance because the house was bigger than usual that night.

The salient factor about this year's Series was that *neither* cast had been in one before. That took care of the stage-fright margin, or old Yankee edge. Maidenhood is everything in these matters. Yet while everyone else talked about money, the players themselves talked about character, as millionaires are wont to do. The word must have a special meaning for them. Because as soon as a team begins to win it *believes* it has character. Just let a couple of lucky hits fall in and the guys will say, "Yeah, we're that kind of team." The rhythm of streak and slump is so wild and unfathomable that the men riding it feel compelled to assert some kind of control over it. Contrariwise, in defeat the players "get down on themselves," search for scapegoats, question their own character. "We *proved* we had character," said the Phillies. Obviously. To win *is* to have character.

Morale also is more a function of winning than a cause of it, but it's a necessary function. It prolongs the streak from six wins to seven, and picks up the junk game that could go either way, that magical third game in five.

There are some teams that sin against the Holy Ghost and reject the energy that victory brings. The Phillies were felt to be one of these, like the Red Sox. Pampered by country-club ownership, went the talk, they could not rise to the myth of team spirit, the sense that the Collective can somehow coordinate its private streaks and slumps to squeeze the extra game. Too rich, not hungry enough, injury prone (injuries strangely are no excuse: character is supposed to thrive on them); teams like the Phillies are the pouting villains we need for our annual play-in-the-round.

Yet give one of them a hot hand—the Red Sox in '75, the Phillies last month—and you'll see who's pouty. Philadelphia did all the things rich brats are expressly supposed not to do. They came from behind four times in a row, counting the playoffs. Outfielder Bake McBride, the brat of brats, turned his orneriness into pure menace, treating the enemy as if they were his manager. Shortstop Larry Bowa, the team cynic, started seven double plays (a record) and cried with joy when it was all over. Pitcher Steve Carlton, who won't even talk to his friends, popped his fast ball so hard that the catcher's mitt sounded like a bat. (I've never heard this effect before.)

Perhaps the best symbol was third baseman Mike Schmidt, because he seemed to personify defeat, almost to anticipate it, *without* being obnoxious, a more evolved mutant. Some dismal playoffs in the past had made him a loser in a Sartrean sense: i.e., *first* you lose, *then* you are a loser, you have defined yourself.

Yet suddenly he had his touch, and he seemed like a different man. And one realized how much one's concept of a team is a problem in perception, or propaganda. Because all the Phillies looked better in victory. For instance, that surliness in the clubhouse—was that really because they were counting their money, or was it because they just don't like reporters, the old-fashioned way? Being civilized to the press is often the only clue we have to these guys' personalities, and it isn't a bad one. But ballplayers from the outback can be unduly disturbed the first time they see themselves misquoted or laughed at in a big newspaper. (And what kind of a man would do that for a living anyway?) A team, like an administration, is as lovable as its press corps makes it.

Baseball is pre-eminently the country game, because it takes up so much space, artificially transposed to the city where strangers boo you; the suspicious, uncommunicative rube has graced every clubhouse since Ring Lardner. In fact, you can probably find Steve Carlton himself somewhere in Lardner, right down to the hideous grimaces.

One of baseball's charming legends has Whitey Ford of New York City playing Henry Higgins to Mickey Mantle of Oklahoma and practically turning him into a boulevardier. Pete Rose struggles to perform the same task for the Phils, but it's tough work Higginsing half a squad. And of course the black styles of resentment practiced by McBride and Garry Maddox were undreamed of in Lardner, and will presumably have to be resolved outside the clubhouse.

As to those miserable objects, "today's kids," who allegedly can't stand discipline from an old-school manager—what about yesterday's kids, the Cleveland crybabies of 1940, or the Dodgers of '43, one of whom (Arky Vaughan) flung his uniform at Leo Durocher's feet? Ballplayers, rich or poor, have always been hard to handle—it is one of the few real tests of great managing—and a flinty-eyed brute like Roger Hornsby had as little luck with it way back when as he would today.

On second thought, has anything changed as little as a major league ballplayer, unless it be the game he plays? Babe Ruth holds a mirror to the 1920s, and the gas house gang might be said to reflect the Okie spirit of the 1930s. But it's a weak reflection. You might have guessed from the hairdos in the 1960s that *something* was happening in America, but what?

You can't deduce much about an era from its ballplayers. Solitary men in a solitary game, they make their way one by one into the big leagues and out again, always slightly to the side of normal society. The team spirit they invoke so fervently is always ad hoc, always this gang this year. Their teammates while they last are closer than family, but they are always being ripped apart and replaced. No wonder some players are withdrawn, and others full of empty good cheer. A barmaid in Lindells of Detroit told me that ballplayers were the stingiest and least friendly of all the athletes who traipsed through the place. Yet there are the Tug McGraws and Pete Roses who thrive on the change and uncertainty of the gypsy life, and who can briefly ignite the rest— as long as the rest are winning anyway.

Team spirit in baseball follows the percentages, it doesn't cause them, though it can quasi-mystically keep batting rallies going (or is it the rally itself that creates the spirit?). This series came down to Willie Wilson's strikeouts and Willie Aikens' stone glove, and all the character in the world couldn't have done a thing about that. If Wilson never plays another series, he will become another Mike Schmidt, a loser; if the wheel spins right, he will become Mr. October II. He will still be the same player, but he will look different and a new type of legend will form around him.

Otherwise, chalk up a small one for the brat who chews, and file this away under "arrestingly average." Nineteen eighty was the year the percentages came back in the guise of melodrama: In other words, it was baseball at its purest.

Bah, Humbug!

Pete Dexter

◆ ◆ ◆

Before he became an award-winning and best-selling novelist, Pete Dexter of the
Philadelphia Daily News *was probably the most widely read newspaper colum-*
nist in town. And with good reason. When, in Thomas Boswell's words, the
"feudin', wheezin' oldsters from the city of baseball discord managed to wander
into the World Series" to face the Baltimore Orioles in 1983, fans couldn't wait
to read what Dexter would say about it. His last line, of course, was most telling.

Yesterday afternoon I walked into my office and went to sleep. I
don't know how I did that—it's not a quiet place, but, then,
neither is the airport and people sleep there all the time. Where do
you think the ticket agents are when you're 14th in line and your plane
leaves in a quarter of an hour?

Anyway, one minute I was 60 pages into our pre-game coverage of the
World Series—did you know the Phillies were in the World Series?—the
next minute my forehead was nestled into the computer I work on, making fields of green zzzs across the screen, as far as you could see.

And as I slept, the elevator door opened, and a translucent old man
in a Phillies uniform got off and came over and shook my shoulder, He
had confetti all over his head. "Peter," he said, "wake up. I have places
to take you."

"What?" I said, blinking. "Who are you?"

The translucent old man smiled wisely. "Look carefully," he said.
"You know who I am," he said. And as he said that I realized he was
right. It was the Ghost of Series Past. Except for being translucent, he
looked a lot like Danny Ozark.

"Oh, no," I said. "Look, can we do this another time? I'm kind of tied up right now with work."

He smiled wisely again. "Work?" he said, "or greed? You have lost the meaning of the World Series, Pete Dexter, and I am here to fly you all over town, back and forth through time, and show you things you need to see."

And before I could recommend McMullen, before I could even groan, the translucent old man in the Phillies uniform had me under his arm and we were flying down Broad Street toward Vet Stadium and 1980. Tug McGraw was out on the mound, finishing off the last Kansas City batter in the sixth game of the World Series.

"Do you see that fellow pitching?" he said. "Do you know what he stands for to all the thousands of people here?"

"Yes," I said. "Tomorrow or the next day he is going to tell the city of New York to take the 1980 World Series and shove it."

As I said that, the game ended. Fans poured out onto the field, running past policemen holding attack dogs. All of them who were not being bitten were holding the same finger in the air, shouting, "We're number one!"

"Now I want to show you the dressing room," the old man said.

I begged him, "Please, not the dressing room . . ." but he took me under his arm, and we flew over the attack dogs and the mounted police, and right into the familiar smells and echoes of that damp place. Players were praying and pouring champagne over each other at the same time, and the television lights were everywhere.

"All this," the translucent old man said, "and you couldn't write a couple paragraphs? Not even a note?"

"I was in Michigan," I said. "Drunk, in the Upper Peninsula. You can ask my cousin . . ." The old man smiled wisely. I was getting tired of that smile. He put me under his arm again and took me out onto Broad Street. Time had passed, it was the victory parade.

People were all holding the same finger in the air shouting, "We're number one," while the players came by in convertibles. The translucent old man pointed out a small boy with one crutch, standing at

Broad and Washington in a Phillies hat. "Oh, Daddy," the boy said to his father, "I'm so happy. I can't wait to read what Pete Dexter says about winning the World Series."

Before I could open my mouth to say that wasn't fair, it was two days later, and the old man and I were in the poor but tidy rowhouse where the boy lived, waiting for the Daily News.

"I didn't know the Daily News delivered," I said. The old man smiled. The paper came, and the boy turned to page 4. This was before you needed a computer and a calendar to find the columnists.

"Daddy!" the boy screamed, "it's not here. Pete Dexter didn't even write a single word . . ."

"He's drunk in Michigan," I yelled, but the old man shook his head. "He can't hear you," he said. The boy had begun to cry, and his leg was getting worse, and I begged the translucent old man to take me back.

"Not quite yet," he said. He took me away, but to a room I had never seen before. An old man was lying in a bed, near the window. There was a baseball game going on outside, but the old man didn't move. He was trying to read his way through the huge stacks of unopened mail surrounding his bed. "Who is that?" I said.

"Look at him closely," he said.

"My God," I said, "it's, it's . . ."

And the translucent old man smiled wisely for the last time. "We got you a place right next to Veteran's Stadium."

I covered my eyes. "No, no, no."

"And look what you're reading," the old man said. It was press releases. "That's right," he said, "that little boy with the crutch forgot about the Phillies and grew up to become a press agent for the Housing Authority."

I began to cry. "Please, I can't look at any more . . . Please." And that's how I woke up, the mark of the Z in my cheek, crying, "Please, please . . ."

I looked at the clock and then at the calendar. "It's not too late," I shouted. "It's not too late to love the Phillies." And I ran into the street and bought Phillies pennants and Phillies T-shirts, and held my finger in the air, shouting, "We're number one." Then I wrote this column. I can't tell you how good it feels.

A weight has been lifted from my heart and a fog has been lifted from my eyes. And in the new clarity, a vision.

The Orioles in five.

The Amtrak Series

Roger Angell

◆ ◆ ◆

Readers of good baseball literature know Roger Angell as one of baseball's most eloquent, graceful writers. The New Yorker *fiction editor, now in his seventies, has contributed "Sporting Scene" baseball columns to the magazine since the early 1960s and collected them over the years in five books of prose. He is also an astute baseball analyst, as the following piece on the uneventful (despite the benching of Pete Rose in Game Three) 1983 World Series demonstrates, particularly his interpretation of the Oriole victory in Game Four. Thomas Boswell didn't bother to include his account of this World Series in any of his books. "Some defeats are worse than others," Boswell wrote after Game Three, "and a few are the absolute pits." This whole series, John Denny's first-game masterpiece notwithstanding, as historian Charles Alexander notes, "was the most one-sided since 1976."*

The World Series, so clear in form and outcome, will be revisited only briefly here. Its neighbor-city participants had inspired a few writers to call it the Amtrak Series, and the first two games—a swift, neat opening 2–1 win by the Phillies, followed by a 4–1 Baltimore victory the next evening—went by so quickly that they suggested two Metroliners swooshing past each other in opposite directions on some marshy Chesapeake-side straightaway. Three unencumbered home runs—by Joe Morgan and Garry Maddox, of the Phils, and Jim Dwyer, of the Orioles—produced all the scoring in Game One, in which the Phils' John Denny, their best pitcher this year, threw his curveball on the corners all evening, setting down the O's in neat little packages of three and getting the home crowd home (and out of a drizzly rain) in less than two and a half hours. The jammed-together, cheerful (under the circs) Baltimore fans were again conducted in their noise-making by their self-appointed leader, Bill Hagy, a local cabdriver, who has announced his retirement from the tummler post next season. (Unlike some of his counterparts and imitators in other cities, he is not paid by the team, and, indeed, has refused any emolument for his work.) He is the inventor of the unique Orioles letter-cheer, executed in body language, and I noticed that his handwriting has become minimal and blurry over the years, like the signatures of other famous men. Game Two brought back Mike Boddicker, who outpitched the other junior, [Charlie] Hudson, and won by 4–1—another impeccable outing for him, since the only Philadelphia run was unearned.

And so we went to Philadelphia and to Game Three—the hard game of the Series for both sides, I think—and when it was over, with Baltimore the winner by 3–2, there was a sudden sense in me and many other onlookers about how the rest of the week might go. The immediate problem for Baltimore in the game was Steve Carlton, who had been resting from his winning appearance in the Phillies' final playoff game. On this day, I noticed, he seemed to be missing one part of his repertoire, which is a three-quarter-speed rainbow slider that suddenly drops out of the strike zone like a mouse behind the sink, and he gave up some uncharacteristic hard-hit blows, pulled to the left side (mostly for outs), in the early innings. Carlton, like most great pitchers, is an indomitable closer—very hard to beat in the late innings no matter what stuff he may have—and it seemed forehanded and lucky that the O's got him out of there in the seventh, with a double by Rick Dempsey and a pulled hard single by pinch-hitter Benny Ayala, which tied the game at 2–2. (Ayala's stated batting philosophy, by the way, is a bit simpler than Yaz's multipart cogitations: "I look for something white moving through.") Ayala then became the winning run, scoring a moment or two later when Dan Ford's hard grounder skidded on a wet patch of the infield carpet and ricocheted off shortstop Ivan DeJesus's glove: a no-fault error. One prime recipient of this gift was Jim Palmer, who was in the game in relief of Mike Flanagan and thus gained the win. He had endured a difficult season, suffering back problems and tendinitis, and at one point had been sent down to the Orioles' Class A Hagerstown team to recover his form. He took this all in good part, becoming a standby bullpen operative in the postseason, and his work in this game, by his own admission, looked more like throwing—*careful* throwing—than pitching, but he was delighted with the win. When he and Carlton were in the game against each other for a few minutes there, we were looking at five hundred and sixty-eight lifetime victories.

The particular problem for the Phillies—or a symbol of the problem, at least—was Pete Rose, who got into the game as a pinch-hitter in the ninth after spending most of it sombrely watching the proceedings from the top step of the dugout, with his white-gloved fists tensely clenching and unclenching. He had been benched by Philadelphia manager Paul Owens, who put Tony Perez on first in hopes of getting a little sock into the lineup—not an inconceivable turn of events, since Pete had had one single to his credit so far—but Rose was at no great pains to conceal his distress and irritation over the demotion. The press hordes made much of the little scandal, of course, and Joe Morgan uncharacteristically lost his temper in the postgame clubhouse when the reporters, after Rose's swift departure, turned their questions toward the gentle Perez. Morgan's sense of propriety was offended; he felt that professionals (including Rose, although he did not say so) should have handled all this more calmly. Rose, in fact, had previously embarrassed the club by not admitting a fielding lapse in Game Two, when he left first base uncovered in a bunt situation that specifically called for him to stay in place: no play was made, the bunt helped win the game, and the fans mistakenly blamed Morgan for the uncovered base.

These trifling contretemps are set forth here because they tell us about a much deeper problem that afflicted the Phillies all year. Paul Owens became the Philadelphia manager in the middle of July, replacing Pat Corrales at a moment when the club was in first place in the flaccid N.L. East but scraping along just one game above the .500 level. Owens, the incumbent general manager, took on the field directorship because the Philadelphia front office foresaw that only a man with his authority and reputation would be able to enforce some difficult alterations in the Phillie lineup of famous and very well-paid older stars, who by now had made it plain that they weren't good enough to win. Owens installed a platoon system of his own, resting Pete Rose and veteran outfielders Gary Matthews and Garry Maddox whenever it seemed advantageous to do so, and reshuffling his batting order. Everyone in the lineup but catcher Bo Diaz, third baseman Mike Schmidt, and shortstop Ivan DeJesus became a replaceable part, in fact, and Owens made frequent use of the lesser-known outfielder Joe Lefebvre and, later on, of a rookie first baseman, Len Matuszek, and outfielder Sixto Lezcano. None of this was easy (Rose's first benching ended a seven-hundred-and-forty-five-consecutive-game streak for him), and no one on the club took it with particular grace. In September, Mike Schmidt indulged himself in a public outburst of criticism of Owens' managing (it came at the moment when the club was embarking on its eleven-game winning streak), and even during the Series, after it had become plain to everyone that the changes had worked and that the team had outdone itself at the end, there were mumbles and grousings from some of the famous principals. Owens himself—he is a tall, stooped, gentle-spoken man, with odd white eyelashes, who carries a packet of Gelusil in his uniform pocket—summed up his club during the playoffs with a musing little aside: "We have an old team and a middle-aged team and a young team." Three teams from which to make one—to make a Baltimore, say. Pete Rose and Joe Morgan were given their release by the Phillies in the week after the Series ended.

Rose, in any case, was back in the lineup for Game Four, and had two hits and scored a run and batted in another—not quite enough to win it. You could say that the Orioles' pitching (Storm Davis, plus Sammy Stewart and Tippy Martinez) won again, or else that it was Orioles second baseman Rich Dauer who did it, with his three hits and three runs batted in and a neatly turned double play to stop a big Philadelphia inning. It was a taut, hard game, in any case, with the Orioles pulling it out by 5–4, and if I believed that managers ever actually win ballgames I would say that Baltimore manager Joe Altobelli won this one, because of what he and his accomplished bench (the "role-players," as they like to call themselves) pulled off in the sixth inning. Trailing John Denny (a right-hander, remember) by 3–2, with Oriole base runners at second and third, he unexpectedly wheeled in the left-side-swinger Joe Nolan as a pinch-hitter; when Nolan was intentionally walked, Altobelli produced Ken Singleton, who switch-hits and was thus proof against any Philadelphia countermove to a lefty pitcher. Singleton walked, driving in a run and tying the game (Sakata came in to run for him), and when Hernandez, a left-hander, did at last come in to pitch, the batter awaiting him was John Shelby, who also switches, and who now, batting right-handed, hit a sacrifice fly that drove in the lead run. Baltimore's fourth successive pinch-hitter, Dan Ford, fanned for the last out, but the marionette show was not quite done, since Altobelli, by moving one incumbent fielder, Dauer, from second base to third base, found room in his defensive deployment for two of the pinch-hitters and for Sakata, too (but none at the same position as the man he had replaced), in the bottom half of the inning. I apologize for this digression, which perhaps needs an accompanying flow chart, but for those of us who were keeping score Altobelli's moves suddenly looked like the moment onstage when the shining red balls vanish from the cup and reappear—count them!—in the magician's fingers, and there was a further glow of pleasure when we suddenly realized that Altobelli somehow still had his three best right-handed backup hitters—Roenicke, Ayala, and Landrum—available on the bench for later use, if needed. Managers try this sort of stuff all the time, but rarely does it work out as elegantly and inexorably as it did here.

In the Series, Eddie Murray and Mike Schmidt each ran into oppressive difficulties in trying to do what he had been doing all year, which was to hit the ball to distant parts and win ballgames. Schmidt talked at length with the writers about his failures (he was batting .063 after four games), and said that the Orioles pitchers were making him chase a lot of pitches that were up and out of the strike zone, and that he was making adjustments in his swing; Murray, for his part, said nothing and made no adjustments (he had had two singles so far, for .125), as is his custom, but it seemed certain that he was unhappily thinking back to the World Series of 1979, when he failed repeatedly at the plate while the O's dropped the last three games in a row and lost to the Pirates. Now he came up in the second inning of the fifth game and whacked a monstrous homer into the upper tiers in right field—"It would have been a homer in Grand Canyon," Pete Rose said later—and followed up in the fourth with an even longer, two-run job that bounced off the center-field scoreboard, where the ball just missed hitting the "M" of his own name up there at a moment when the message screen was listing the American League R.B.I. leaders. Rick Dempsey hit a home run and also a double, and scored the last run, and the O's, behind McGregor's 5–0 shutout, were World Champions.

Long-Haired Aliens
Cross the Border

George Vecsey

◆ ◆ ◆

So much for 1984–92—but say what you want about the Phillies of those years, the team was building in the right direction (enough to go from last place to first in one year). There has been much written about the fast and furious pennant of 1993 and the grungy, gung-ho ballplayers who won it (see this publisher's Phillies '93: An Incredible Season *by the able Rich Westcott). So I present here a couple of off-beat twists on the subject, starting with some acute observations from the pen of George Vecsey of the* New York Times.

The United States is committed to entertain Iran or Iraq should they qualify for the 1994 World Cup of soccer. And Canada was obliged to accept the Phillies for the World Series of baseball. It says so in the contract.

"We had to be semisociable coming across the border so they'd let us all in. I didn't see anybody not get in," John Kruk said, quite proudly.

If innocent Marines could fly the Maple Leaf upside down during the 1992 World Series in Atlanta, imagine what the raffish Phillies could perpetrate in the next few days. If American singers habitually butcher the lyrics and the music to "O, Canada," imagine what international incidents the swaggering Phillies could touch off.

They came clamoring into the Skydome for a workout yesterday, every man jack insisting they're not as oafish as their reputation. You be the judge.

The first sound you heard was a bleat from one corner of the club-house. "Pitchers don't get World Series bats?" screamed Mitch Williams, the relief pitcher known as Wild Thing.

"Oh, shut up," yelled Pete Incaviglia.

Wild Thing was jealously observing Chuck Schupp and Kelley Richards of the Louisville Slugger Company presenting handsome new World Series bats to all the hitters. Somebody broke the news to Wild Thing that pitchers are not allowed to bat in American League ball parks because of the absurd designated hitter rule.

Wild Thing put on a red and white bandana with the word "Fear" inscribed on the front. "You gotta have a strong stomach," Wild Thing said of all his managers. He said he had been hyperactive when he was a child. Did he take medicine? "Nah, my father moved us out to the country."

There was a commotion across the clubhouse. Incaviglia had just discovered there was no smokeless tobacco in his locker. This is a team that was visited last spring by a man who had lost half his jaw to bone cancer. A dozen Phillies gave up chewing on the spot, but they all went back to chewing eight innings later while Wild Thing frittered a lead. Somebody found Incaviglia his dip. He was placated for the time being.

An acrid cloud drifted from another corner. Len Dykstra was smoking in the crowded clubhouse, a plastic spittoon at his feet. "Gotta check my weapons," Lenny said. A few of us looked ready to duck for cover. Fortunately, he was referring to his World Series bats.

"No hangers!" Dave Hollins screamed. He had the clenched jaw of Faye Dunaway playing Joan Crawford in "Mommie Dearest." Dykstra had commandeered all the hangers for his T-shirts.

Some reporters asked Darren Daulton if he had ever been to Toronto. "We were going to come up in February, but we decided to stay home," he said with a straight face. Daulton lives in Safety Harbor in the state of Florida.

Unshaven John Kruk slouched into his locker, his hair tumbling around his shoulders. "This is the worst day of my life," Kruk announced. "You guys gonna watch me get undressed?"

"What kind of dress code we got today?" Kruk yelled. "Pants? I ain't gonna wear pants." When last seen clinching the pennant Wednesday night, Kruk had a huge rip down the back of his pants. He said he had not changed because "Greene was pitching too good."

Somebody asked Kruk about the Phillies' image. "I don't think you're gonna find any Rhodes scholars in here," he said. He skipped over the incongruity of a dozen sportswriters in sneakers and jeans and sweatshirts asking him about his slovenly image.

"I'm not a slob," Kruk said. "I'm not a model. I don't get paid to look good. You go to a rock concert and a lot of people look like that, but they can't play ball."

He seemed bewildered by the attention the Phillies were getting. "This isn't how we intended it to be," he said. "Nobody wrote about us when we stunk."

He was uncomfortable with the concept that the Phillies might be seen as representing the United States. "We ain't gonna start a war," he said. "Clinton's doing a pretty good job of that."

Wild Thing lurched across the clubhouse, waving a couple of Big Macs at Kruk. "Not now," Kruk hissed. "They'll get a picture of me eating."

The Phillies stuffed their mouths full of tobacco. It was time to work out on the artificial turf of the Skydome. The other Phillies had red caps on. Kruk pulled on a white cap that said "America's Most Wanted." He looked like a placard in the post office. Kruk remembered he was in another country and put on his pants. The two countries were still on speaking terms. But it was still early.

Game Four:
When Four Hours, 14 Minutes and 14 Runs Weren't Enough

Bruce Buschel

◆ ◆ ◆

I would like to take this opportunity to thank my friend Dr. Paul Steinfield, an orthopedic surgeon, for inviting me to this game, and those two folks in Section 629 who decided not to attend, thus leaving us two better seats than the ones we were supposed to sit in. As Bruce Buschel, whose work has appeared in GQ *and the* New York Times Magazine, *makes painfully obvious, Game Four was sui generis to the 1993 World Series (maybe to all World Series), and perhaps no one but the Phillies could have lost it the way they did. By Game Six everyone (except maybe manager Jim Fregosi) seemed to know that Mitch Williams had nothing left. But the big move—and the one that will be hot-stoved ad infinitum—came in the eighth when Fregosi decided to play the percentages and removed right-handed reliever Roger Mason for lefty David West to set up the shell-shocked Williams in the ill-fated ninth. Mason (who was pitching $2^{1}/_{3}$ innings of shutout baseball, with a 1.17 series ERA) had a hot hand all right, and in a short series, as Jimmy Cannon once observed, always "bet the hot hand before the cold wind freezes your fingers." Ironically, Cannon wrote those words about the hot hand of the 1955 World Series—Johnny Podres, the Phillies pitching coach. You'd think someone would have known better. But Game Four . . . Game Four. This piece originally appeared in* Philadelphia Magazine, *for which Buschel is a contributing writer.*

I had nightmares all winter, Doctor. They always started the same: I am watching television, when out of the screen march Beavis and

From *Philadelphia Magazine*, March 1994. Reprinted by permission of Bruce Buschel.

Butt-Head. Only they're not really Beavis and Butt-Head, they're Kim Batiste and Mitch Williams. Batiste stands in the corner. I throw him the remote control. He drops it. Mitch Williams, in his tattoos and skivvies, sits down, shakes his head and says over and over again. "I'm not going to commit suicide. It's only a game."

He's right, of course; it is only a game. So how come I keep having these nightmares about this one game, the longest nine-inning night game in the history of baseball? It wasn't long enough? It has to continue in the dark, dank Vet of my unconscious, played and replayed, extended and altered by irrational substitutions? Johnny Callison plays right, Stu Bykofsky pinch hits, Lenny Dykstra hits two two-run homers. Wait—that really happened, the Lenny Dykstra part. Didn't it? Is Incaviglia still waiting to pinch hit?

Eventually, I wake up. Usually screaming the number *four. Four!* Not as in golf, Doctor, as in baseball. As in Game Four. As in four hours and 14 minutes. As in 14 runs being too few. It wasn't the worst game ever played, nor the most painful, but it was the worst most painful game in memory. Why not Game Six, I hear you asking. (Not really asking, not verbally, just thinking.) Game Six was no bargain, believe you me, but Four was a water torture, a blue-ball tease, a world-class roller coaster choke job. Six? Four? What's the diff . . . you see what just happened? Six . . . four . . . Doc, we're getting somewhere already. Somewhere I didn't want to get.

There is every possibility that Game Four, that malefic contest, could take on an afterlife as miserable and unexpungeable as 1964 itself. You know about 1964, doncha Doc? Only the greatest collapse in the history of sports, a collapse that helped (de)form a generation's view of life and hope and fatalism, that's all. I know—it was a long time ago. Perhaps the upcoming 30th anniversary has it weighing on my mind.

The summer of '64, lest we forget, followed the winter of '63 as surely as the Phils' demise followed JFK's. In the mind's eye, these two saturnine events occurred seconds apart, like frames of a home movie. (Was Zapruder spotted anywhere near Connie Mack Stadium?) Everything was radiant, dappled with good humor and great promise. Kennedy's first 1,000 days. The Phillies first 150 games. Wasn't that John Callison's wife in the pink pill-box hat? Didn't Richie Allen break the color barrier at Ol' Miss? Everything was beautiful and then it was all over. *Bang!* Lee Harvey Oswald. *Whoosh!* Chico Ruiz. With accomplices on grassy knolls and dusty pitching mounds. Life was good and then life was bad, bereft, never to be the same.

Some of us entered neither voting booth nor baseball stadium for years after. I don't want to horn in on your profession, Doctor, but I've been thinking about starting a self-help group where baby boomers could gather with transistor radios and Tony Taylor cards and remember exactly where they were the moment Chico Ruiz stole home. It couldn't be a 12-step program, no sir, too cruel a reminder of the Phils' own 12 steps to infamy.

"Hi, my name is Bruce B., and I still have tickets for the 1964 World Series . . ."

I wouldn't want, three decades down the road, to be haunted by this Game Four the way I am '64. Maybe if we go over it, put it into perspective, we can diminish its power, pry loose its talons from the psyche. Hell, it's not as if the season wasn't great fun—it was! it was!—and the Phils weren't a wildly lovable bunch of motherkrukkin' misfits—they were! they were!—and they didn't play with such *joie de dirt* and wag their tongues with such abandon that they made you forget all about money—they did! they did!—it's just that, in the end, no matter how talented or tantalizing, regardless of the depth of your belief, in the bitter end, the Phils, the Fated Phils, will, inevitably, one way or another, break your heart.

It has been otherwise but once in the last century. Them odds are tough to buck, buckeroos. So the lesson is loud and clear: Don't count your gonfalons before they unfurl.

If we can take this slowly, please, inning by inning, I'll try to remember that, as the Wild Thing warned, it's only a game.

Top One

The Vet looks like an Orson Welles production, fog rolling in, ceaseless drizzle, cast of thousands. And Steve Carlton on the mound, the Ghost of Pitching Past, as ruminative and private as the current gang is impulsive and open. The ceremonial first pitch is a presentiment: low and in the dirt. No one swings. Thousands boo. Can Philly fans see the handwriting on the scoreboard? They see it everywhere.

Tommy Greene is a wreck. Before an usher can dry your seat, the Jays have loaded the bases, and Paul Molitor, the debonair hitting machine, is at bat. He walks on four frightened pitches. If Greene can just retire the next hitter . . . Tony Fernandez immediately drives in two runs with a sharp single to left.

Get Carlton up in the bullpen.

The sky is falling. **3–0, Jays**

Home One

As Lenny Dykstra waddles to first base—after his 3 millionth leadoff walk—you think maybe he's been spending too much time with his Thighmaster or Stairmaster or some master. He runs like a pygmy rhino. Arriving at first, he daintily removes his red gloves, finger by finger, hands them to his gentleman-in-waiting and then spits a wad of chaw that doesn't quite clear his lower lip, causing a piece of tobacco leaf to hang precariously from Mr. Dykstra's open mouth. All eyes are on him. This does not dissuade him from stealing second.

Symmetrically, the Phils too load the bases, with walks to Hollins and Daulton. Jim Eisenreich steps up. Jim Eisenreich used to react quite poorly to far less nerve-wracking environments, like 20,000 polite fans in Minnesota in mid-June. Thrown a genetic curve called Tourette's syndrome, he has to ingest various pharmaceuticals every day to stop himself from doing precisely what his teammates have become famous for doing—cracking wise and cursing blue streaks, indulging tics, twitches and unnameable eccentricities. Over all this and more Eisenreich has control. He walks on four pitches from Todd Stottlemyre. Dykstra waddles home. The bases are still jammed. The Vet is jammin'. Their chant sounds like "Hooton, there he is!"

On the mound, Todd Stottlemyre turns into Burt Hooton.

In the box seats, several occupants have drug flashbacks.

That the Phils have scored without a hit should surprise no one.

They talk the talk, they take the walk. These fat, undisciplined, white-trash weisenheimers are secretly well-schooled and bright. (And, according to Bill Conlin, who should know of such things, one of the best-conditioned teams he has ever covered. Kruk, he simply has a body structure similar to, dare we say, another pregame-multiple-frankfurter-eater who wore darker pinstripes. David West, he's fat. Everyone else pumps iron from morn till midnight.) The Phillies led the world in walks. For the first time ever, three players on the same squad—Dykstra, Kruk and Daulton—had over 100 bases on balls, and Hollins, missing nearly a month, had 85.

Stottlemyre is meat. Of his 27 first pitches, Phils will swing at just two.

Milt Thompson lines a screamer to deep center, above Devon White's glove, high against the padded wall. The bases are cleared. The Phils take the lead. One hot dog, please. And a beer.   **4–3, Phils**

Top Two

The designated hitter was adopted in 1973 when the American League thought more runs would draw more fans. If it were true then, and there are doubts, it is no longer. The National League has no trouble attracting fans or double-digit tallies. The Phils outscored every team in baseball except the bandbox Tigers, 877–899.

Because AL pitchers have to hit in NL towns, Todd Stottlemyre has his inaugural major league at bat. He walks. Which means he has to run the bases now. (It also means Tommy Greene should be shot.) Rickey Henderson fouls out on a fine, running catch by John Kruk, proving one shouldn't judge a Kruk by its cover.

When Alomar singles to right, Stottlemyre the Virgin rounds second and heads toward third and, being out by a mile, compounds his wrongheadedness with a face-first dive into the third base bag. *Bag* is a misnomer. It is 15 square inches of stuffed, unforgiving canvas. Blood drips from the Virgin's chin. He lies supine, motionless. The trainer runs onto the field. What Phillies fans are saying is best left unsaid. (They really do want him back in the game.) Groggily, Stottlemyre stands and counts the outfielders to prove his senses have returned.

Forsaking bandages for the hockey folks back in Toronto, his chin looks great on television—raw, red, oozy.

Speaking of television, despite artificially reduced ratings because one home team is Canadian, despite the absence of a red-hot superstar, despite no national audience connected to a superstation team, the 1993 Fall Classic outdraws the 1993 NBA Finals. Say what? Yes, the Phils and Jays surpass the Bulls and Suns and their ultimate Nike matchup of Jordan vs. Barkley.

No matter how hard the owners try, they cannot maim this game.

Home Two

Stottlemyre must be dazed: Tommy Greene singles. Lenny Dykstra will make certain that Greene is tempted to slide into nothing. Lenny points the bat to the ground like a divining rod, then cocks it into position, his gloved fingers tapping the handle as a court stenographer types a sudden confession. The flight of a Stottlemyre fastball is redirected out of the park. Not a wimpy, wind-blown, little-guy dinger, but a manly four-bagger. Fast and far. Like Barry Bonds or Fred McGriff. Will this muscular shrimp ever fail? You need a walk and steal? Dial D-Y-K-S-T-R-A. It's late and you desire a protean shot? Dial D-U-D-E-H-I-T. You gotta love this guy.   **6–3, Phils**

Top Three

They score four times, the Blue Jay way, walks and singles, singles and walks, like an obstinate drizzle—they annoy and accumulate and finally drown you. They will, as you know, tally 15 runs this night without benefit of a single home run. Sounds illegal.

When the starters depart simultaneously (Greene makes way for a reliever, Stottlemyre for a pinch hitter), they have pitched more balls than strikes, sanctioned more baserunners than outs. Had they pitched underhand, floating the ball right down the pike, they would have fared no worse.

The Phils, meanwhile, have blown a four-run lead. And it's only a dress rehearsal. **7–6, Jays**

Home Three

Al Leiter retires the side in order, including hot Milt Thompson.

Milt Thompson is the only African-American-Philadelphian Phillie on the field. Damn, the Phillies are white. The whitest team in baseball. (Can't you have a discussion about *anything* in this country without mentioning race? No.) Name another team whose four best players are white; whose first six hitters (when Morandini plays) are white; that fields eight white players when facing a righty? The black players are part-timers and backups who know their places: Jordan, Chamberlain, Thompson, Batiste. It took Mariano Duncan, a Dominican, years to prove himself a starter, if he has yet achieved that status. The pitching staff has Ben Rivera. Big Ben notched one inning in the Series.

Is all this mere happenstance? You want history? We got history. The 1950 Whiz Kids were the last all-white team to win a pennant. The Phillies were the last team in the National League to integrate, in 1956, ten years after Jackie Robinson—who singled out Shibe Park as the lion's den—first played just 100 miles north. The Phillies passed on Willie Mays. And Roy Campanella. And traded Fergie Jenkins for two old suitcases. That short, celebrated list is but the snowy tip of the iceberg.

After the Whiz Kids, the Phillies languished in or near the cellar for decades, except in '64, when Richie Allen arrived. They were, went the euphemism, slow to integrate. As late as 1980, the world championship team had only three blacks on the roster for most of the season (Garry Maddox, Bake McBride and Lonnie Smith). But that was long ago and far away, right? This can't apply to the enlightened 1993 edition of the Phils.

It is widely accepted that the Phils reflect their city, blue-collar, hard-working, neighborhood stiffs who would play ball in Fairmount Park if the Red Man were plentiful and the beer cold. Since the Phils don't mirror the city's multicultural diversity or racial makeup, they must mirror the city's attitude toward color. Exclusionary.

Does anyone really think the Phillies play harder than the Giants or the Orioles or the Angels? Aren't there union guys and truck drivers in Chicago and Milwaukee and Pittsburgh?

Maybe it's me, but there always seemed something racial, something coded, in the terms *hard-working* and *blue-collar* and *throwback*. How can a black player be a throwback to a time when there were no black players? Or is that the point?

White people are tired of seeing, and competing with, rippled hard-bodies named Deion and Barry and Rickey, guys who look as if they can do anything they please on the field. White people attribute these sleek physiques to Darwin or God (not Nautilus or Universal) when, in fact, it is the John Kruks of the world who have all the God-given talent—it is Kruk who refuses to lift anything unattached to a cheese-burger in the off-season. John Kruk, bless his soul, may be the whitest man on earth. Overweight, overachieving and over-tressed.

As for the long hair, what else can a white boy do? He can copy high-fives and mimic end-zone demonstrations, he can turn his cap back-ward and point his index finger derisively, but a shaved head makes him look like a neo-Nazi or a chemo patient or a swimmer. So he cultivates his hair. Long hair is the antidote to the shimmering pate. As with Afros of yesteryear, the totally bald black head is sending a mes-sage—just don't ask white people what that message may be: It's clean, it's criminal, it's celebratory, it's talk-show friendly, it's maximum-secu-rity tough, it's something African-Americans can pull off and Cauca-sian-Americans cannot.

A friend from Pittsburgh telephoned last week. "I shaved my head," he said. "I was thinking Kareem or Barkley, maybe a Steeler free safety, but I look like fucking Phil Silvers."

Top Four

Jays out in order. Thank God. This is exhausting. Another beer, please.

Home Four

Disregard the old saw about baseball on the radio—you have to see all this to believe it. Lenny Dykstra bangs Al Leiter for a double, missing another home run by a foot or so, and scores on a Duncan single.

Now 7–7, you have to like your chances. This is a Phillies kind of game, when pitchers can't find the plate, fielders can't find traction, the score is a mixed drink, the clock swears to go past midnight and general weirdness has descended upon the Vet like a Spielberg special effect. You gotta like your chances. **7–7, Phils**

Top Five

The *Toronto Sun* had a contest. Finish this sentence: "The Phillies are so ugly that . . ."

The winner was—you better sit down, kids—"The Phils are so ugly the turf spits back."

Honest. *The turf spits back.* John Kruk gets off better one-liners between Twinkies.

If the Phillies mirror Philly, then the Blue Jays are like their humorless, efficient Toronto. They go about their work like a sequestered jury. As far as one can tell, they are devoid of nicknames. They do not understand that when your own teammates call you Jeffrey Dahmer—as with Jim Eisenreich—then you are beyond the sting of the notoriously bitchy Philly press. What did the newspapers call John Olerud all year long? John Olerud. How about a nickname contest in the *Toronto Sun?*

Even when handed a straight line, the Jays drop the ball. Cito Gaston couldn't figure out Who's on First for a few days and not one clever line ushered forth from any of the involved parties. How could any manager consider sitting down either Olerud or Molitor? One hit close to .400 all year and the other is hitting around .500 in the postseason. Having a predominantly righty pitching staff means the Phils will send up lefties, and few balls will bounce Molitor's way at third. It takes no genius to bench Ed Sprague. If you're managing a team with Rod Carew and George Brett and Puddin' Head Jones, who sits?

Home Five

Dave Hollins said he would never bunt on Molitor. So Dave Hollins bunts on Molitor. In baseball, this is not lying. Ain't baseball great? The drizzle has been upgraded to a genuine rain. Umbrellas dot the stands. Water pours off the roof. Darren Daulton is up. If Dykstra is the Popeye of this animated group, Daulton is the spinach. Though he has been struggling of late, leaving a ton of men on base, you always feel good about him, his accurate arm, his seven-time loser knees, his handling of pitchers.

Larry Andersen, with the Phils in the early '80s and back again, said of Daulton: "He's like E.F. Hutton on this team. When he speaks, everyone listens. Daulton is the leader Mike Schmidt wanted to be, but never was."

Daulton clouts a two-run homer. The Phillies regain the lead, 9–7. All is right with the world.

Presently, Milt Thompson is standing on second base, having doubled in Eisenreich. 10–7. Lenny Dykstra shakes the moisture from his helmet and eyeballs Al Leiter. Leiter delivers. Lenny swings, swiftly, compactly. Holy shit! Another long shot into the right-field bleachers. Poof, just like that! Dykstra trots around the bases, his face impassive, gazing into some private, parallel universe. As he rounds third, quite business-like, one deliriously tabulates:

Four runs, four RBIs, two homers, one double, one walk, one stolen base, and it's the fifth friggin' inning of the fourth friggin' game of the World Friggin' Series. The Babe ever do that? The Mick? Move over, men, here's The Dude, who just passed Joe D. with his eighth and ninth postseason blasts.

Lenny, Lenny, Lenny, Lenny, Lenny, Lenny, Lenny.

When he later tells the media "No big deal, dude, I been doing this all year," it's hard to tell if it is hubris or false modesty or both, if he is still lobbying for the MVP award—which he did shamelessly, and somehow amicably—or just spouting the flat truth.

The numbers, even when familiar, never fail to astonish: most runs scored (143) in the NL since 1932; first player ever to lead a league in hits, walks and at bats in a season; reached base most times (323—

more than twice a game!) since 1929. Of his 19 homers, nine gave the Phils the lead, two tied in the fifth or later, five got to within one run or added an insurance run. It's the greatest run most of us will ever witness, from game one through 172. You can't help but love the Dude.

On his way to the mound to rescue Leiter, Cito Gaston touches his left shoulder, signaling for southpaw reliever Tony Castillo. As for Leiter, rarely has a pitcher been happier about his removal. "I was just hoping to get out of that bloodbath without actual physical abuse," he said. "I was glad I got out without going in an ambulance with a bruise on the forehead. I'm serious." The new pitcher is, huh, Mark Eichhorn? Gaston wants Tony Castillo. Where's Castillo? He is still sitting down, waiting for the skipper's call. The phone service connecting the dugout to the bullpen has been out of order. Communications breakdown. You can dial the offices of the Nippon Ham Fighters in Japan while stuck in traffic on the Schuylkill Expressway, but you can't reach a bullpen in shouting distance from a dugout. Welcome to the information superhighway. One more beer, please.

Can you get picked up for DWI on this new superhighway? **12–7, Phils**

Top Six

David West enters the game. How's that for a Stephen King title? *David West Enters the Game.*

David West is the only pitcher to pitch in the last three postseason games in which a team scored 14 runs or more. David West has, to this moment, faced eight batters in World Series competition and, on 36 pitches, walked four, allowed four hits, given up five runs and permitted three of four inherited runners to score. His ERA is infinity. His blood pressure must be close to that. On David West's first pitch, Devon White doubles. On David West's second pitch, Roberto Alomar singles. A run scores. David West's personal streak is now at ten unsolved batters in a row. It should be noted that David West had a fine first half for the Phils.

Joe Carter flies out to right. David West's ERA plummets to 162. Fans give David W. a Standing O. They needed a sixth-inning stretch anyway.

David West returns to form. Olerud singles. Molitor gets hit by a David West pitch. His numbers now look like this: Of 13 batters faced, four walked, one homered, three doubled, three singled, one was hit and Joe Carter was retired. God bless Joe Carter. Tony Fernandez grounds out, scoring another run. Pat Borders flies out. David West's ERA drops to 63. Just a notch or so above his belt size.

It was a relatively good World Series outing for David West.

This is no joking matter. The Jays are creeping back.   **12–9, Phils**

Home Six

Hollins doubles to center. Daulton finesses a free pass. Milt Thompson singles off Tony Castillo. For the months of August and September, Milt Thompson accrued four RBIs. He has just earned his fifth of the game.

Mitch Williams swaggers to the bullpen, down the right-field line, with his red glove, long hair and farcical goatee. Fans applaud. Curt Schilling reaches for his towel. Fans at home reach for Wild Turkey, Xanax, the neck of the nearest dog.

On CBS, Mike Schmidt is recalling the high-scoring affairs during his tenure with the Phils. Schmidt is an intelligent, articulate man who has been virtually black-balled from the sport at which he excelled. How must it feel to be the Greatest Third Baseman of All Time and unable to secure employment as manager, hitting coach, color man, bat boy? What does it do to him to see ex-teammate Larry Bowa coaching third base and hear that Bob Boone is being groomed as a manager, to visit with Tim McCarver in the booth, to know that Pete Rose, Jim Kaat, Joe Morgan and Tom Hutton all make a living at the mike. Only Mike Schmidt cannot.

He plays golf and fishes for blues in Florida. Seeing the Greatest Third Baseman of All Time does little for the spirit.   **13–9, Phils**

Top Seven

The Jays are down by four runs, and their reliever, Tony Castillo, leads off the inning. Is Gaston watching the game or negotiating with a telephone repairperson? Castillo strikes out.

Rickey Henderson is booed. Rickey is booed most everywhere, being universally disliked. People think he is a hotdog. Lenny Dykstra, on the other hand, is intense. Rickey symbolizes everything wrong with the modern game. Lenny is a colorful character from the golden age. Rickey has stolen more bases than anyone else in history and will be sent to the Hall of Fame one day. Lenny had a near-fatal car crash while driving drunk and he is sent to Europe to represent the game. Rickey is reviled because he plays a black man's game. Lenny is beloved because he plays Rickey's game.

Rickey walks. Rickey steals. Rickey is booed.

Somehow, Larry Andersen is getting outs with one stupid pitch, a slider that either nips the outside corner or misses wide. His 43-year-old arm is completely shot. Could the lu-lu-lu-lu-lu voodoo of the Phillie Phanatic be working? With a backup chorus of thousands, atop the Phils dugout and inside the smelly, soaking outfit, Dave Raymond is hexing, and gracing, his next-to-last game. After 16 years, he is hanging up his flat webbed feet and his big emerald schnoz and his brass balls. Singlehandedly, or schnozzedly, he has made the case for mascots. He's leaving to develop characters for children's television shows. He has had plenty of practice.

Home Seven

Seventh-inning stretch feels gooooood. Before you can buy some peanuts and Crackerjack, the Phils have the bases loaded again. And Daulton is at bat. He slams a ball to right field, way back, way back . . . and . . . foul by feet. Would've been 17–9. Would've been overkill, you say. Save some for tomorrow, you say, when the series is all tied up, you say. On a 3–2 pitch, Daulton gets hit. Kind of. An inside pitch glances off something and the ump waves him to first. The score is 14–9. Another beer, please.

Eisenreich is out. Thompson, the African-American with the white-hot bat, scorches a ball up the middle. Roberto Alomar makes a nice snag, flips to second for the force, retiring the side with the bases still full of Phils. One run, like an impacted molar, has been extracted. Plenty, it's plenty. **14–9, Phils**

Top Eight

It is raining. It is midnight. The Mitching hour. Fans with angina are advised to stop reading here.

Since when does Beavis appear without Butt-Head? Butt-Head without Beavis? Not on MTV. Not in my dreams. Not in three previous victories. No one said they were pretty, all thumbs and gingivitis, but they get the job done. Kim Batiste stays glued to the bench as Mitch Williams is greeted with dubious encouragement—howls, towels, whoomps, beer orders, high fives, low sighs, palms smacking foreheads, and balled-up hot dog wrappers. This will be the last time Mitch pitches at the Vet in red pinstripes. It is quite a finale. Daulton will call it "the perfect ending to a perfect nightmare."

The Wild Thing will be missed. He is the most dramatic one-inning player in the game. Rather than providing relief, he cranks up the tensions. The only thing orthodox about Mitch is his covered head—too much motion, too little balance, too much hair, too little control, and he still protected 43 victories. The Phils had to win every one of those games twice, once in eight innings and then again in a nail-biting ninth. Fans got two thrills for the price of one. Turning a cameo into a starring role was viewed as upstaging by certain teammates, akin to Brando making a huge entrance at the tail end of Act 3. The Wild One didn't much care what anyone thought. At least that's what he said.

"When I walk out of here, I'm gonna forget all about this game. I leave it on the field." He will be saying those lines in about 20 minutes in the locker room, after the deluge. When he gets home to Marlton, he won't be able to forget—he will be greeted by cops and broken glass and death threats. Sleep will be out of the question. He has a 9mm pistol with him, but still feels vulnerable. After he appears in the sixth and final game of the Series, sleepless in Toronto, he will, again, have trouble leaving it on the field. He will say, when no one asks, "I'm not going to commit suicide. It's only a game."

In this particular game, Mitch takes over for a faltering Larry Andersen with the score at 14–10, runners still at second and third. Molitor has just doubled down the line, over and around the glove of a backpedaling Dave Hollins. Would Beavis have caught the ball? Not cleanly, but something positive would have happened. Mitch now surrenders a run-scoring single to Tony Fernandez and walks Borders and strikes out pinch hitter Puddin' Head Sprague. Two outs, a 14–11 lead. Rickey hits a loopy liner to short center that looks catchable until Dykstra spins his wet wheels for a split second and then wants to dive for the ball but the turf is too slick and if he doesn't come up with it it may roll to the wall and Rickey'll round the bases and tie this thing up so Dykstra stops dead in his tracks and plays it on a safe high bounce and two more runs score and Dykstra looks despondent as he soft-tosses the ball back to the infield, second-guessing himself, cursing the conditions, sensing the game slipping away, along with his performance and the season. Shake if off, Lenny, there's more.

Now Devon White hits a fly ball to right-center and Dykstra comes in and over a couple steps and the goddamned thing keeps carrying and carrying and Dykstra has to change directions on the lime-color ice rink and—whoomp!—the ball gets beyond him and skids into the gap and Borders crosses the plate and Lenny keeps chasing and Rickey crosses the plate and White lands at third and I'm stone-cold sober and the Phils are losing and this madness is a time-lapse version of 1964—12 minutes instead of 12 games, but the bloody message is the same.

Things that can't happen happen.

Five-run leads can't evaporate into the moisturized air. Fourteen runs can't go for naught. Not at home. Not before 62,731 screaming meemies. Not in a universe with logic, in a world with compassion, not after Lenny pumps two missiles over the right-field fence. Come on. Not now. Not again. Fuck you.

You think you're watching a game, and then you realize it's your life.   **15–14, Jays**

Home Eight

Mike Timlin pitches the home eight. Kevin Stocker strikes out. And so does pinch hitter Mickey Morandini. Why not Mickey Mouse? Where's Incaviglia? It's a one-run game, Doc, and the ball is flying, and what happened to Fregosi's grand theory about sticking with who brung ya to the big dance? Inky's season was a wonder—24 homers, 89 RBIs in 368 at bats. Now he's buried like an empty marrow bone in the backyard? Just when we need a shot, a quick fix. Doesn't he deserve as much loyalty as Kim Batiste or Mitch Williams? Inky will not appear in this morose marathon. His eight at bats in the Series are fewer than Ricky Jordan's.

Timlin whiffs two and gets yanked for his effort. What the Phils wouldn't have traded for two damn strikeouts. Gaston brings in Duane Ward to face Lenny Dykstra. There are no rabbits left up Lenny's sleeves. For the past two innings, he has looked like anything but the Happy Human of Game Two. Now he's the Pissed Person of Game Four. Disgusted, furious, bewildered. He strikes out looking, and puts up only mild protest about the mildly questionable calls. Timlin runs out of the dugout to congratulate his mates, only to discover the game is not over, not officially, not yet. Who can blame him? It sure feels that way.

What is the sound of 125,000 hands not clapping?

Top Nine

Bobby Thigpen pitches the ninth. 'Twas not so long ago that Bobby Thigpen pitched only ninth innings when his team held slender leads—57 times in one record-setting season. Now, with "Auld Lang Syne" playing softly in the background, Thigpen is a reminder of how these marvelous Phillies were put together, with head cases, medical cases, weight cases, legal cases, briefcases, uppercases and Bobby Thigpen, too.

The Phillies are what Emma Lazarus had in mind when she originally wrote: *Give me your tired arms, your platoonists, your hobbled messes yearning to breathe free . . .*

Home Nine

This inning is kind of a blank, tell you the truth. There was no comeback. **FINAL: 15–14, Jays**

Postgame

With precious little time to file, writers reach in every direction for ready-made metaphors and handy analogies; they compare this to Larsen's perfecto and Reggie's three-ringer night and Mazeroski's ninth-inning shot (if only they knew . . .). ESPN's Peter Gammons says it was the most fun he's ever had in a ballpark. Poor guy.

Ray Ratto, columnist for the *San Francisco Examiner*, gets it right: "This game can't be written. This is one of those nights where you just punch 800 words into the computer, admit that you're ashamed of yourself, then go home and have a beer."

Which is just about what John Kruk does. "I had a sore throat from talking to all of them [at first base] . . . Honest to God, I did the same thing I do every night. I had a couple of beers and went home. It was late, about 5:30—I just sat around and stared."

Players and writers unite! Tipple together! Had Ratto and Kruk been matching ales at sunrise, the world would have less shame and better stories. That task fell into the laps of Lenny Dykstra and Bill Conlin, who had agreed to write a book together. When asked about the game on a New York radio show, Conlin huffed, "That loss cost me $50,000 in book sales. And I need the money!" Dykstra went on a local cable show and declared: "There couldn't be a worse feeling, so we just said 'Fuck it!' "

Which is apparently what Dykstra later told Conlin. The book is dead. Long live conflicts of interest.

The Day After

The next afternoon, at the press conference, Joe Carter wants to meet a certain *Daily News* columnist, face to face, pronto. He wants to see what kind of lowlife would write that he and two teammates were at Delilah's Den.

Joe Carter wants Stu Bykofsky.

Imagine, Doctor—with Game Four barely in the books, Carter focuses on a tabloid gossip columnist who placed him at a legal, upscale strip joint on Delaware Avenue. Since there were no reports of bartenders beaten or explosive devices hurled, where's the damage? Just being seen at Delilah's is a defamation of Blue Jay character? Hell, after last night's loss, you might find half the Phillies team sleeping behind the bar. Did the Phils turn into Broad Street Bellyaches when the Atlanta press suggested locking up their women and children (particularly blond pubescent girls) when the playoff-bound sybarites arrived from the North? Is Joe Carter really threatened by a bespectacled rumormonger who brandishes an automatic-firing ellipsis?

Joe Carter is a Christian. A decent man who was having a decent postseason—nothing spectacular, mind you. Though he believes both sloth and taking the Lord's name in vain are sinful, being around the Phils did not offend his righteousness. Stu Bykofsky, however, has sent him over the precipice. Bearing false witness against a neighbor is bad enough, but putting him in a house of lewdity when he was with his family, well, all hell will surely break loose. Verily, the Series took on biblical proportions.

When the person of Joe Carter stepped up to the plate in the ninth inning of the sixth game, it was not the strength of a mere mortal swinging mere lumber, nay, but the very wrath of a vengeful God. After giving up the fatal home run to Carter, all Mitch Williams could say was, "Life's a bitch."

Punchline

There's my story, Doc, the whole *megilla*, summed up nicely in three little words: Life's a bitch. Four words, technically, if you're a stickler on contractions. Four little words, four hours, 14 minutes, 14 runs. There it is. Finally, Game Four is over.

And the doctor says, "It is spring. Perhaps vee can begin again, yes?"